Participation and Non-Participation in Student Activism

Radical Subjects in International Politics

Series editor: Ruth Kinna

This series uses the idea of political subjection to promote the discussion and analysis of individual, communal, and civic participation and activism. 'Radical subjects' refers both to the character of the topics and issues tacked in the series and to the ethic guiding the research. The series has a radical focus in that it provides a springboard for the discussion of activism that sits outside or on the fringes of institutional politics, yet which, insofar as it reflects a commitment to social change, is far from marginal. It provides a platform for scholarship that interrogates modern political movements, probes the local, regional, and global dimensions of activist networking and the principles that drive them, and develops innovative frames to analyse issues of exclusion and empowerment. The scope of the series is defined by engagement with the concept of the radical in contemporary politics but includes research that is multi- or interdisciplinary, working at the boundaries of art and politics, political utopianism, feminism, sociology, and radical geography.

Titles in Series:

Taking the Square: Mediated Dissent and Occupations of Public Space, edited by Maria Rovisco and Jonathan Corpus Ong.

The Politics of Transnational Peasant Struggle: Resistance, Rights and Democracy, Robin Dunford.

Sustainable Urbanism and Direct Action: Case Studies in Dialectical Activism, Benjamin Heim Shepard.

Participation and Non-Participation in Student Activism: Paths and Barriers to Mobilising Young People for Political Action, Alexander Hensby.

Participation and Non-Participation in Student Activism

Paths and Barriers to Mobilising Young People for Political Action

Alexander Hensby

ROWMAN &
LITTLEFIELD

INTERNATIONAL

London • New York

Published by Rowman & Littlefield International Ltd.
Unit A, Whitacre Mews, 26-34 Stannary Street, London SE11 4AB
www.rowmaninternational.com

Rowman & Littlefield International Ltd. is an affiliate of Rowman & Littlefield
4501 Forbes Boulevard, Suite 200, Lanham, Maryland 20706, USA
With additional offices in Boulder, New York, Toronto (Canada), and Plymouth (UK)
www.rowman.com

British Library Cataloguing in Publication Data
A catalogue record for this book is available from the British Library

ISBN: HB 978-1-7834-8693-9
PB 978-1-7834-8694-6

Library of Congress Cataloging-in-Publication Data is Available

ISBN 978-1-78348-693-9 (cloth: alk. paper)
ISBN 978-1-78348-695-3 (electronic)

∞™ The paper used in this publication meets the minimum requirements of American
National Standard for Information Sciences—Permanence of Paper for Printed Library
Materials, ANSI/NISO Z39.48-1992.

Printed in the United States of America

For Susan, mother and proto-sociologist

Contents

Preface

This book is about student activism, and why some students convert their political interests into forms of action, and why others do not. These are in many ways timeless questions for social science research, but they have taken on a new potency in recent years due to the remarkable 'movement of the squares' protest cycle (Biekart & Fowler, 2013; Gerbaudo, 2013; Kavada, 2015), as well as the mobilising powers of information communications technologies and social media networks (Bennett and Segerberg, 2012; Castells, 2012). While recent scholarship has devoted much of its energies to the new mobilising opportunities these movements and technologies have created, relatively little attention has been paid to *non*-participation in this context. Beyond critiques of the professionalisation of party and activism politics (e.g. Hay, 2007; Dauvergne and LeBaron, 2014), there have been few attempts to understand the sociological factors which may promote and sustain non-participation in contemporary society.

In exploring these questions, this book draws on the case study of the 2010/11 UK student protests. Although preceding the aforementioned protest cycle as per Kavada's (2015) definition, the protests shared many of its characteristics and repertoires. The UK Government's proposal to treble the cap on tuition fees for students in England prompted large-scale regional and national demonstrations, and the formation of a network of multiple, simultaneous university occupations. Taking place across seven weeks in autumn 2010, the protests arguably generated a greater scale and diversity of participation than had been seen on UK campuses for more than a generation. Yet this moment of agency was short lived, as activists struggled to sustain the momentum of the campaign once the fees increase was passed in Parliament. Using original survey data of students from 22 UK universities, and 56 in-depth interviews with students from six universities, this book explores the protests' rise and fall. This reveals important insights about the different layers of engagement and identification among participants, as well as the social and political characteristics of non-participants.

Student activism, of course, has its own distinct protest tradition, and this book also seeks to frame and contextualise the case study within the unique properties of the campus field, as well as the modes of organisation and participatory repertoires central to its history. In so doing, it brings together three relevant, yet often divergent, literatures of political science, social movement studies, and sociology. This allows analysis to take full account of the relationship between formal and contentious politics, and the intersections between social and political dynamics. In sum, this book seeks to contribute to a more general *sociology of politics*, incorporating a sociological analysis of the identities, value formations, and subcultures that are found in political groups, parties, and networks.

ACKNOWLEDGEMENTS

The writing of this book would not have been possible without the invaluable support of some very important people. This partly reflects the project's unusual evolution: when I began my PhD at the University of Edinburgh in September 2010, the student fees protests – upon which the thesis would be based – was yet to happen. Already committed to a case study for researching political participation and non-participation, I quickly became distracted by the sudden and incredible surge of movements, campaigns, and revolutions occurring across the world during this time. Each of these – from the Arab Spring to the Indignados, from UK Uncut to Occupy – represented a potentially fascinating topic for research, encompassing as they did the embrace of new technologies and the radical rejection of the political status quo. For any PhD student, ditching preconceived plans to pursue unfolding events can be a risky business, and to this end I wish to thank my supervisors Hugo Gorringe and Michael Rosie for their advice and mentorship. Not only did they encourage me to follow these movements and assess their research potential, they crucially pulled me back into reality once it was time to commit to a single case study. Moreover, throughout fieldwork and the writing-up process, Hugo and Michael provided regular feedback and advice. In short, this research simply would not have been possible without their continual hard work and support.

For the realisation of the research design, there are many people I must thank, albeit anonymously. The distribution of the survey across 22 universities would have been impossible were it not for some 90 staff members from across the UK who agreed to forward my email to students in their schools, departments, and colleges. The scope and depth of this project owes a great deal to their generosity. I am also indebted to student interview gatekeepers at University of Edinburgh, University College London (UCL), and University of Warwick, all of whom went out of their way to put me in touch with members of each campus's activism network. Of course, I must also express my deep gratitude to the 56 students who agreed to be interviewed for this research. In sharing with me their time, insight, honesty, and humour, they have made this book what it is.

As my analysis and arguments developed, I was fortunate to draw on a number of stimulating conversations with activists and academics working on social movements and radical politics. I would particularly like to thank Colin Crouch, Cristina Flesher Fominaya, Peter Hopkins, Joseph Ibrahim, Dan Mercea, Christopher Rootes, Clare Saunders, and Dave Tinham for their wise words and valued insights. Special mention should be reserved for Bram Meuleman and Joanne Sibthorpe, both of whom acted as enthusiastic co-conspirators during some of my more impulsive forays into activism ethnography. I am also grateful for the advice provided by Ross Bond, Paul Norris, and Taylor Spears on the research's quantitative aspects.

For the transition from thesis to book, I must thank Nick Crossley and James Kennedy, who as examiners presided over an unexpectedly enjoyable viva, and were both enthusiastic about the research's publishing potential. I am once again indebted to Anna Reeve, who, as senior commissioning editor, encouraged me to bring the book to Rowman & Littlefield International and ensured that its initial development proceeded swiftly and painlessly. Since her departure, I have been grateful for support from Dhara Snowden, who has provided me with a necessary blend of encouragement, sympathy, and coercion. I would also like to thank my series editor, Ruth Kinna, for her supportive words and helpful comments as the manuscript took shape.

For their editorial support throughout the book's development, I would like to express my gratitude to Lucy Bond, Emile Chabal, Janet Fearnley, Lois Lee, Allen Simpson, Mike Slaven, Matthew Warren, and Mike Watson. Finally, I would like to thank my family for keeping me going through this long, arduous, but ultimately rewarding process of scholarship. For this, I am eternally grateful.

Chapter 1

Introduction

MILLBANK TENDENCY: A TALE OF TWO MARCHES

On 9 November 2011, approximately 2,000 students marched through London to protest the Government's Higher Education White Paper and its proposed marketisation of the sector. University funding had been a campaigning issue for more than a decade, but this was no ordinary demonstration. Despite the modest turnout, the Metropolitan Police deployed twice as many officers for the event as there were marchers. Moreover, Scotland Yard announced in the days beforehand that police were authorised to use rubber bullets, baton rounds, and water cannons on students – a threat which reportedly had the blessing of Prime Minister David Cameron (*Daily Mail*, 8 November 2011). On the morning of the march, police distributed flyers at tube stations warning marchers to avoid 'outbreak[s] of violence and disorder', as being caught in the wrong place at the wrong time might lead to arrest and a criminal record that 'could seriously affect your future employment or educational opportunities'.

Unsurprisingly, these threats contributed to a tense and paranoid atmosphere as the march progressed through central London. Demonstrators were effectively encircled by a police line throughout its four-hour duration, with every side street closed, barricaded, and patrolled by officers. As the march crossed into the city's financial district – a pointed gesture in its own right – office workers from the overhead buildings peered from their windows at the marchers below – some cheered, one or two flicked V-signs, while others took photos on their smartphones. Students kept up their spirits by singing and chanting, even if their repertoire had started to shift away from the familiar campaign slogan 'No Ifs! No Buts! No Education Cuts!' to commentaries on the march itself: a group of female undergraduates chanted at police officers, 'You're sexy! You're cute! Take off your riot suit!', whereas others sang, 'You can shove your rubber bullets up your arse'.

Meanwhile, on the event's Twitter hashtag (#nov9), activists were monitoring the demonstration and its media coverage: some blamed the police for being too aggressive; others criticised the marchers for being too timid, stressing the need for direct action to attract more press attention. On the ground, however, opportunities for disruption were limited: with each passing barricade, tension built between marchers and police, boiling over on some occasions into direct confrontations and arrests (videos of which were soon posted on YouTube). By the time they reached London Wall, a police dispersal order saw marchers tightly encircled by a fixed police line – a tactic known as 'kettling' – with small numbers allowed to filter out at set intervals. By 5:00 p.m., the demonstration was over. The general feeling was that the protest had been snuffed out: aside from the left-leaning *Guardian*, there was very little coverage in the national press. In the now-opened side streets, union representatives took roll-call of names before boarding their minibuses back home.

Among attendees interviewed for this book, Yvonne, a first-year undergraduate at the University of Warwick, admitted that she had also been partly attracted by a union-subsidised trip to London. Ronnie, a Warwick postgraduate and experienced activist, recalled enjoying attending because it ultimately represented 'a day out with people who I get on with'. For many participants, however, the march was recalled with much negativity, described as 'unpleasant' (Peter, Edinburgh), 'really bad' (Marianne, Cambridge), 'disempowering' (Brett, UCL), and 'the worst demo ever' (Rhiannon, Edinburgh). Clearly, the police tactics were designed to stifle any confrontational or spontaneous actions. For Edinburgh student John, there was no question as to why this was the case: 'It was because of Millbank. No-one was pretending it wasn't. It was because of Millbank, and they didn't want it to happen again'.

Rewinding one year, the landscape of student activism in the United Kingdom (UK) looked quite different. Having recently abandoned its free education doctrine, the National Union of Students (NUS) had not organised a national demonstration for four years. The early 2000s had seen students mobilise in large numbers against the Iraq War and variable tuition fees, yet by 2010 their campaign agenda had fragmented, with some favouring Climate Camp activism while others engaged in actions with Students for Justice in Palestine (SJP). Nevertheless, the financial crisis of 2007/8 had begun to engineer a change in activists' focus, as did the newly formed Conservative-Liberal Democrat Coalition Government's 'austerity agenda' to cut public spending and control the UK's national debt. Its first major expression came in the form of a proposed bill to treble the tuition fees cap for students in England – due to be voted in Parliament seven weeks later.

The proposed increase incurred widespread opposition from students, and though the policy would not affect current undergraduates, their hostility was intensified by the controversial position of the Liberal Democrats. In the preceding election, many had voted for the party because it pledged to oppose any tuition fees increase in Parliament, while promising to abolish fees altogether if elected to government. Given this twin grievance, the NUS arranged a national demonstration for 10 November 2010. Although London had seen violent protests during the previous year's G20 summit, the Metropolitan Police anticipated little in the way of disruption from students. With around 10,000 expected to attend, 225 police officers were deployed for the event. Instead, it drew 52,000 students, with over 100 universities represented from across the UK (*The Guardian*, 10 November 2010). As the march began to progress from Horse Guards Parade, the scale of turnout was as much a shock to students as it was to the police:

> I came out of the train station and literally just stood for about ten minutes doing a whole 360, like, what the hell's going on? It was very positive – there was a sense of pride that this many people had come together to support the campaign, so there was a sense of 'I'm really proud to be a student – so many people here!' (Hayley, Roehampton)

> I'd been on a few demos before but it was absolutely incredible, like, the streets being packed with students – everywhere you looked, there were people. And I guess there was that degree of optimism as well, you know – this is huge, this is the biggest demonstration that's happened in years, we can actually achieve something! (Andrew, Cambridge)

For experienced and first-time marchers alike, partaking in this spectacle generated feelings of pride, empowerment, righteousness, and community – a combination almost unique to protest, and perhaps validating Jasper's (1997: 220) claim that it provides 'virtually all the pleasures that humans derive from social life'. Yet events were about to take an unexpected turn. Some activists had covertly planned a number of potential 'escalations', and with the demonstration route unusually short, many marchers felt a surplus of energy as they approached its rallying point outside Tate Britain. Police officers had been guarding nearby Liberal Democrat offices in anticipation of vandalism attempts, yet few paid any attention to the looming presence of Conservative Party HQ as the march proceeded down Millbank. At approximately 1:30 p.m., a small group broke off from the main route, urging marchers via SMS, leaflets, and word-of-mouth to 'follow the red flags'. As they made their way into the offices of 30 Millbank, police, and NUS stewards were unable to prevent thousands of students from surging towards the lobby. With windows smashed, smoke bombs thrown, and bonfires of placards being lit in the surrounding courtyard, events quickly descended into carnage:

> It escalated very quickly. People had smashed windows, someone threw a sofa. ... People just went absolutely bananas, absolutely crazy. (Hayley, Roehampton)

> We took Millbank, we got in through the doors, and there were thousands
> of people outside. ... The police had batons but they didn't use them, partly
> because they realised they were hopelessly outnumbered. (Anon)

Around 50 students made it onto the roof of Millbank Tower, whereupon they
hung banners and waved anarchist flags. Meanwhile, large numbers were
departing NUS's rallying point to watch events unfold in the courtyard. Until
Territorial Support Group (TSG) officers arrived approximately 45 minutes
after the initial attack, protesters were virtually given free rein. For many
involved, this engendered a sense of empowerment that surpassed the scale
of the demonstration itself: in occupying Conservative HQ, they were defy-
ing the Government *and* the police. Once the TSG arrived, however, the
costs and risks to participation soon became apparent. Students outside were
kettled, while 35 people were arrested and later charged with criminal damage and/or trespass. Most controversial of all, one protester threw an empty
fire extinguisher from the roof, narrowly missing students and police officers
in the courtyard below:

> What was amazing for me standing there watching was the fire extinguisher
> coming down from the roof. I have a particularly distinct memory of me and
> this guy – who's a revolutionary socialist – saying 'fuck, this is a bit much!'
> (*laughs*). (Lindsey, Edinburgh)

Although quickly condemned by activists, the incident was arguably symptomatic of the chaos that had enraptured the demonstration. Much of this
was uncoordinated and impulsive, but as an overall spectacle it had not been
entirely accidental. With little time to pressurise Parliament into voting down
the fees bill, activists recognised the importance of generating actions that
would attract the interest of the UK press. In this respect, the Millbank attack
was a conscious attempt to create a radical, almost certainly divisive, yet necessary, 'moment of excess' (Free Association, 2011). Not only did it create
new possibilities for collective self-expression that transcended the sum of
its parts, it also succeeded in hijacking the mainstream media narrative. For
media-savvy students especially, seeing themselves on the front pages of the
newspapers and broadcast live on television represented a moment of true
agency. *Millbank* was the news, and they were the ones making it happen:

> There was a TV in the lobby [of Millbank] showing Sky News, and suddenly
> just seeing the Skycopter filming this massive crowd that were outside – it was
> like, 'oh, I'm stood inside there! That's a lot of people!' (Anon)

> There were two issues of the Evening Standard that day: in the first, the protest
> was on page four and it was, like, a picture of two pretty girls holding a placard,

and a little piece about, like, 'twenty thousand students went on a protest ...'
And then two hours later, it was, like, front page, with a picture of a boy smash-
ing up Millbank, and '50,000 students on the protest ...!' (Donna, UCL)

With mainstream media firmly focused on students, it is fair to say that
'Millbank' – as the event became known – provided the campaign with its
'scale shift' from campus grievance to national talking point (Tarrow and
McAdam, 2005). Moreover, it imbibed the rest of the campaign with a radical and provocative ethos: three more large London demonstrations followed,
as well as a coordinated day of lecture walkouts, and a reported 51 occupations of campus buildings across the UK. In other words, for seven weeks in
autumn 2010, UK students evoked – and arguably, surpassed – the actions
and radicalism of their 1960s predecessors.

Yet despite this scale of anger, media attention, and participatory opportunities, the protests mobilised only a fraction of their student support base.
Although it is questionable whether a higher turnout would have overturned
the fees bill – which Parliament passed, albeit narrowly, that December – the
failure to achieve this certainly contributed to student activism's almost-
as-rapid *downward*-scale shift shortly after. By the time of the 9 November
2011 demonstration, activists were struggling to mobilise even a tenth of what
they had achieved the previous autumn. The event's organisers, the National
Campaign Against Fees and Cuts (NCAFC), blamed low participation on the
lack of leadership from the NUS, which had distanced itself from campaigns
post-Millbank. Ideological fault lines also seemed more manifest than the previous year, with students unsure over whether they should be campaigning for
'free' or 'affordable' education. In the end, the strongest uniting factor was, as
Ronnie put it, to 'remind people that we hadn't forgotten about last year'. Yet
this was not a strong enough reason to mobilise students en masse – indeed,
many seemed unaware that the demonstration was even taking place.

Of course, non-participation has always been a feature of social movements, and the student protests of 2010/11 were no different. Nor should 'participants' be taken as a homogenous category: after all, the vast majority of
students did not occupy Millbank, nor did they join the NUS demonstration,
well attended though it was. Even at its autumn 2010 peak, most students
did *nothing at all*. This is not to belittle the campaign's mobilising efforts:
rather, it is to draw attention to its value as a case study. On the one hand,
those who took part participated in different ways, be it signing petitions or
occupying university buildings. On the other hand, it cannot be assumed that
those who did not participate were not engaged in the fees grievance: Opinion Panel (2010) surveyed students shortly after the fees announcement and
found that 81 per cent opposed the increase. In sum, the student protests make
for an ideal opportunity to study the relationship between participation *and*

non-participation: Why did participants participate in the way they did, and why did so many supportive non-participants not participate at all?

STUDENTS, PROTEST, IDENTITY, AND DEBT

These are curious times to be a student. The expansion and professionalisation of higher education has transformed the sector, so that today, universities enrol in greater number and diversity than ever before. Students have a wider range of institutions, courses, and qualification levels to choose from, and can opt to study part-time, overseas, or online. Yet these transformations have come at a cost. Across the world, declining government subsidisation requires that students pay considerably more for their higher education than in the past. In the UK, graduates owe tens of thousands of pounds via decades of fees and loan repayments on a scale increasingly comparable with those in the United States (and without the scale of endowment funds and scholarships). Furthermore, they enter a labour market that rewards undergraduate qualifications far less than in previous generations, often necessitating taking on additional work experience, unpaid internships, vocational training, or further study to progress towards their chosen career.

Such is the importance placed on the governance, finance, and administration of higher education that we are left unsure as to *why* students come to university, and – in the words of Stefan Collini (2012) – what universities are *for*. Emphasis on producing an educated, flexible, and creative workforce that will generate economic growth has seen higher education transformed into a competitive marketplace. Given this rationale, universities are repositioned as 'service providers', and students as consumers. Any commitment to universities delivering a *public good* is increasingly compromised, as the provision of courses which are not deemed to directly serve the interests of the economy are now placed under greater scrutiny.

In this context, students perhaps have more *and* fewer reasons to protest than ever before. On the one hand, the emphasis on maximising employability while meeting living costs through part-time work or commuting affords little time and energy for extracurricular activities, let alone those which may contribute little to one's career development. On the other hand, activism participation not only offers a means of speaking out against the pernicious effects of higher education marketisation, but also provides opportunities for a *political* education, including the pursuit of new ideas, values, and participatory experiences. Indeed, this political education is seen as something of a rite of passage for undergraduates, reflecting student activism's tumultuous, uneven, yet often inspiring history. According to Rootes (2012: 4864), its emergence is predicated on students amounting to a critical mass in modern societies. Since then, in Europe, Asia, Africa, and the Americas, they have been capable of creating attention-stealing moments of agency. As well as representing their own interests, students have also played important roles in wider social movements – whether they are challenging authoritarian states, opposing wars, advocating civil rights, or proposing ethical alternatives to globalisation (McAdam, 1988; Boren, 2001; Hoefferle, 2013).

The campaigns and protests of the 1960s have cast a long shadow in student activism history – particularly in Europe and North America. Drawing as they did on an 'extraordinary conjunction of demography and social change' (Rootes, 2012: 4867), their counter-cultural legacy has set high expectations for student protest as a generation-defining force. In the years since, protests that have gained media traction have seldom escaped comparisons with the 1960s, including narratives about reclaiming the 'spirit of 1968'. This has perhaps contributed to a nagging sense of disappointment in the perceived efficacy of contemporary student activism. Certainly, large, residential universities afford numerous opportunities for political engagement and the building of campaigns. With students 'structurally freed up for activism' (Crossley, 2008: 29), the campus 'affords mechanisms which allow the politically motivated to find one another and form networks'. Together with its foci of political groups, societies, and the student union, campuses arguably represent an ideal field for generating campaigns and mobilising large numbers. At the same time, however, efforts to sustain activism and build wider movements is permanently hamstrung by the constant turnover of student cohorts, thereby limiting the retention of skills, experiences, and institutional memory.

Student activism also has a complicated relationship with the general public – especially in the UK. With its tendencies towards opposing authoritarianism and illiberalism, and the advocacy of progressive and alternative political ideas, students have been positioned in wider society as an 'incipient intelligentsia' (Rootes, 1980: 475). This has contributed to long-standing characterisations of the student activist not only as moral, idealistic, and righteous but also as arrogant, dogmatic, and naïve. Consequently, their public symbols and depictions – be it Tariq Ali, Camila Vallejo, or Rik from *the Young Ones* – can easily fluctuate from inspiring to ridiculing. Activists' public profile sometimes leads to divisions within the wider student body, as their public voice and actions opens up questions of representation, and who may legitimately 'speak' for students. This, of course, also reflects the fact that activism is historically practised by a small minority of students overall (Clarke and Egan, 1972; Hoefferle, 2013). While the low rate of conversion is at least partly attributable to the aforementioned costs and risks to participation, it may also reflect trends in young people's engagement in politics and activism more generally.

STUDYING PARTICIPATION AND NON-PARTICIPATION

Political participation has long been a subject of theory and research in political science, sociology, and social movement studies, though these literatures interact and intersect far less frequently than they should. Within political science, studies have often reflected a broad desire to improve state-citizen dialogue, as well as measure the democratic health of a society longitudinally. More recently, scholars have sought to rethink how we *define* participation, with analysis demonstrating how individuals express their dissatisfaction towards the participatory system as well as its decision-makers. On the other hand, sociological approaches (to which social movement studies arguably lean), are more focused on capturing the *experience* of participation, including the identities, cultures, and meanings generated through these actions. In studying participation as a social interaction, this goes some way to explaining some of the motivations, expectations, and identifications that encourage and sustain involvement in everyday life.

Political science research on participation is typically large scale and quantitative in nature. In the UK, prominent studies include Parry et al. (1992), Jordan and Maloney (1997), Pattie et al. (2004), as well as the Hansard Society's annual Audit of Political Engagement (2004–16). Results tend to claim that only around 10–15 per cent of the UK population can be considered 'politically active', and that traditional indicators of participation such as civic and party memberships are in terminal decline (Hansard, 2010; see also Norris, 2002). This has led to non-participation being represented through basic quantitative ideal types, ranging from the 'alienated/hostile' (Hansard, 2010) who are mostly disconnected from the political process, to the 'concerned, unmobilised' (Jordan and Maloney, 2007), whose political engagement and concern go unconverted due to a lack of confidence in the efficacy of available participatory repertoires.

It is also commonly found that young people are over-represented among non-participants, with 18–24-year-olds the least active age group, and displaying relatively little interest in politics. This has been challenged by researchers who contend that young people are politically engaged and active in more 'cause-oriented' ways that are not so easily captured in mass surveys (Bang, 2004; Marsh et al., 2007). Arguments have also been made that young people have had little encouragement to get involved, since their interests have been mostly ignored in electoral politics for many years (Henn et al., 2002; Cunningham and Lavalette, 2004; Hay, 2007; Henn and Foard, 2012).

Sociological approaches to political participation have generally favoured a more qualitative approach, seeking to explore the interactions, cultures, and identities associated with parties, social movements, and civic associations.

Unlike in political science, this has generated a miscellany of methodological approaches and case studies. Some researchers have taken an interest in how politicisation is shaped by family background and schooling, including the accumulation of knowledge, norms, and skills that encourage active engagement later in life (Bourdieu, 1984; Coles, 1986; Braungart and Braungart, 1990). Beyond primary socialisation, others have highlighted the importance of social networks and microstructures for creating opportunities for, and expectations of, activism participation (McAdam, 1986; Crossley, 2008). Drawing more from elements of social psychology, authors such as Gamson (1992) and Jasper (1997) have studied individuals' emotional responses to political grievances, and how their social framing may stimulate forms of action. Finally, research by Touraine (1981), Snow (2001), and Melucci (1988) have considered why individuals may engage with a particular issue or cause, and socially associate themselves with a group or movement's collective identity.

In both political science and sociology, however, studies of non-participation as a category in its own right have generally been few and far between. Aside from the aforementioned participation surveys, political science approaches have tended to favour thinking of non-participation as the outcome of an individual's rational deliberation process (Olson, 1965; Whiteley and Seyd, 2002) or as the resultant failure of certain mobilisation strategies (Verba and Nie, 1972; McCarthy and Zald, 1977). Sociological approaches are again more varied, with research drawing attention to how people collectively manage negative emotions of powerlessness (Norgaard, 2006), or the role of networks in overruling or providing insufficient pathways to mobilisation (Oegema and Klandermans, 1994). On both sides of the literature, however, each approach arguably offers what the other does not: whereas sociological case studies highlight the experiences and interactions that shape non-participation, political science research offers an institutional context and the ability to apply these trends more broadly.

Considering these gaps in our knowledge, there are strong reasons for studying participation and non-participation in student activism. In so doing, this book seeks to draw these different literatures together, with quantitative measurements and classifications complementing qualitative research into the experience of participating in different activities. It also takes the view that processes of engagement and participation in activism – especially student activism – draw from the same well as formal politics. For undergraduates in particular, university can play a defining role in shaping an individual's political interests, beliefs, and sense of identity. Furthermore, the unique social and spatial resource of the campus environment provides a greater range and concentration of participatory opportunities than most students are likely to have experienced before. Given this context, studying student *non*-participation allows one to analyse more closely the reasons why young people may feel reluctant to engage in politics and activism today.

STUDENT ACTIVISM AND THE CASE STUDY

Using the 2010/11 student protests in the UK as a case study, this book sets out to explain why certain individuals mobilise for forms of activism participation and why others do not. As well as comparing the different levels and experiences of participation – from hardened occupiers to occasional petitioners – it also seeks to analyse non-participation as a more general social phenomenon. Of particular interest are students who self-identified as activists prior to the protests and came to play an important role in the mobilisation of others; students who were mobilised (and radicalised) by the protests but had previously been mostly inactive; and students who, while sympathetic to the protests' aims, took little or no part in them. These questions also carry relevance to issues of youth engagement more broadly.

Although there is much potential for analysing the 2010/11 student protests, as a case study it remains relatively under-researched. This is partly due to the fact that from January 2011 onwards, they were quickly usurped by a number of high-profile activism events, including the Arab Spring, anti-austerity protests in Greece and Spain, the English riots, and, of course, the global Occupy movement. This does not mean that plenty has not already been written on the subject, however. At their autumn 2010 peak, the protests received extended coverage in newspapers and magazines, with notable pieces including Laurie Penny's (2011) report on the UCL occupation for the *New Statesman* and Paul Mason's (2011a) article for the BBC website, 'Twenty Reasons Why it's Kicking off Everywhere'. The latter was later expanded into a book (2011b), which attempted to trace organisational commonalities between the student protests and uprisings in France, Greece, and North Africa, particularly in their use of social media and network technologies. The same year also saw the publication of two edited collections – by Hancox (2011) and Palmieri and Solomon (2011) – featuring articles about the student protests from activists and journalists. In late 2011, a group of students produced *The Real Social Network*, a film which chronicled UCL's campus occupations, which was screened at universities, activism conferences, and festivals.

Perhaps inevitably, these outputs tended to take a largely normative analysis of student protest participation, written as they were by activists and supportive co-travellers. Many were published at a time when the protests were still taking place, thus reflecting activists' *esprit de corps* in seeking not only to inform readers but also to inspire them into taking further collective action. Consequently, they offer relatively little analysis of why the protests failed, or why supportive non-participants could not be mobilised. Academic publications from this time took a similarly critical view, though most turned their attentions to the grievance of higher education funding (e.g. Molesworth et al., 2010; Holmwood, 2011; Bailey and Friedman, 2011; Docherty, 2011; Collini, 2012; McGettigan, 2013). Studies of the protests focused mainly on students' democratic organisation of campus occupations, covering events at Newcastle University (Hopkins et al., 2011), UCL (Aitchison, 2011), and University of West of England (Salter and Kay, 2011), as well as students' use of social media (Theocharis, 2012). With the exception of Crossley and Ibrahim's (2012) contemporaneous study of activism networks at the University of Manchester, however, empirical studies of student mobilisation, participation, and non-participation have been lacking.

In filling this gap, this book's original research comprises of two distinct but interrelated forms of data. First, it draws on a survey of students in the 2011/12 academic year, from 22 UK universities (N = 2,485) to measure students' participation and non-participation in the 2010/11 protests, along with their attitudes and experiences of politics more generally. Second, it makes use of 56 interviews with students – ranging from highly active participants to non-participants – from a subsample of six universities. The triangulation of these methods allows for participation to be measured quantitatively by mapping trends of thought and action, and understood qualitatively through capturing students' reflections on their personal experiences of politics and activism at university. The choice of these methods also allows for data to be analysed in comparison to similar studies, notably Hansard's (2004–16) participation surveys, and qualitative case studies of student activism and other protest groups (e.g. McAdam, 1986; Eliasoph, 1998; Norgaard, 2006; Crossley and Ibrahim, 2012).

Through its data and research, this book seeks to develop our understanding of participation and non-participation across the political science, social movements, and sociological literatures. First, it advocates a network approach for studying activism participation and non-participation. This incorporates a critique of classical rational choice theories in favour of one emphasising the *subjective* rationality of political decision-making. Building on network approaches within social movement studies (i.e. McAdam, 1986; Oegema and Klandermans, 1994; Diani, 2000), as well as political science research into the social motivations of individuals (Whiteley and Seyd, 2002), it considers the social environment and available conversations that shape individuals' actions. This rests on a broadly Bourdieusian approach, where politicisation is a process predicated on the accumulation of knowledge, capital, and self-confidence, and access to networks and fields where participation is valued and encouraged.

Second, research draws attention to the importance of identification and dis-identification in individuals' participation and non-participation. This emphasises the enmeshing of the social and political, where the conveyance of morals, values, and ideologies is often bound up in the identities, aesthetics, and lifestyles associated with the people practising them. Mobilisation and politicisation are thus partly shaped by a desire to conform and associate socially with a distinct group, as is common to sociological studies of subculture (e.g. Becker, 1991). Conversely, dis-identification may inform an individual's decision to *not* participate, as the social identity of a group's participants may overrule his or her sympathy or support for the political values they espouse. This employs collective identification analyses found in the work of Melucci (1988), Snow (2001), and Saunders (2008), but this approach is extended to consider how identities are also externally ascribed and perceived by outsiders. In addition to analyses of non-participation cultures by Norgaard (2006) and Eliasoph (1998), these conceptions incorporate sociological processes more commonly found in research on social class (e.g. Skeggs, 1997; Savage et al., 1992).

Third and finally, it is argued that non-participation should be studied not only as a response to specific grievances and mobilisation drives but also as a social phenomenon in its own right. As with participation, non-participation is partly produced and sustained through social networks. Further developing the work of Oegema and Klandermans (1994) in particular, these 'counter-networks' consist of socially connected individuals for whom non-participation (or at least, limited participation) is considered a normal and legitimate non-activity. During specific grievances and collective action frames, this status quo might be maintained and strengthened by the sharing of a number of 'self-preservation narratives', be it members' concerns over the costs and risks to participation, 'counter-grievances' that take issue with a campaign's goals or tactics, or dis-identification with the image and character of the activists themselves. For many students, these self-preservation narratives are symptomatic of deeper uncertainties over their performance as political actors, leaving them feeling 'caring but not committed' about politics more generally (see also Hensby, 2014; 2015).

Of course, one must also acknowledge some of the limits and boundaries to this book's research case. First of all, it should be pointed out that students are not necessarily a typical subsection of young people, nor are all students necessarily 'young'. Given its emphasis on knowledge acquisition, and the networks and resources provided by the university campus, the extent to which this book's analysis of participation and non-participation can be applied to young people in general is at least partly restricted. Another unavoidable limitation of this research is that it focuses primarily on a case study that is rooted in the politics and activism of universities in the UK and grievances associated with its higher education funding system. While similar anti-fees campaigns have recently taken place in Bangladesh, Canada, Chile, New Zealand, and South Africa, it is open to question how pertinent this book's findings are to student activism in other countries, including those predicated on unrelated grievances.

In terms of the case study's framing, among its most prominent absent populations are the students who came to university after the £9,000 fees cap was put in place. This cohort was not yet at university when data was collected, though some would have participated in protests the previous year: school and college students attended the national demonstrations in London in large numbers, and were arguably a key element to Mason (2011b) and others' portrayal of the protests in generational terms. Also missing from the data are students from the 2010/11 academic year who were no longer at university in 2011/12. This creates a slight disjuncture between the principal period of study and the available research population, particularly in the case of final-year students who graduated before data collection began. It should also be pointed out that while the survey closed in June 2012 and the last interview was conducted that October, higher education campaigning continues to be a fixture on campuses across the UK. Consequently, subsequent student occupations and demonstrations, as well as the ongoing campaign work of NUS and NCAFC, fall outside the narrative covered in this book.

One final point about the book's limitations concerns its overall purpose. The research does not seek to offer a critical analysis as to why the student protests failed to prevent the fees bill being passed in Parliament, or whether this was even a realistic possibility. Certainly, none of its analysis intends to challenge any of the political values underpinning the fees campaign, nor dismiss normative critiques made by others on the subject. The focus is on participation and mobilisation – clearly essential aspects to making any movement successful – but it is for others to judge whether the evidence presented suggests that increased participation or different tactical decisions might have produced a different outcome.

THE STRUCTURE OF THIS BOOK

The book consists of eight chapters, combining theory and research on political participation and activism with analysis of the 2010/11 student protests case study. Given the aforementioned disconnections across sociology, political science, and social movement literatures, chapter 2 seeks to bring all three together in a comprehensive account of existing theory and research in political participation and non-participation. It details long-term civic engagement trends in Western societies, including the effects of individualisation on

young people's politics. The chapter also unpacks the activities and repertoires associated with social movement participation, incorporating debates
over the value and efficacy of online activism. Finally, it evaluates different
theoretical approaches for understanding participation, before advocating a
field and network perspective that emphasises the social embeddedness of
political actors. Chapter 3 follows this up by applying a network approach
to the study of student activism. This involves an analysis of the campus
as a field for generating activism cultures and participatory opportunities,
including its foci of groups, societies, and unions. The chapter also traces the
specific history and traditions of student activism, from the 1960s to the present. This leads on to a deeper exploration of the 2010/11 fees case study, and
its contextualisation within contemporary trends and campaigns in student
activism today.

Chapters 4–7 constitute the book's original research and analysis.
Chapter 4 maps out basic trends from the survey, measuring engagement
and participation for the student population as a whole. Results are used to
consider whether majority student attitudes towards the efficacy of electoral
and protest politics conforms to a 'participatory ideal'. The chapter then
measures student engagement, knowledge, and participation in the 2010/11
protests. These trends are explored in more detail in the following chapters,
which introduce student interview accounts to trace the narrative of the case
study. Chapter 5 focuses on the paths and barriers to participation for different types of students, spanning their political socialisation from family
upbringing to their arrival at university. This also incorporates the analysis
of non-participants' political background, and the acquisition of norms and
values that sustain their limited engagement. The second half of the chapter
traces the narrative of the fees and cuts protests from the fees announcement to the NCAFC's 'National Walkout and Day of Action'. In addition to
mobilising agencies such as NUS and local student unions, analysis shows
how social networks played a pivotal role in generating paths *and* barriers to
students' participation.

The case study narrative resumes in chapter 6, spanning the development
of campus occupations to activists' efforts at resuming protests in 2011 and
building a durable student movement. Through this part of the story, the
chapter analyses students' *experience* of protest participation and the formation of different layers of collective identity. This also takes into consideration activism identities as perceived by non-participants, and how narratives
of dis-identification reinforced their decision to not take part. Analysis of
non-participation is expanded further in chapter 7, which compares supportive, unsupportive, and undecided non-participants, focusing on differences
in students' political background, invitational connectedness, and social
network memberships. The second half of the chapter extends this analysis

to take account of non-participants' disengagement with politics more generally. This emphasises the importance of not only knowledge and confidence in discussing politics but also the network factors that socially sustain and legitimise non-participation in everyday life. Finally, chapter 8 draws conclusions from the analysis conducted in chapters 4–7, thereby highlighting the explanatory power of networks, counter-networks, and collective identifications for explaining participation and non-participation in student activism. This is followed by an evaluation of the 2010/11 protests and reflections on the future of student activism.

Chapter 2

Theorising Political Participation and Non-Participation

To understand student activism within the broader context of political participation, one must go deeper into the trends, conflicts, and innovations that have shaped politics and civic engagement in Western societies over the past 50 years. Key to this is the decline of 'mass society' via the disembedding effects of market-driven individualisation (Beck, 1992). This runs parallel to similar changes in mass politics, including party dealignment, low voter turnout in elections, and decline in party and civic memberships (Norris, 2001; 2002; Skocpol, 2003). These trends form the backdrop to Robert D. Putnam's (2000) famous 'Bowling Alone' thesis, in which he argued that American citizens' social capital has been eroded by their increasing disconnection from traditional political and civic institutions, and the individualising effects of modern media technologies.

Decline in mass politics does not necessarily entail decline in political engagement; however, it may instead reflect changes in how we define (and measure) participation. Authors such as Giddens (1991) and Inglehart (1977) have claimed that the narrow and inflexible formal channels of old have slowly given way to increased choice in how citizens can legitimately express themselves. This owes much to increases in literacy, wealth, and education which drive patterns of political participation (Norris, 2002), but also the decoupling of identity from collective traditions (Beck, 1992). This has enabled citizens to pursue new political interests and activities in addition to their basic material interests, including identity-based and single-issue politics. Protest and activism have been a key part of this transformation, exemplified in the rise of environmental, LGBT, and human rights movements since the 1960s. Although it is disputable whether these 'new' social movements can be considered as distinct from the long history of contentious politics (see Calhoun, 1993), compelling arguments have been made

17

that protest is now a key part of the political process, even if depictions of a 'social movement society' (Tarrow, 1998) render protest functionally wedded to Western liberal democratic structures.

Despite this, the study of activism as a form of political participation draws on a fractured and sometimes messy academic literature. As noted in chapter 1, political science approaches remain mostly committed to measuring participation using formal definitions of politics. Although useful for producing measurable data that can be repeated and compared over time, it arguably does so while flattening out social, historical, and generational distinctions. Conversely, social movement-specific approaches are more case study oriented and often produce rich sociological findings, but researchers are sometimes reluctant to apply them to wider participation and mobilisation trends. Moreover, activism case studies tend to centre on significant upsurges in protest activity (of which this book is no exception) rather than the spaces in between. In other words, the assembled literatures provide a wealth of social and political movement analysis, but in isolation each lacks a crucial analytical ingredient. In bringing these literatures together, this chapter reviews political science approaches to measuring political participation, before introducing the repertoires commonly associated with social movement activism. It then provides an analysis of different theoretical approaches to understanding political mobilisation across the social sciences, before considering their usefulness to the field of student activism.

MEASURING POLITICAL PARTICIPATION AND NON-PARTICIPATION

The inclusion of activism in political participation research presents a number of dilemmas to scholars seeking to measure it. Political science approaches have traditionally focused on formal processes of engagement and civic behaviour using large-scale survey datasets. This allows for participation to be compared longitudinally and between countries, as exemplified by scholars' use of Hansard's Audit of Political Engagement in Great Britain, the General Social Survey (GSS) in the United States, and the European and World Values surveys (e.g. Inglehart and Baker, 2000; Kirbiš, 2013).

These surveys tend to paint an underwhelming picture of contemporary political participation. Findings from the GSS, for example, provided much of the evidence for Putnam's 'Bowling Alone' thesis, whereas Hansard's 2010 audit of political engagement classifies 16 per cent of British citizens as politically active, and only 10 per cent as 'politically committed'. Hansard also finds that the politically active and committed tend to be white, middle-class, university-educated, and more politically knowledgeable than the UK average. As figure 2.1 shows, participation for most citizens involves signing petitions and forms of ethical consumption. Repertoires that might be considered higher in personal cost and risk (McAdam, 1986) are generally less popular, with only 4 per cent claiming to have taken part in a demonstration, picket, or strike in the past three years.

Figure 2.1 also shows that almost half of UK citizens have participated in *none* of the listed activities in the past three years. Of course, to automatically categorise this as 'non-participation' is a misnomer since respondents may be involved in activities absent from the survey's criteria. In fact, one of the major disadvantages of longitudinal surveys is that in seeking to draw historical comparisons, the need for consistency tends to produce static and inflexible definitions of political action (Marsh et al., 2007). This is arguably borne out in Hansard's definition, with all forms of protest seemingly amalgamated into a single category of equivalent weighting to 'urging someone to get in touch with a local councillor or MP'. Of particular concern is its definition of 'being active'. In the 2009 audit, respondents who had undertaken three or more activities were classified as 'activists' – a moniker which was revised to 'politically active' in the 2010 audit. In either case, calculations prioritise range above frequency, which means committed, frequent protesters who

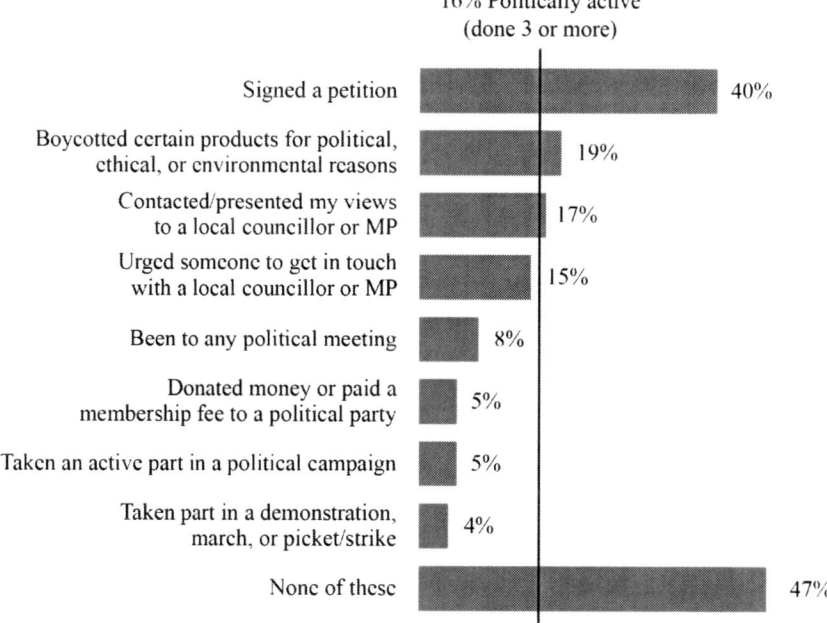

Figure 2.1   Selected percentages of forms of political activity among GB citizens from the 2010 Hansard Audit of Political Engagement. *Source*: 2010 Hansard Audit of Political Engagement.

eschew formal political processes might not even qualify as 'active'. While this might be partly attributable to the historical bias towards governmental systems as the more 'legitimate' avenues of participation, it also reflects more practical methodological constraints: voting and membership are easily stud-ied quantitatively, whereas the more amorphous and evolving world of social movements is harder to integrate into these sorts of measurements.

What these measurements do at least capture is the large proportion of citizens' inactivity in electoral and civic forms of politics. Hansard usefully distinguishes between different types of non/underactive citizens, including 'detached cynics' (17 per cent of British adults), 'disengaged/mistrustful' (24 per cent), 'bored/apathetic' (8 per cent) and 'alienated/hostile' (9 per cent). These categories are calculated using respondents' knowledge of electoral politics, participation, and sense of 'civic duty'. The high percentage points of the first two categories in particular echoes concerns raised by Hay (2007) about citizens' dissatisfaction with the *quality* of politics on offer. Explana-tions for this include governments' separation of public debate and private decision-making (Gripsrud, 2002), which also relates to critiques of parties' preference for delivering image above content to the voting public (Hay, 2007; Cunningham and Lavalette, 2004; Henn et al., 2002).

Although one might be wary of extrapolating too much from these catego-ries without the support of qualitative data, they nevertheless represent useful ideal types which go beyond simple participant/non-participant distinctions. Of particular interest are the categories that indicate engagement *without* participation, as the issue is not so much the valuing of politics than the inability or unwillingness to convert this into political action (at least accord-ing to the survey's definition). In their study of interest groups, Jordan and Maloney (2006; 2007) identify a similar intersection called the 'concerned, unmobilised'. Drawing on the same survey as Pattie et al. (2004), they found that only a third of respondents who felt strongly about environmental politics were members of environmental organisations (Jordan and Maloney, 2007: 37). Some questioned the efficacy of such memberships, though others may instead have lacked certain pathways or resources to become more active and consequently remained 'unconverted'.

MEASURING YOUTH PARTICIPATION

One of the most common findings from political participation surveys is that young people are more disconnected from politics than any other age group. This can manifest itself in a number of ways, with 18- to 24-year-olds found to be less active (Hansard, 2010), less interested in formal politics (Heath and Park, 1997), and less likely to identify with any particular party (Furlong and

Cartmel, 2012). This has led to (or perhaps reinforced) political commentators' portrayal of contemporary youth as an 'apathy generation' (Hiscock, 2001) who 'plug in, recharge their batteries, and bop along giving not a damn about the burning world around them' (Agger, 2009: 49). To understand the causes of such trends requires a careful avoidance of such normative depictions, not least as there are problems disentangling specific generational or cohort properties from more regular 'lifecycle' effects.

Despite these concerns, survey research by Henn et al. (2002) indicates that the majority of young people discuss politics with their friends and family at least some of the time. A follow-up study by Henn and Foard (2012) supports these findings, with two-thirds claiming to have some interest in politics. This calls into question the notion that youth non-participation in formal politics is synonymous with apathy: certainly, as Eden and Roker (2000) point out, one can be cynical and engaged at the same time. Moreover, it raises the question of how political engagement is measured: Marsh et al. (2007) argue that the inflexibility of many surveys to incorporate new repertoires of participation (especially online) is likely to affect young people's results the most, particularly those below the voting age. Henn et al. (2002) agree, arguing that surveys presuppose a common understanding between researcher and respondent, allowing for the reproduction of certain assumptions about what politics *should* mean, regardless of their applicability to all cleavages in contemporary society.

Interestingly, Hansard's 2009 audit reports that younger people (18–24) are more enthusiastic about the effectiveness of 'campaigning' (broadly defined) than other age groups: 57 per cent see it as effective, compared with the overall average of 47 per cent. This creates a contradiction between young people's attitude towards activism, and their apparent qualifications as activists: nearly half of 18- to 24-year-olds have signed a petition and the majority are enthusiastic about the efficacy of campaigning, yet they are apparently less active than any other age group. This raises the question that if young people are broadly receptive to activism, what are they doing exactly?

Drawing on data from the 2002 European Social Survey, Norris (2003) concludes that young people are increasingly favouring 'cause-oriented' styles of politics. This is distinct from 'citizen-oriented' actions in that they are as likely to target corporations and communities into enacting change as they are to governments. Bang (2004: 14) takes this further, claiming that contemporary young activists are more interested in enhancing their capacities for *self-governance* and *co-governance* than 'submitting themselves to an abstract social norm or mode of state citizenship'. In this sense, political identity is acquired through being 'ordinarily engaged in the construction of networks and locales for the political governance of the social', making them 'everyday makers' of politics (Ibid.: 26). Significantly, this entails a political engagement more on individuals' own terms: unlike the consistent, long-term commitments of party membership, everyday makers are more likely to switch their engagement on and off depending on their own personal interests and availabilities. This emphasis on flexibility and short-termism not only runs parallel to the greater demands for mobility in the labour market but also complements Bauman's (2000) observation that individualisation has transformed identity from a given into a 'task'.

Young people's apparent disconnection from formal politics is understandably an issue of concern for politicians and officials, who fear that this attitude will persist as they progress through their adult lives. Yet, as Howker and Malik (2010) argue, contemporary British youth have much to be concerned with when it comes to their material interests. Whereas the so-called 'baby boomers' were well placed to prosper from post-war opportunities such as free university education, affordable housing, and the services of a burgeoning welfare state, Howker and Malik argue that today's youth have become 'lab-rats in a decades-long economic experiment' of neo-liberal policy (2010: 76). They depict a 'jilted generation' of young men and women burdened by student debt, their earning opportunities stunted by a depressed and risk-conscious employment market, and ultimately expected to make up the difference in public sector costs as their parents' generation grows older.

Less clear, however, is the extent to which these grievances translate into a measurable 'generational consciousness'. In their survey data, Henn and Foard (2012) find that British youth are especially concerned with issues related to the economy, education funding, and unemployment. Furlong and Cartmel (2012) find similar results, but note also that the political concerns of so-called 'Generation Y' are not particularly different from older generations. Certainly, it is clear from both surveys that young people are untrusting of politicians and cynical towards the efficacy of the democratic process. This can be seen as rooted in experience as much as perception, with Marsh et al. (2007) noting how young people have tended to be treated more as 'political apprentices' than citizens in their own right. Kimberlee (2002) traces the growing marginalisation of youth access in UK political parties, noting the scaling down of the major parties' youth wings, as well as the sharp decline in parliamentary candidates under the age of 30. Roberts and Sachdev (1996) point to parties' reluctance to target young people electorally as it runs the risk of alienating their larger and more reliable core of older voters. Marsh et al. (2007: 117) also note how attempts to bring youth back into the political process – such as the Young People's Parliament model – are based on a didactic model of participation that possess little or no binding effect on policymakers.

In the UK, perhaps the most prominent recent example of state attempts to enhance youth political engagement concerns the introduction of compulsory citizenship classes in secondary schools. Despite the Government-commissioned Crick Report's recommendation that classes should promote 'political engagement' and 'concern for the common good', Cunningham and Lavalette (2004) argued that the citizenship curriculum instead prioritised civic duty and obedience. This distinction was made all the more manifest by the fact that the classes were introduced around the same time as Britain's decision to support the United States and invade Iraq in 2003. Protest against the war was large in scale and reach across the world, though in the UK protests became notable for their youth involvement: according to journalist Libby Brooks, the protests featured 'the most significant child-led campaign for a century' as 'schoolchildren as young as 10 walked out of their classrooms to attend what were, for most, their first political demonstrations' (Brooks, 2003; quoted in Cunningham and Lavalette, 2004: 259–260). While Cunningham and Lavalette's interviews with school protest participants suggested that they were 'showing an awareness of international issues and events' and a 'concern for the common good' as originally envisaged by the Crick Report, they found that local authorities and teacher associations tended to view the protests instead as a disciplinary issue.

In summary, youth political participation is subject to life-cycle effects, generational effects, and also broader trends and attitudes that transcend age groupings. All of these impact on how we might measure youth participation. There is evidence to suggest that part of the reason young people appear disconnected from formal politics is that they are afforded very little attention from government and policymakers, whereas research by Bang (2004) and Marsh et al. (2007) indicates that young people are less likely to perform well in participation surveys because they favour a cause-oriented politics that does not necessarily conform to consistent, repeatable forms of civic engagement. Many of these activities fall under the moniker of activism, which as noted earlier remains a form of politics underrepresented in large-scale participation surveys. This necessitates further investigation of the different types of social movement participation, what impact they have, and the social context that surrounds them.

SOCIAL MOVEMENT REPERTOIRES: COSTS, RISKS, AND EFFICACIES

Protest might be the most obvious form of social movement participation, but not all forms of social movement participation necessarily qualify as an act of protest. The basic objective of protest is to give what Tilly (2004) calls 'WUNC displays', that is, displays of worthiness, unity, numbers, and commitment directed at holders of power and influence (or society more generally). This obviously requires *protesters*, and though it is common for organisers to set themselves mobilisation targets, one should be wary of automatically equating size with success. It is not necessary, for example, that all three million Greenpeace members take part in the shutting down of a power station for the protest to be considered successful. For a whole host of reasons, protest rarely attracts anything close to a 100 per cent turnout of its sympathetic public, although the inability to do so is seldom used to explain a protest's failure. Of course, ensuring and increasing protest turnout is undoubtedly extremely important to its success, but participation recruitment should ultimately be seen as a means to an end rather than an end in itself.

To successfully mobilise a suitable number of participants, protest usually requires organisers with the knowledge, skills, and resources for planning and publicising an event and defining its political purpose. This is certainly the view of social movement scholars associated with 'political process theory': Tilly (2004), for example, argues that social movement campaigns are often the work of 'social movement entrepreneurs', for example individuals or small groups who identify issues or grievances in need of public attention, synthesise ideas, and deploy them in a way that can stimulate social and political change. As this illustrates, social movement participation is more than just protesting, though the precise nature of 'leadership' and 'organising' roles varies greatly according to a group's structure. In certain cases, a group's founder(s) might become its de facto leader(s) via a central committee, whereas others might seek to disperse power democratically throughout its participants, with decision-making decided upon by vote or consensus (Pickerill and Chatterton, 2006). This impacts on how an individual might be expected to participate more generally: it may involve holding an elected position, playing an active part in consensus meetings, or simply being willing to muck in with various aspects of day-to-day organisation.

It should also be noted that most political groups do not expect equal participation from all members. Not all prospective participants necessarily have the same time and resources to devote to activism, and so must choose ways of participating to suit their own 'biographical availability', that is, personal constraints that 'may increase the costs and risks of movement participation, such as full-time employment, marriage, and family responsibilities' (McAdam, 1986: 70). This is easier when protest campaigns offer a range of protest repertoires, though differences in how individuals participate may become problematic when they are seen by some as reflecting differences in *commitment*. This is more likely to cause tension among participants in smaller groups where social ties and affinities are strong, as they tend to rely more on the regular participation of core members for the group to continue. Moreover, as Crossley (2007: 228) observes, 'High density tends to produce trust', and consequently conflict may arise if certain individuals are judged to have compromised this trust in some way.

A further source of potential tension comes from variability in the *length of time* individuals are prepared to devote to participating in an activist group. 'Participation' might of course entail a single, one-off act of protest, or it might amount to an entire activist 'career'. While attracting dedicated participants might be less of a concern for campaigns that have a relatively brief lifespan, social movement groups and organisations tend to think in the long term. This usually reflects the enduring nature of campaigning issues – the identity politics of gender, race, and sexuality; global concerns such as poverty, war, and the environment; and the ebb and flow of partisan politics is not going to go away anytime soon – and so groups seek to recruit participants that will help build or maintain a group's stake as a mobilising and influencing force.

So what might social movement participants actually *do*? McAdam (1986) offers a useful starting point with his distinction between activism repertoires which are low or high in cost and risk. Cost refers to the 'expenditures of time, money and energy that are required of a person engaged in any particular form of activism', and risk refers to the 'anticipated dangers – whether legal, social, physical, financial, and so forth – of engaging in a particular type of activity' (McAdam, 1986: 67). Such distinctions are obviously useful, but categorising activism repertoires according to these measurements raises the important question of context, especially in relation to risk: for example, in most cases signing a public petition will be low risk given the lack of immediate physical interaction involved, but such actions might prove dangerous in the long run if one is living in certain political contexts (such as totalitarian states, or to use McAdam's own example, the United States at the height of McCarthyism).

The examples of high- and low-cost/risk participation shown in table 2.1 are presented as extreme ideal types. Tarrow (1995: 98) notes how the more 'confrontational' and 'violent' forms of protest tend to be higher in cost and risk, and consequently harder to mobilise large numbers for. Low-cost/risk forms of participation, on the other hand, tend to be more 'conventional' in character and attract large numbers more easily – a trend that is reflected in the participation percentages shown earlier in figure 2.1. Of course, there are many forms of participation not included in table 2.1 that might shift according to context or sit somewhere in between, such as attending demonstrations, giving speeches, or participating in vigils.

Given their long-standing popularity among student activists, it is useful to focus on two established protest repertoires – demonstrations and occupations/sit-ins – and consider when and why they might be used by activists. Demonstrations are perhaps the most commonly recognised protest

Table 2.1   Examples of high- and low-cost/risk social movement participation in a generalised Western context

High-cost/risk participation	Low-cost/risk participation
Leading/organising a protest	Signing a petition
Direct action (e.g. shutting down a meeting)	Writing a letter
Taking part in a strike	Boycotting consumer products/ethical shopping
Staging an occupation/sit-in	'Liking' a political campaign/group on Facebook
Hacking/distributing classified information	Joining a social movement organisation

repertoire. As Tilly (1976; 1995) argues, the idea of taking to the streets to make collective claims has existed for thousands of years, though the modern demonstration of organising public marches to protest on behalf of a specific grievance has its roots in eighteenth- and nineteenth-century Europe. Demonstrations became more frequent during the interwar years of the twentieth century, and later gained widespread prominence in the civil rights, student, and anti-war protests of the 1960s, a prominence enhanced by the growth of mass media news coverage, which often gave demonstrations a real-time *mediated* (as well as physical) audience. According to Meyer and Tarrow (1998: 4), public demonstrations have now become a 'perpetual element in modern life', a point exemplified by the fact in many countries they are now written into state law and policed accordingly (see also McCarthy and McPhail, 1998).

Using Casquete's (2006: 47) definition, a demonstration is 'a collective gathering in a public space whose aim is to exert political, social, and/or cultural influence on authorities, public opinion and participants through the disciplined and peaceful expression of an opinion or demand'. In this sense, demonstrations embody Tilly's 'WUNC display' very clearly. Demonstrations do not really seek to achieve their aims through the *act* of demonstrating: rather, their power depends on their visibility, mediation, and symbolic salience to force *others* – usually institutions of authority, or society itself – into meeting their demands. Moreover, finding oneself surrounded by a multitude of like-minded people may provide separate 'process' benefits to demonstrating, both strategically – participants having opportunities to sign up to campaign mailing lists and gain new activism contacts – and emotionally insofar as that protesting can be exciting, empowering, and fun (Jasper, 1997: 197).

When considering the cost of participating in a demonstration, one should acknowledge that demonstrations are a diverse tactic and certain cases will demand more from participants than others. In general, though, demonstration participation takes time out of one's day, requires a certain amount of physical exertion, and obliges its participants to physically identify themselves with the cause in question. In the latter case, it should be noted that the cause may also end up identifying *them*, since the visibility of their actions might result in activists having to defend their beliefs and actions to others. Beyond these basics, however, the potential for increased costs and risks depends on a range of factors, including where and when the demonstration is taking place, the extent to which the demonstration co-operates with police provision, the contentiousness of the issue, the numbers of participants involved, and even the weather conditions on the day. Nor are risks and costs necessarily dependent on *how* one participates in the demonstration: large, uncontrolled demonstrations with too much or too little police provision may become intimidating and dangerous places to be, whereas small, carefully organised, and peaceful rallies might in contrast demand relatively little from participants.

If the goals of demonstrations ultimately depend on their ability to pressurise others to meet demands, the goals of occupations are more closely tied to the *process* of protesting (Pickerill and Chatterton, 2006; Hopkins et al., 2011). Put simply, occupations are predicated on a desire to physically reclaim space and, in so doing, remind authorities or society at large of the power of individual agency. Although there are numerous different types of occupations, they tend to recall one of two distinct protest traditions (and sometimes both). The first is the *occupation-as-strike*, which draws on the history of labour movements and is thus predominantly demands based, for example calling for better pay or working conditions. Combined as they often are with strikes and walkouts, the taking of the space becomes a bargaining tool, that is, 'we are not leaving until you do *this*', and consequently locations are chosen on the basis of their capacity to disrupt the normal running and output of the organisation. Historical examples of this include the Alfa Romeo car plant occupation in Milan in 1920, the UAW Flint Sit-Down Strike in Michigan in the 1930s, as well as student sit-ins to protest against separate male and female dormitories at UK universities in the 1960s (Mason, 2008: 249–250; Fine, 1965; Crouch, 1970).

The second tradition is *occupation-as-camp*, which takes a more long-term, communal approach to claiming space. These are seldom framed by demands placed on *others*, but are arguably more politically ambitious through their desire to build 'futures in the present' (Pickerill and Chatterton, 2006). In practice, this may involve practising alternative democratic systems, living according to certain moral and ethical ideals, or experimenting with autonomous and sustainable lifestyles 'between the cracks of capitalism' (Holloway, 2010). The liminality of these spaces can transform the consciousness of its participants, as they create opportunities to 'meet, build trust and develop shared goals and strategies' free from the constraints of mainstream society (Schein, 2012: 337) and thereby build a 'revolution from below'.

Camp occupations can take place in a range of different locations: those requiring little more than planning and discussion spaces may choose to occupy empty buildings as de facto squats, whereas occupations targeting specific locations with a view of shutting down certain facilities and activities in the process are more resolutely protest oriented. Examples of this include Faslane and Greenham Common anti-war camps in the 1980s (McKay, 1996), and the Camp for Climate Action, which took place at numerous UK power station sites in the late 2000s (Saunders, 2010). More recently, the occupation repertoire has been used for occupying public spaces to visualise the 'emancipatory possibilities' of new political subjectivities, as evidenced in citizens' occupation of Tahrir Square in Egypt, which later inspired Occupy Wall Street and the subsequent global Occupy movement (Kerton, 2012; Pickerill and Krinsky, 2012; Graeber, 2013). Although not a new tactic (Tiananmen Square in 1989 being perhaps the most notable historical example), public square occupations have succeeded in giving radical politics a great deal of coverage, evoking Lefebvre's (1996) formulation of citizens' 'right to a city' in a manner that through their global mediation dramatises ideals of autonomy and agency in ways that might otherwise go unnoticed.

Occupations can be considered high-cost/risk due to the time, energy, and commitment they generally demand from participants to establish and maintain camps, especially when under the threat of forced eviction or arrest. These costs and risks might deter some from getting involved, but participation can also produce an 'affective commitment' among members which encourages continued participation (Klandermans, 1997). In contrast, *low*-cost/risk participation tends to be more individualistic in character. Although not best suited to demonstrating protest commitment, activities such as petitions, coordinated letter-writing campaigns, or social movement organisation (SMO) memberships can provide quick and efficient displays of support for a cause through what Della Porta and Diani (2006: 171) call 'the logic of numbers'. Alternatively, repertoires such as wearing badges, consumer boycotts, and ethical shopping can be useful for raising awareness of an issue, promoting a cause or campaign, or helping to challenge certain everyday practices and assumptions.

In many ways, petitions have much in common with demonstrations, as much of their traction derives from the ability to provide evidence of the *scale* of public feeling. Unlike demonstrations, however, petitions are an object that can be physically handed over to a target. Through such actions, petitions can function as effective snap polls, which expose democratic deficits in an authority's decision-making. Power often comes from the speed and the scale of the response; whereas demonstrations typically require time to organise, petitions can mobilise more people into registering their views without them having to do so simultaneously (see Kaldor, 2000: 112). Petitions also have a clarity and sincerity in which their purpose can be articulated – whereas demonstrations can sometimes become receptacles for multiple groups campaigning with different aims, the aims of a petition are usually fixed and clearly stated from the outset, giving signatories a clear, collective focus.

ONLINE ACTIVISM: CREATING NEW REPERTOIRES?

Much of the discussion so far has centred on repertoires conducted 'offline'. Until recently, this distinction would be of little significance, but there is mounting evidence to suggest that a fair amount of political consumption, debate, and action now take place online – particularly among young people (Banaji and Buckingham, 2012; Coleman and Blumler, 2009; Anduiza et al., 2009). Broadly speaking, the Internet has three main uses for activists: as a means of organisation, a means of producing and consuming information, and as a field for political action. Increasingly, however, distinguishing between these uses has become difficult, especially since the advent of the user-as-producer world of 'Web 2.0' (Hands, 2011). This section focuses on online repertoires of protest, including repertoires of 'communication power' (Castells, 2009), which arguably blur the lines of media production and protest participation.

To begin, one should acknowledge the significance of the Internet for increasing the reach of existing protest repertoires. Perhaps the most prominent example of this is the e-petition. E-petitions are capable of speeding up the process of petitioning while reducing organising costs, enabling them to be created and distributed with such speed that they can provide almost immediate feedback to an issue of concern as it unfolds. These attributes are borne out in recent research data: for example, the Oxford Internet Survey found that between 2007 and 2011 the percentage of people who had signed an online petition doubled to 14 per cent, whereas those doing so offline fell from 20 to 18 per cent (Dutton and Blank, 2011).

The proliferation of e-petitions is aided by the fact that they can be built using freely available multi-access software. In recent years, however, e-petitions have also become useful tools for bringing multi-participatory citizenship into the governmental process: Adams et al. (2005) note how Scottish Parliament pioneered the use of e-petitions by integrating them into the political process via a Public Petitions Committee, who screens and forwards them to relevant departments. This initiative was then introduced by the UK Government in 2006, with the attached promise that petitions with over 100,000 signatories would be debated in Parliament. By 2012, its website had received over eight million signatures from over five million unique email addresses (Hale et al., 2012). Similar to this initiative are online groups and pages on the social networking site Facebook, where users are invited to register their support by joining or 'liking' them. Although primarily used to distribute information and invitations to offline protest events, the act of 'liking' a politics page has begun to gain significance through its capacity to generate eye-catching numbers. Each of the main UK political parties now has its own official Facebook page, with figures usually matching their own formal party memberships (Bartlett et al., 2013).

More expressive forms of online activism have emerged since the advent of 'Web 2.0', broadly defined as 'the proliferation of user-created content and websites specifically built as frameworks for the sharing of information and for social networking, and platforms for self-expression' (Hands, 2011: 79). Web 2.0 represents a significant step in the rise of what Castells (2007; 2009) calls 'communication power', which has emerged from the exponential increase in peer-to-peer communications technology usage, from mobile phones to Wi-Fi networks, and now serves as a platform for individuals to produce forms of 'counter-power' via social networking, blogging, and file sharing. Counter-power emerges from the establishing of new norms of interaction – particularly among young people – as online platforms provide network access on a global scale for users to find forms of information they wish to receive and engage with like-minded people (Nah et al., 2006; Bennett, 2008; Theocharis, 2012).

Web 2.0 is capable of creating spectacles through mass actions. Campaign groups encourage social media users to attach logos to their avatar in much the same way as they might wear a campaign badge, though arguably the more powerful repertoires emerge spontaneously. Most notably, activists can generate mass actions through the distribution of Twitter hashtags or 'memes' – videos, photographs, and quotations – which are then shared and adapted by other users. This process of 'going viral' reflects the blurring of user and content provider so central to Web 2.0. Its creation of so-called 'prosumers' has transformed media consumption to the extent that institutional, mainstream media increasingly looks to independent content providers for its information: either as smartphone-equipped 'monitorial citizens' who act as 'witnesses at the scene' (Banaji and Buckingham, 2012: 168) or as 'participatory journalists' (Deuze, 2003).

There is some debate as to whether social media production is a facilitator to protest, or a form of protest in itself. Certainly, it has long been part of the *culture* of protest, from the Walter Benjamin-inspired proliferation of radical 'zines' in the 1960s and 1970s, to the autonomist 'be the media' sloganeering of the alter-globalisation movement in the 1990s (Lievrouw, 2011). It is clear that participatory journalism has a political objective within the media itself – namely, providing first-hand accounts of events otherwise ignored or given one-sided coverage – but its efficacy as a form of protest in its own right is more questionable. It can clearly 'raise awareness' and influence public opinion into taking action, but taken in isolation participatory journalism is perhaps overly dependent on a Habermasian faith in the potential of online communication networks to operate as a newly virtualised public sphere, facilitating the free distribution of information and ultimately enabling the better argument to come out on top.

VALUING PARTICIPATION: ACTIVISM OR SLACKTIVISM?

Questions about the purpose of certain protest repertoires can easily lead to debates over what constitutes 'good' or 'effective' activism. Although social movement scholars try to avoid such judgements, attempts to measure protest repertoires in terms of the costs and risks they demand from participants can be easily misconstrued as reflecting a normative protest 'value'. For example, high-cost/risk repertoires are usually practised by groups and movements who advocate a hitherto-marginalised politics, necessitating more radical and eye-catching ways of garnering attention. Because of the commitment involved, participants might make value judgements on groups and individuals who appear less committed than themselves (e.g. Saunders, 2008: 247). On the flipside, Bobel (2007) found in his interviews with feminist group members that some felt they had failed to live up to the 'perfect standard' of participation as practised by others, and consequently felt self-conscious about self-defining as 'activists'.

If high-cost/risk participants brood about whether their involvement reaches these perfect standards, those involved in predominantly low-cost/risk participation are sometimes questioned about whether their activities constitute activism at all. For mobilising agencies such as Avaaz.org, which deal mostly in petitions and coordinated template letter-writing campaigns, low-cost/risk activism is considered both efficacious in its own right, and important for mobilising individuals who do not have the time or resources to be more physically active (Patel, 2007). This defence is questioned by Morozov (2009), who claims that these repertoires have a more nefarious effect, namely creating the *illusion* of having a more valuable impact while reducing motivations to engage in higher-cost/risk (and thereby more effective) forms. In other words, 'slacktivism' promises all the glory and personal satisfaction of social movement participation, but with none of the engagement, endeavour, or responsibility that should come with it. Furthermore, authors such as Putnam (2000) and Gladwell (2010) argue that low-cost/risk forms of activism on their own are too individualised and non-committal to build the necessary strong social ties that are integral to successful campaign groups and social movements in the long term.

Of course, low-cost/risk repertoires have their limitations. Social media campaigns such as KONY2012 are arguably geared more towards kick-starting a wider debate than achieving activism goals on their own (Madianou, 2013). E-petitions, on the other hand, generally work best when targeting an achievable goal and have a particular audience in mind. This is not to say petitions cannot be deployed for the 'big issues': as the alter-globalisation and Occupy movements have demonstrated, petitions can operate as a useful auxiliary to other, more high-cost/risk repertoires (Della Porta and Diani, 2006: 165). They can help illustrate a population's broader support and solidarity for activists engaged in high-cost forms of protest, as well as enable individuals unable to physically take part to register their support in a meaningful way. 'Slacktivist' arguments also imply that low- and high-cost/risk participation is a zero-sum relationship, meaning that individuals who 'like' a cause on Facebook automatically feel extricated from the need to attend demonstrations and suchlike. This, however, makes the dubious assumption that both are subject to equivalent recruitment processes. The issue of *mobilisation*, and the context through which individuals are invited to participate, is a key focus for the next section.

THEORISING POLITICAL MOBILISATION

Explaining *how* people might come to participate is a separate question to explaining *why* people participate – after all, most activists will likely state that they share a movement's grievances and wish to help it achieve its goals. Yet sharing grievances is not necessarily enough to inspire individuals into participating. Given that social movements require collective action, explaining how people participate requires studying mobilisation processes. This might be self-determined (where groups of actors collectively decide to do something) or it might be brought about via invitations and call-outs from existing political agencies. Approaches to mobilisation cover a variety of different fields of research, though each is worthy of discussion here for their variety of theoretical and empirical approaches, as well as how they conceptualise non-participation.

Rational Action Theories

The first major approach to explaining political mobilisation draws on economic theories of voter and citizen behaviour in US political science in the 1960s, most notably Olson's (1965) theory of collective action. Olson firmly held the view that mobilisation was not a natural or spontaneous process for individuals. Rather, members 'will not act to advance their common or group objectives unless there is *coercion* to force them to do so, or some *separate incentive* distinct from the achievement of the common or group interest, is offered to the members of the group individually' (Olson, 1965: 2, original emphasis). Whereas the former stimulus referred to action determined by belonging to dense social collectives such as trade unions, the latter opened up a more cynical aspect of mobilisation: that, assuming a group is likely to be successful in achieving its goals, an individual's incentive to participate is *reduced*. This is because his or her contribution is not vital to the group achieving its objectives, nor does it promise any cost-benefit value beyond those derived from the group's objectives, which are likely to be achieved anyway. In this context, the rational choice is to *not* participate and 'free-ride' on the group's successes.

Olson's theory is useful for understanding mobilisation strategies employed by political agencies that in the pursuit of consistently high membership strategies clearly have incentives of their own. However, its theorisation of *individual* participation has been criticised for employing a fixed definition of rationality which disregards the specificity of a group's aims, strategies, and repertoires. Participation might also appear rational for reasons other than the realising of explicit political goals, including more intangible social or moral benefits. Moreover, Olson's depiction of the decision *not* to act has little grounding in any sort of social and cultural context. As Crossley (2008) argues, the theory assumes that people only participate on the condition of equal involvement, which might not be necessary or relevant to a movement's organisation. Additionally, participating actors may not have the resources to make an 'equal' contribution to the group's activities.

An attempt to provide a more relational context to the individualistic drives depicted by Olson can be found in resource mobilisation theory (McCarthy and Zald, 1977). It takes the view that contentious politics is really played out by those who are the most socially *connected* rather than disaffected, given that most people sympathetic to a cause seldom convert this into sustained action. This again places the onus on mobilising agencies for explaining participation. Groups and campaigns advertise events through the production and distribution of flyers, leaflets, posters, or news articles so as to access a critical mass of individuals, some of whom might be predisposed to take part. Acts of protest, too, may serve partially as means of recruitment, attracting intrigued onlookers who though conversation with activists and/or receiving leaflets might feel like getting involved.

The argument put forward here is that mobilising agencies seek to present joining their group or campaign as the rational choice for politically minded individuals who are unsure of how best to act. This approach succeeds in opening up mobilisation as a two-way relationship, but like Olson's theory, it implies a process divorced from any social or cultural context such as

biographical availability or information access. Recalling the earlier discussion of online activism repertoires, it is also questionable how relevant
this theory is to a new, more networked context where social movement
entrepreneurship is less dependent on professionalised mobilising agencies.
Furthermore, mobilisation is also depicted mechanically and even cynically,
assuming that the likelihood of mobilisation is somehow *calculable* – a view
not necessarily applicable to all protest repertoires.

Attempts to provide a more nuanced definition of rationality can be found
in Verba and Nie's theory of 'civic voluntarism' (Verba and Nie, 1972;
Verba et al., 1995). This theory identifies three factors that account for political mobilisation and non-mobilisation. First, access to resources (defined as
time, money, and skills) determines whether an individual is *available* to
participate. Second, psychological factors related to the individual's sense of
political efficacy determine whether he or she *wants* to participate. Third, formal and informal recruitment networks – be they social networks of friends,
family, and colleagues, or the recruitment strategies of political agencies –
determine whether he or she has been *asked* to join. The core idea of this
model, therefore, is that resources facilitating participation are the product of
social structures of class and education, and that individuals in possession of
these resources are more likely to participate. This model is convincing insofar as socio-economic status broadly correlates to levels of political participation, with high-status individuals over-represented in the category of very
active participants (Verba and Nie, 1972: 131–133). However, as Pattie et al.
(2004) point out, using socio-economic status as a predictor of participation
and civic values fails to explain why large numbers of high-status individuals
also do not participate in politics. Moreover, the theory does not account for
why countries with higher educational rates do not have consistently higher
civic participation and voter turnout. In other words, political engagement
requires explanation beyond the economic capital of participants.

To counter this 'incomplete mechanism', Whiteley and Seyd (2002) adapt
Verba and Nie's approach to account for multiple incentives to political participation. This incorporates both tangible and intangible benefits. Whatever
the achievability of a campaign's collective goals, an individual might also
be mobilised via the promise of selective incentives, which refers to the benefits he or she might receive as a consequence of participating. These come
in two forms. On the one hand, *process incentives* are incentives derived
from participation itself, such as entertainment or catharsis (Opp, 1990).
Outcome incentives, on the other hand, relate to motives concerned with
achieving specific private goals, such as advancing career prospects. In both
cases, selective incentives may be drawn from a basic social desire to meet
new people and forge new meaningful relationships independently of a campaign's political goals.

In sum, rational incentive models are undoubtedly useful for expounding the many non-material benefits individuals might gain from political participation, but successive authors' efforts to incorporate more sociological factors arguably reveal fundamental limitations with the concept of rationality itself. In each approach, there remains an assumption that individuals consciously choose whether to participate or not from the options presented to them. As noted by Marsh et al. (2007), this presupposes politics as an identifiable 'arena' that one consciously enters into (along with an awareness of, and respect for, the rules of the game), rather than as an evolving, multifaceted *lived* experience. This arguably reflects the theory's case bias towards electoral politics: unlike parties or civic agencies, social movements are often more fluid and unpredictable. Participation comes in many different forms, making participatory incentives difficult to predict, especially in newly formed movements. This fluidity and unpredictability is perhaps more easily captured in alternative mobilisation theories.

Emotional Cognition Theories

In general, rational choice perspectives have little to say about the mobilising power of political issues themselves – after all, if grievances alone explained participation, there would be no such thing as non-conversion. Authors such as Gamson (1992), Jasper (1997), and Goodwin et al. (2001) have argued for the need to look deeper at how certain grievances might generate particular emotional responses that become significant for mobilising individuals into taking action. To clarify the relationship between emotion and mobilisation, Jasper (2006) adapts Giddens's (1991) distinction between practical consciousness, discursive consciousness, and the unconscious. Whereas the first relates to reflexive thought and action, the other two are more instinctive and harder to articulate. Jasper's key argument here is that emotions originate not singularly from the discursive level (as is perhaps assumed in rational choice approaches), or the unconscious level (as found in Freudian psychology), but from *all three* levels, often simultaneously.

Furthering his argument, Jasper claims that this produces a range of different emotional responses – urges, moods, reflexes – but it is *moral* emotions that are of most interest here. These often arise out of individuals' reactions to and beliefs about the world we live in: a sort of 'moral habitus' that we carry around with ourselves and add to through experience. Emotions play to our internalised sense of reason and justice, and these 'moral shocks' can lead to action. According to Gamson (1992: 32), this is because moral emotions provide 'the righteous anger that puts fire in the belly and iron in the soul'. Moreover, acting according to one's own moral code (especially in the face of opposition) 'feels good *directly*' (Jasper, 2006: 167, original emphasis).

In contrast, those who do not perceive pleasures and satisfaction in such actions, or perhaps have a more distant engagement with such moral emotions, are less likely to mobilise.

Emotions do not only come into play through individual responses to events; they can also be used as a mobilisation device by social movement groups to appeal to individuals' sense of morality, particularly when the intended audience is not materially affected (Goodwin and Jasper, 2006). Emotions can also be used to sustain participation through forging relations of solidarity and trust among activists, along with the enjoyment, pride, and sense of identity one might gain through belonging to certain activism cultures. As Jasper (1997: 220) asserts, 'Virtually all the pleasures that humans derive from social life are found in protest movements: a sense of community and identity; ongoing companionship and bonds with others; the variety and challenge of conversation, co-operation and competition'.

Using emotions alone to explain mobilisation leaves some discernible gaps, creating opportunities for it to be used in tandem with other approaches. First, more needs to be said about the role of *knowledge* in emotional and discursive engagement with a political issue. Converting initial moral outrage into action often entails a deliberation process that opens up a multitude of further choices: Does one choose to participate in the first available opportunity presented to them, or do they consider other options? If participation becomes a question of choice, by what criteria is this decision made? Echoing the arguments of Morozov (2011) and Putnam (2000), low-cost/risk participation often has the reach and the resources to get to the front of the queue when individuals are seeking opportunities to convert their moral outrage into action: Does this represent the most effective form of participation, or simply the most accessible? Deciding which form of participation might be a daunting task, especially where certain choices are high in cost and risk. Consequently, the acquisition of knowledge to decide on the best form of action can be a never-ending process: unless one makes a leap of faith, one can end up doing precisely nothing.

As this suggests, emotions can also have a *demobilising* effect on potential activists. Political issues worthy of our attention might create feelings of helplessness, guilt, insecurity, anxiety, and fear – negative emotions which may not necessarily be resolved by any of the available choices for action. This is especially prevalent in political issues that do not lend themselves easily to goal-oriented campaigning – Norgaard (2006), for example, found in her study of non-participation in climate change activism in Norway that negative emotions were often *collectively* managed by individuals through certain shared narratives. This is because of the significant social gap between emotional cognition and political action, making emotions 'deeply embedded in and reflective of social structure and culture' (Norgaard, 2006: 379).

An example of this was citizens' use of 'selective attention strategies' to negotiate anxieties over climate change. For some, this involved engaging in certain environmentally friendly activities so as to at least be seen to be doing *something*. For others, even face-saving acts of tokenism represented a leap of faith too far, preferring instead to 'protect themselves' emotionally by controlling their exposure to information on climate change. Others adopted a 'perspectival selectivity' to deflect personal responsibility in favour of narratives that express either an individual's powerlessness to effect meaningful change (i.e. 'my participation doesn't make a difference, so why bother') or the supposed neglect and culpability of others (i.e. 'we might not be perfect, but *they* are far worse').

Certainly, the act of protest involves putting oneself politically 'out there', and this commitment has consequences for how individuals choose to present themselves publically. The desire to maintain favourable images of the self in front of others recalls the social psychology of impression management (Goffman, 1971), which, in the case of politics, can work both ways – in some contexts, political participation can be viewed extremely positively, as individuals' desires to act upon their moral code might draw admiration from others. In other contexts, however, political participation may prove more troublesome. If, as Bauman (2000) claims, identity has become a 'task', then political identities are 'stickier' – demanding greater commitment from owners – than the floating, flexible, and short-term 'consumer identities' he identifies in *Liquid Modernity*. This, of course, remains context dependent, and Eliasoph's (1998) study of the American Buffalo community illustrates how in fields where narratives of apathy dominate, the idea of being politically active invites ridicule rather than admiration:

> Buffaloes ... equated citizen involvement in toxics, disarmament, and foreign policy with 'protesting', which meant 'carrying a sign', 'standing out in a parking lot with a sign', 'wearing sandals': making a fool of oneself, ineffectually standing out in the middle of nowhere. People who think they can have an effect on politics are fools, who are puffing themselves up – and that would seriously violate country-westerners' political etiquette. (Eliasoph, 1998: 135)

In sum, it can be argued that emotions are an important and often-overlooked raw material for explaining social movement mobilisation and demobilisation. This raises important questions about expectations of efficacy in political campaigns, as well as how apathy is socially produced. Nevertheless, converting instinctive emotional responses into collective action (or inaction) requires broader cultural contextualisation, which returns us to the social level. For this reason, discussion of mobilisation theories will close on two final themes: theories of collective identification and theories of mobilisation fields and networks.

Collective Identification Theories

In the theoretical approaches discussed so far, the concept of 'collective identity' exists as an assumed byproduct of other processes than one possessing its own explanatory power. Although not strictly a theory of mobilisation, authors such as Klandermans (1997) posit that identity functions as an important bridge between grievance and agency. Collective identification approaches draw on social psychology, particularly theories of symbolic interaction: Melucci (1988), for example, argues that political ends and means are decided collectively by actors, which involves considering the limits and possibilities provided by the environment in which they find themselves. From this, a sense of the collective 'we' is produced. At a strategic level, this determines the goals and repertoires a movement might adopt, and at an interactional level it initiates a collective evolution in the beliefs, norms, and attitudes of its participants. It is out of these social, strategic, and emotional experiences among participants that a sense of *collective identity* can be produced, which helps to strengthen and sustain movements beyond their initial mobilisation.

There is some disagreement among scholars as to the significance of collective identity in social movement studies. Typically, collective identity refers to both social and practical relationships in the present, though Polletta and Jasper (2001) extend this to also include shared *imaginaries*. It is also unclear whether the concept should be applied at a group or movement level. Certainly, Melucci (1996), Klandermans (1992), and Diani (1992) are all of the view that a stronger collective identity produces a stronger and more productive group. However, beyond a basic shared interest, collective identity is more difficult to apply at a *movement* level, as individual groups and networks might feature significant ideological, organisational, and tactical variation (Saunders, 2008). Furthermore, McDonald (2002) claims that anarchist networks associated with the alter-globalisation movement reject the principle of collective identity as infringing on activists' individual autonomy. Consequently, collective identity is produced not by its interpersonal relationships but by its actions – a distinction that might also be true for many protest camps.

While McDonald's refutes notions of collective identity for its perceived political uniformity, the visibility and importance of a group's actions (especially direct actions) may still operate as a necessary part of a collective identity *product*. According to Snow (2001: 4), this can act as 'a powerful impetus to collective action', and 'the constructed social object to which the movements' protagonists, adversaries, and audience(s) respond'. A good example of this would be Occupy Wall Street, which positioned the occupation tactic as a central part of its protest identity. This identity was then adopted by copycat camps across the world, helping inspire a global Occupy movement (Gitlin, 2013). As this suggests, collective identity products may also be co-produced by actors *outside* of the initial movement – be they political allies, opponents, or the media – though this raises the possibility of a semantic struggle over what a movement's collective identity 'product' should look like.

It can also be argued that McDonald's emphasis on individual activist autonomy does not necessarily refute Melucci's (1988) depiction of collective identity as the *outcome* of a group's interpersonal connections and shared experiences. Although not necessarily integral to the group's overall decision-making, occupations and protest camps benefit from building relationships of mutual trust, respect, and commitment between participants. Moreover, even while upholding a strong sense of individual autonomy, Saunders's (2008) research indicates that groups may still coalesce around certain related social activities and cultural 'lifestyles'. In this sense, they are not dissimilar from the 'shared meanings, experiences and reciprocal emotional ties' which Flesher Fominaya (2010: 397) sees as defining outcome-based group collective identities. Exploring this further arguably requires a closer analysis of the nature of these interactions, especially when considering how product and outcome collective identities might facilitate (or prevent) mobilisation. This is the subject of the final theoretical approach.

Field and Network Theories

This discussion draws on two interrelated approaches to studying social movement participation. The first is Crossley's (2002) adaptation of Bourdieu's (1977) theory of practice to bring concepts of habitus and field into social movement analysis, and the second concerns Diani and McAdam's (2003) efforts to combine a unified theory and method of social networks. Although possessing different theoretical backgrounds, both are ultimately trying to achieve the same thing, namely a microstructural approach to social movement mobilisation. Bourdieu's theory holds that individuals make themselves in response to the conditions they find themselves in, and become characterised by the knowledge and dispositions they acquire and the concrete preferences they make. This reflects the interaction and negotiation of one's personal 'habitus' – the ongoing acquisition of schemas, interests, and dispositions that inform our social instincts – and the particular fields we enter, which have their own norms and hierarchies of knowledge and behaviour.

Applied to social movements, Crossley (2003) argues that this proposes an intuitive rather than rational basis for mobilisation, with individuals acting according to what feels appropriate personally and socially. Being an activist therefore requires a 'radical habitus' which is acquired through sustained engagement with activism fields. There are two significant points here. First, the theory places important emphasis on the *process* of acquiring an activist identity or disposition. One does not become an activist simply by choosing to be one – he or she is expected to acquire distinct forms of political knowledge (why one is supporting a cause, and the ideals behind it), the social and cultural capital that generate opportunities to participate, and the practical knowledge and experience of participating. Second, the theory highlights the *embeddedness* of social agents, with choices, priorities, and opportunities framed by the fields and networks they belong to. These help develop an individual's 'cognitive toolkit' through the everyday resources they are exposed to, be they conversations, books, or social activities (Passy and Monsch, 2014). This directly challenges the rational choice assumption that decision-making processes are highly individualistic, while breaking down activism mobilisation opportunities to a more interactional, microstructural level.

For many activists, embeddedness in activism fields has its roots in their family and upbringing, enabling politics to become part of their habitus at the earliest stages. Key family relations are sustained by what Putnam (2000: 23) calls *bonding* social capital. This is the 'sociological superglue' that maintains a degree of stability and conformity through members' adherence to shared values and practices. For example, Coles (1986) observes how children learn about the political world through the experiences and attitudes of their parents and family. Political socialisation can develop in various ways: in their life-course study of youth activist leaders from the 1960s, Braungart and Braungart (1990) found that most had followed the political direction of their parents' politics, albeit in different ways and to different degrees. Some reflected on the influence of their early exposure to activism through parents taking them picketing, whereas for others a more general inspiration came from activism having played a part in their family history. In other words, be it an early familiarity with political texts and ideologies, the emotional inheritance of a family political history, or the practical experiences gained through participating in protest activities, political socialisation equips activists with a habitus that gives them a head start for acquiring activism opportunities later in life.

Of course, there is a need to explain mobilisation beyond simple cultural reproduction, and this is where social networks come to the fore. Complementing Putnam's (2000) bonding social capital is the concept of *bridging* social capital. This draws on what Granovetter (1973) famously called 'the strength of weak ties'. These ties offer scope for individuals to take advantage of new social opportunities and thereby develop a broader range of interests and resources not provided by his or her immediate social circle. In this way, bridging capital is vital for those from non-political backgrounds to develop a political socialisation via means other than family.

Network ties – both strong and weak – are important for converting predisposition into action. A good illustration of this is found in McAdam's (1986) study of the conditions that facilitated high-cost/risk participation in the 1964 Freedom Summer project. McAdam argued that applicants were more likely to take part if they already had memberships with other political organisations, had prior activism experience, and knew other people involved in the project. This places greater emphasis on the social costs of decision-making, where fulfilling social obligations and expectations might initially seem more important than the politics of the issue itself. McAdam found that applicants with personal links, a political background, and prior experience of activism were better equipped to perceive and prepare for participation, especially when it is high-cost/risk. In contrast, those without such attributes were more inclined to lose their nerve and withdraw their application, which, given their lack of social ties, carried less of a social burden of 'letting the side down'. This case study led McAdam to theorise a model of recruitment for high-cost/risk activism (see figure 2.2).

Although individuals already equipped with an activist habitus via family socialisation might be fast-tracked through this recruitment process, McAdam's model is useful for visualising the paths (and barriers) to activism mobilisation, as well as how participants develop into committed activists. Contemporaneous studies indicated that this model could be applied more

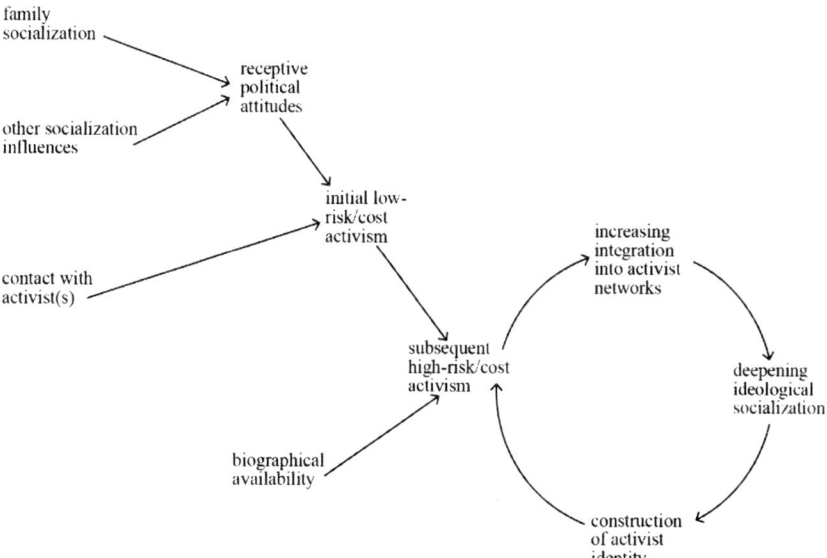

Figure 2.2 McAdam's (1986) model of recruitment to high-cost/risk activism.
Source: American Journal of Sociology.

widely: in their research on Italian environmental activists, Diani and Lodi (1988) calculated that 78 per cent had been recruited through private or associational networks, a finding supported in similar work carried out by Della Porta (1988). Nevertheless, scholars have pointed out potential weaknesses in McAdam's model, notably that the recruitment process appears to exist in isolation from other networks. The network properties of an individual's 'biographical availability' also warranted further exploration. This led McAdam to qualify his position somewhat by arguing that commitment to a *particular* identity, reinforced by ties to participants, was a stronger predictor of participation than prior organisational involvement on its own (McAdam and Paulsen, 1993).

As noted in the previous discussion, 'outcome' collective identities play a key role in how individual protest networks *sustain* participation and membership. Returning to figure 2.2, high-cost/risk activism enters the participant into a cycle of network integration, which increases the chances of deepening ideological socialisation and identification, leading to further participation. From a network perspective, this entails the accumulation and strengthening of ties with other activists while simultaneously diluting the effect of non-network ties that might discourage activism. Consequently, the overall network becomes *denser* as individual ties strengthen, producing relations of trust which set the foundation for further acts of high-cost/risk participation (Crossley, 2003; 2007) and deterring members from leaving (McPherson et al., 1992). Dense networks clearly have their advantages for building and sustaining movements, but they also carry risks if networks start to operate as 'cliques'. For example, Saunders (2008) found in her study of radical environmental groups that networks can incorporate unspoken social dynamics – such as informal hierarchies and language choices – which help maintain group relationships and boundaries. These elements add up to a form of bonding capital as per Putnam's definition, though this might make a group seem inaccessible to newcomers.

Network approaches can also explain aspects of non-participation. First, a primary socialisation that pays little or no attention to politics, or perceives social movement activism to be illegitimate or dangerous, is likely to discourage individuals from participating unless they encounter weak ties promising otherwise. Second, individuals with political interests but no network context through which to participate might find it difficult to seek out protest opportunities, and if they do, the experience of protesting alone might seem boring or alienating (McAdam, 1986). Moreover, activism participation draws on knowledge and debate to help form individuals' opinions. Oegema and Klandermans (1994) surveyed individuals in the Netherlands to find whether they planned to sign a national petition against cruise missiles. For those who had expressed an initial willingness to sign but ultimately failed to do so,

Oegema and Klandermans identified two explanations – 'nonconversion' and 'erosion'. The first can be explained by individuals' lack of opportunities to convert their support into action. This might include not being targeted for an organisation's campaign drives, as well as lacking access to networks in which members might discuss the issue and what they might do about it. As a result, the *lack* of social pressure to think or act results in non-conversion. Erosion, on the other hand, might be caused by facing the 'reality' of partici-pation, which might stimulate the sorts of negative emotions described earlier in Norgaard's work. Alternatively, erosion might be the result of network 'cross pressures' where cynics or opponents of the issue might dissuade or discourage individuals from acting upon their original willingness. In other words, participating might cause *too much* social pressure and antagonism, resulting in non-participation appearing the easier option.

In sum, network and field approaches provide a microstructural theory of participation and non-participation where the taking up of protest oppor-tunities is largely dependent on the social circumstances individuals find themselves in. As a method of research, these approaches pose challenges for how networks can be identified as providing greater explanatory power than other variables used to explain mobilisation. This is no easy task, and as Diani (2004) admits, network approaches risk providing tautological analy-sis, especially when using protest case studies. In other words, if one looks for networks in protest groups, it is likely that networks will be found, but this alone does not prove that any causal mechanism. Diani notes that, a bet-ter testing of the theory might be found by looking for cases where activism networks *do not* produce participation. Analysing the network properties of non-participation will be a key theme for the rest of this book.

CONCLUSION

This chapter began by noting how the study of political participation draws on a fractured and messy literature across the social sciences. As the discussion has shown, this is partly reflective of the wide range of activities which may qualify as 'participation' – from writing letters to politicians, to occupying public squares. With this is mind, the range of methodologies employed is somewhat inevitable, though it is still important to avoid ghettoising differ-ent forms of participation analysis as opportunities for critical dialogues and methodological innovations may be lost as a result. Definitions of 'politics' should not be ghettoised in this way either. Certainly in the case of student activism, its grievances, targets and repertoires span electoral and social move-ment politics: in the UK, the role of public funding in most universities serves to underline the fact that student activists are citizens as well as protesters.

It is therefore important to develop a theoretical and methodological framework for understanding student activism: one that best captures how individuals are mobilised for activities typical to the field, while recognising the relationship between formal and informal politics. The relative lack of institutional control in student activism, together with the range of repertoires favoured, renders rational choice approaches largely unsuitable. That said, Whiteley and Seyd's emphasis on selective incentives – particularly of a social nature – are arguably useful for studying student mobilisation, even if the rationalist language of incentives is not. In cases where campaigns and movements are embryonic, sparsely organised, and still unfolding, the manifest goals and outcomes of participation might be difficult to perceive. For this reason, it is important to think about initial triggers to participation, even those that may have little political drive. Conversely, the work of Jasper et al. highlights the importance of emotional responses to political grievances, and actors' almost impulsive desire to convert these feelings into something satisfying and meaningful.

In rejecting individualistic theories, however, these triggers to participation require a wider social context to be properly analysed. For this reason, this book advocates a field and network approach for studying student activism. University campuses are inherently social spaces, and following the work of Crossley (2002; 2008), can be seen as comprising multiple overlapping networks of students. More broadly, campuses may operate as nodes within a broader national (and even international) network of universities. Campus networks coalesce around different groups and societies, which for those of a political nature provide resources and numerous participatory opportunities. Within this context, networks can facilitate the satiation of moral emotions (both online and offline), as well as promoting an image of student activism which may encourage identification and ultimately, participation. As McAdam shows, initial participatory triggers may be followed by further participatory opportunities, which encourage a deeper commitment through the social bonds they create, giving activists access to new experiences, knowledge, and resources. The densely networked context of the university campus also provides such an opportunity to study participation and non-participation side by side.

In taking this approach, further exploration of the essential properties of the campus field is required: the resources it offers, the culture of activism it facilitates and its historical relationship with the wider political process. This will be the focus of the next chapter.

Chapter 3

Student Activism Past and Present

Opportunities, Constraints, and Repertoires of Contention

Student activism has long been a significant form of social movement participation – indeed, its prominence in the 1960s was a key factor in establishing social movements as a field of study through the work of Touraine (1971) and others. Its power owes a great deal to the unique spatial properties of the campus, as well as the lifecycle position of the majority of its students. Consequently, student activists have undertaken significant campaigns and protests over the past 50 years, from the 1968 revolts in Paris to Quebec's mass strikes in 2012. Despite this, the amorphous and transitory nature of the student population restricts their capacity to sustain groups and campaigns across successive cohorts. Moreover, protest campaigns sometimes lead to disputes within this population over who can legitimately speak on behalf of students. As a result, there have been disagreements among scholars over whether even peak periods of protest activity can be understood as the product of an overarching student *movement* (Hanna, 2008; Rootes, 2012; Hensby, 2016b).

Studying the university campus as a field for protest participation requires an understanding of its past. Activism from the 1960s especially has been subject to numerous histories and memoirs, with many reproducing the view that protest in the UK was a poor relation to more dynamic events taking place elsewhere in Europe and the United States. While it is true that UK students were seldom at the forefront of the major student uprisings of the time, recent studies by Hughes (2015) and Hoefferle (2013: 7) have found it to have been a 'vibrant, globally conscious movement with its own unique blend of issues, strategies and theories'. The prominence of protest and activism on UK campuses today consequently owes a great deal to the legacy of student campaigns and actions in the 1960s and 1970s.

This chapter provides a basic overview of the history of student activism in Europe and North America while paying close attention to its development in the UK. It traces the evolution of modern student activism repertoires, including the goals, tactics, and forms of organisation typically employed by students. Building on this, the chapter then considers the state of student activism today, responding in particular to the recent and ongoing expansion and marketisation of higher education. This provides the narrative background for exploring in detail the 2010/11 UK protests against fees and cuts, which will form the basis of the empirical study covered in the following four chapters. Finally, the chapter considers the university campus as a field for activism research. This applies network approaches advocated by McAdam and Crossley et al. to explain how the campus generates participatory opportunities, as well as sustain specific activist cultures. Drawing on the chapter's historical cases, the chapter concludes with an analysis of the strategies and outcomes of student activism, raising the question of what might be considered 'successful' or 'effective' student protest today.

A HISTORY OF STUDENT ACTIVISM IN EUROPE AND NORTH AMERICA

Student protest has existed for as long as there have been students, but as an organised and influential form of political contention student activism is a relatively modern phenomenon. In Europe and North America, student activism tends to be left leaning or liberal in nature, and usually falls into one of two distinct but interrelated traditions (Yettram, 1981; Barker, 2008). The first concerns students as an *interest group*, focusing on political matters related to the university campus and higher education more generally. The second concerns students as de facto *vanguards*, which more often relates to campaign issues that transcend the campus, be they matters of government policy, foreign affairs, or identity politics. Through these campaigns, students have acquired some degree of political significance as an 'incipient intelligentsia', representing society's progressive (if not always appreciated) moral arbiters (Rootes, 1980: 475).

Prior to the Second World War, occurrences of student unrest usually reflected the uneasy birth of universities as institutions, with protests developing out of disputes with a university's townspeople, or from students' dissatisfaction with their social power relative to the administration (Boren, 2001). In certain historical cases – notably the 1848 revolutions in Europe – students played a supporting role in wider political movements, though on some occasions they were also found on the 'reactionary' side (Barker, 2008: 47). The rise of student activism as we recognise today has its roots in the standardisation of the university system in the mid-twentieth century. The integration of universities with government, state, and society formalised the hierarchy of university governance, leaving students cast as too transient a population to warrant a role in decision-making processes. With student numbers increasing both on campus and in wider society, these systemic tensions began to take on broader social properties.

The emergence of the post-war 'baby boomer' generation saw students in the 1960s become increasingly frustrated with the values of its elders, who they considered morally conservative, politically authoritarian, and socially paternalistic. This found expression in a number of ways. In the United States, the civil rights movement became a major campaigning issue on campuses, with students playing a significant role in the 1964 Freedom Summer campaign (McAdam, 1988). This issue, together with growing opposition to the Vietnam War, gained sympathy and support from students in Europe, whose own discontent towards government owed more to a desire for liberation from the traditions and conventions of the university system (Rhoads, 1998; Ellis, 1998). For many on the left, this was also expressed in an ideological shift: inspired by writers such as Herbert Marcuse and E. P. Thompson, students began to favour a more humane 'New Left' politics, which not only broke with the Soviet Marxism of their elders but also recognised students' potential as agents of revolutionary change.

Despite these intellectual stirrings, students' protest tactics during the early 1960s were not especially different to those employed by broader social movements, though their prominence grew steadily on campuses. British students became more familiar with demonstrations through the spread of Campaign for Nuclear Disarmament (CND) branches, and the anti-apartheid movement helped popularise the use of pickets and boycotts. By the mid-1960s, media coverage of the civil rights movement, Berkeley's Free Speech Movement, and the work of Students for a Democratic Society (SDS) in the United States was giving greater visibility to teach-ins, sit-ins, and other forms of nonviolent direct action to a national and international audience.

This steady building reached a sudden and spectacular eruption in May 1968. Student protests in Paris against university authoritarianism forced campus closures, which in turn provoked mass demonstrations, occupations, and radical clashes between students and police. Students gained support from schools, factories, and trade unions, triggering protests and occupations for an increased minimum wage across France. With students and workers united in a nationwide strike against the Government, President Charles De Gaulle – who at this point had fled Paris – was forced to call an election. Although this move would eventually quell revolutionary fervour in France, images of student barricades and police clashes were mediated through internationally televised news across the world. This appealed to students on the New Left in particular, who felt that state repression of provocative, Situationism-inspired protest events would stimulate a revolutionary consciousness among citizens and inspire them to take action in their own countries. The cross-national diffusion of ideas and repertoires saw students play a part in anti-state uprisings in Czechoslovakia (the famous 'Prague Spring') and Yugoslavia, as well as campus-based protests in West Germany, Italy, and the United States throughout 1968 and 1969 (McAdam and Rucht, 1993; Tarrow, 1998; Gordon, 1998; Boren, 2001).

Student activists in the UK also mobilised in large numbers, though protests were generally less violent than their international counterparts (Ellis, 1998). Campaigns during this time were hampered by the lack of organised leadership comparable to the SDS in the United States and West Germany, as the NUS's constitution forbade it taking specific political stands.[1] Nevertheless, this created a vacuum for alternative organisations to mobilise on a range of local, national, and international issues. Students at the LSE, Hull, and Essex organised sit-ins in solidarity with those in Paris, and activists at Hornsey Art School used the international context as a platform to organise their own rights-based protests. National networks such as the Radical Student Alliance (RSA), the Revolutionary Socialist Students' Federation (RSSF), and the Vietnam Solidarity Campaign (VSC) set up branches on campuses across the UK, with the latter helping organise three anti-Vietnam War demonstrations in London's Grosvenor Square between 1967 and 1968.

For many in the UK, student protest was a new and alarming development. The October 1968 Vietnam demonstration drew a crowd of around 100,000 people, but was condemned by the NUS for being led by 'political hooligans' seeking a 'weekend revolution' (Ellis, 1998: 66). To the national press, the rise of activism was characterised as another example of the nefarious influence of 'Americanism' on British youth (Hoefferle, 2013: 205–206). This sidestepped the fact that student activism overseas spoke of a wider politics – namely, opposition to paternalistic authoritarianism and the right to freedom of speech – which British students recognised in their own universities. Such hostility would take its toll, however, and by the end of the 1960s activists' use of increasingly radical tactics was being met with increasingly repressive sanctions. Globally mediated events raised the perceived costs and risks of protest participation, and with students cited in conservative critiques of the 'permissive society', mounting tactical and ideological disputes saw activism organisations such as SDS and RSSF soon fragment (Ibrahim, 2010; Rootes, 2012).

Student activism in Europe and North America consequently lost much of its revolutionary zeal in the 1970s, though it arguably gained greater organisational consolidation through the rise of national and local unions

(Hoefferle, 2013). As a result, students moved from being a 'politically marginalised grouping' to gaining recognition 'as a main constituency in university governance' (Luescher-Mamashela, 2013: 1444). Having amended its constitution in 1969, the NUS would become a key organisational force within UK student politics in the 1970s, co-ordinating national campaigns through its member unions. This helped students make tangible gains on a number of issues, including representation on university governing bodies, modernising campus facilities, and even forcing university divestments in Rhodesian and South African companies.

This period also saw the broadening of students' campaigning interests. Local branches of organisations associated with the burgeoning environmental movement such as Greenpeace and People & Planet became a fixture on many campuses (Rootes, 1997; Hensby et al., 2012), along with groups and societies promoting identity politics such as feminism and gay rights. With female activists often marginalised in male-dominated student groups and unions during the 1960s, the women's liberation movement was significant for establishing women in political leadership roles. Moreover, with women having suffered the worst of universities' *in loco parentis* principle,[2] its campaigns were crucial in fighting paternalistic conventions within universities, as well as raising awareness of feminist politics more generally (Hoefferle, 2013: 191). By the end of the century, gender politics and LGBT activism were arguably as prominent as any campaigning issue on British university campuses.

STUDENT ACTIVISM IN THE TWENTY-FIRST CENTURY

The powerful legacy of student activism in the 1960s and 1970s is perhaps a mixed blessing for students today. On the one hand, achievements from past campaigns can be found on most modern campuses: students are represented on university councils and committees and have access to facilities and support services of a range and standard far beyond those available to the baby boomers. The history of student activism has also helped establish protest as a legitimate part of a student's university experience: most campuses feature a student union with campaigning interests and resources, as well as numerous groups and societies affiliated to political parties and SMOs. On the other hand, its legacy can sometimes be difficult to live up to. Relative latency periods offer opportunities for veteran *soixante-huitards* to lament the 'apathy' of today's students (e.g. Agger, 2009; Spanier, 2008), and whenever student protest achieves a level of public prominence, the mainstream media is prone to hailing the 'return' of student activism or invoking 'the spirit of '68' (Dean, 2016). Comparing generations in this way can be problematic insofar as it risks overlooking students' current grievances, though in seeking to position themselves as part of a historical movement activists are not always averse to drawing these parallels themselves.

Of course, one should not underestimate the 'extraordinary conjunction of demography and social change' that occurred in universities during the 1960s (Rootes, 2012: 4867). This placed a generation of young people at the vanguard of many of the international political struggles of the time – a phenomenon which some authors consider unlikely to be repeated (Anderson, 1999–2000; Rootes, 2012; Ibrahim, 2010). Its declining influence also owes to further transformations in higher education in the intervening years: although in many ways a continuation and acceleration of processes beginning in the 1960s, universities have undergone significant expansion in the past two decades. Today, around 45 per cent of the British age cohort goes to university, compared with 6 per cent in the mid-1960s (Collini, 2012: 28). In the UK and France especially, this expansion has been partly accommodated by the formation of 'new' universities, which were designed to offer a more vocational and business-oriented range of courses.

As well as expanding in number, today's student population is also becoming more heterogeneous. Once the preserve of white, male, and affluent students, government-sponsored widening participation programmes have extended access to higher education for women, ethnic minorities, working class, and older people. This has been complemented by the introduction of part-time and online programmes, making it easier for students to study while living off-campus or working in paid employment. The expansion and internationalisation of degree programmes – particularly at postgraduate level – has also increased the number of overseas students in most universities. Of course, none of these factors impede students' political engagement as such – indeed, they can be seen as helping broaden activists' campaigning portfolio. However, authors such as Klemenčič (2014) have noted that the diversification of the student population challenges long-standing assumptions of a 'common' or 'typical' student experience, making it more difficult to establish a collective student identity, or shared grievances.

Despite this seeming fragmentation, activism and protest continue to play a prominent role on university campuses, as well as contribute to national and international political debates. Students across the world are prominent players in environmental movements, with activists in the UK recently running successful campaigns to force universities into divesting from fossil fuels. Universities have also hosted groups affiliated to the Free Palestine movement – notably through the international group SJP – and were responsible for a high-profile network of campus occupations in the UK and North America in 2008. Students also continue to promote forms of identity politics, and have campaigned in recent years on transgender rights, the legacy of colonialism (notably the 'Rhodes Must Fall' campaign in South Africa and the UK), legal protection for sex workers, and the elimination of 'rape culture' on campus.

Many of these identity-based causes have more recently fed into activists' advocacy of a 'safer spaces' policy, which typically sets ground rules against forms of discrimination while promoting inclusivity and respect for individuals' physical and emotional boundaries. In practical terms, this involves identifying instances of symbolic violence (or 'micro-aggressions') and promoting the use of 'trigger warnings' in advance of sensitive content. The policy has its roots in protest camps and LGBT groups, but more recently has been extended to apply to the campus as a whole. This has generated a number of controversial incidents, notably the 'Halloween costume drama' at Yale (see Friedersdorf, 2015), and numerous protests in the UK against invited speakers whose views were seen as violating the safer spaces principle.[3] Variations of 'no-platforming' have existed in student activism since the 1960s – witness the sustained picketing of speeches on British campuses by Conservative MP Enoch Powell – but critics have claimed that its more recent application has morphed into a form of censorship, with damaging consequences for free speech on campus (see Lukianoff and Haidt, 2015; Dunt, 2015; Williams, 2016).

While some of these actions have a divisive effect on the student community, one grievance that continues to speak to the majority is the cost of studying. Tuition policies vary considerably across Europe and North America: universities in France and Germany, for example, charge only nominal fees, whereas graduates from private institutions in the United States can incur debts of up to $60,000. Fees are only one part of the picture, however. The legacy of the 2007/8 global financial crisis and resultant 'austerity agenda' of many governments has disproportionately affected young people, as the depression of graduate-level employment opportunities and rising rents, together with the demands of fee repayment programmes, have left many students resigned to a career mostly spent 'in the red' (Howker and Malik, 2010; Giroux, 2013; Graeber, 2013).

Rising student debt is also symptomatic of the effective retrenchment of the state from higher education funding across Europe and North America (Giroux, 2013; Klemenčič, 2014). This trend towards 'marketisation' is geared to driving up standards in all universities, reflected in the rise of senior management structures and quality assurance schemes, as well as the professionalisation of student services. In this context, students are effectively repositioned as 'consumers' of higher education, encouraged to choose which dispenser offers the best service and value for money. This has major consequences for how activism is organised, as the student voice within universities is increasingly co-opted into forms of consumer feedback, such as the survey-based 'satisfaction' metrics which feature in league tables and assessment frameworks. Studies by Klemenčič (2012) and Brooks et al. (2014) also find that student unions are increasingly governed by an unelected, non-student senior management team. This has led some authors to voice concerns over the 'domestication of the student voice', with unions' campaigning agenda marginalised in favour of consumer-focused service provision (Morley, 2003; Williams, 2013).

Despite this seemingly bleak prognosis, students across the world have not been deterred from organising large-scale protests against higher education costs. Admittedly, these tend to fall into sporadic cycles of defensive campaigning, with mass mobilisations occurring when funding conditions are about to be made appreciably worse. These protests have at least benefitted from their relevance to the wider political context of the global financial crisis and austerity politics, enabling students to foreground *generational* grievances in a fashion arguably not seen since the 1960s. Debt and funding protests have occurred on varying scales in Canada, Chile, the United States, New Zealand, the Republic of Ireland, and South Africa in recent years, but it is the 2010/11 UK protests that form the key empirical focus of this book. The following discussion explores this case study in more detail.

FEES, DEBT, AND RESISTANCE: THE 2010/11 UK PROTESTS

Students in the UK have witnessed one of the most dramatic transformations in higher education funding policy, evolving in less than 20 years from a system of government-paid tuition and maintenance grants to £9,000 tuition fees and 30-year loan repayment programmes. As a case study of contemporary student participation and non-participation, the 2010/11 protests require a basic framework for identifying its grievances, goals, and repertoires of contention. To this end, it is useful to consider the protests as the product of a 'collective action frame' (Snow et al., 1986; Gamson, 1992; Tarrow, 1992; Klandermans, 1997). Although its application varies across social movement studies, a collective action frame can be broadly defined as 'a set of action-oriented beliefs and meanings that inspire and legitimate social movement activities and campaigns' (Gamson, 1992: 7). Collective action frames consist of three key components: feelings of injustice, a construction of identity, and the emergence of agency. These components shall be used to unpack the case study.

Higher Education Funding and Injustice

Since the late 1990s, university funding for students in the UK – and specifically, in England[4] – has provided a regular cycle of grievances with each new round of legislation. This can be divided into three distinct phases. Until 1998, university education was funded by a 'block grant' from government, with students granted maintenance costs during study. In the 1980s and 1990s, this funding block was slowly reduced by successive governments while at the same time university participation doubled (Collini, 2012: 105). In 1997, the Conservative Government-commissioned Dearing Report recommended the introduction of means-tested tuition fees to help universities cover their increasing costs. This was acted upon the following year, as the newly elected Labour Government introduced upfront tuition fees of a maximum £1,000 per year and replaced maintenance grants with government loans to be repaid as a percentage of income following graduation. These reforms chimed with Labour's desire to see 50 per cent of young adults going into higher education in the next century, but critics such as Barr and Crawford (1998: 81) voiced concerns that introducing fees and saddling students with long-term debt would put off students from poorer backgrounds.

The second policy phase began in 2003, when the Labour Government announced proposals for 'variable fees' with a maximum figure of £3,000 per year (indexed to inflation). Unlike before, fees would now be paid after graduation via an expansion of the student loans repayment scheme, with repayment deferred until graduates' annual income exceeded £15,000. While these proposals brought extra income to universities, this again came from students rather than the state. Admittedly, students no longer had to pay fees upfront and outstanding payments were to be written off after 25 years, but the increase nevertheless represented a controversial policy U-turn on Labour's 2001 election manifesto. The bill passed by a majority of only seven MPs in 2004 and the new system was introduced in the 2006/7 academic year. Despite the promise of variable fees with universities encouraged to 'compete on price', all universities almost immediately elected to charge the maximum amount (Collini, 2012: 106).

Built into the 2004 legislation was the instruction that the £3,000 fee cap would be independently reviewed after three years. This paved the way to a third policy phase. In the wake of the global financial crisis, the Department for Business, Innovation and Skills (a telling departmental shift) announced plans to develop a more 'entrepreneurial' higher education sector that was less dependent on public funding. This led to the commissioning of the Browne Review in November 2009, which was tasked with designing a sustainable system of financing higher education while continuing to meet demand for undergraduate education (McGettigan, 2013: 20). Its final report was published in October 2010 and recommended the abolition of the cap on tuition fees, allowing universities to set their own costs (subject to a progressive levy issued by government). Repayments were pushed back to once graduates were earning over £21,000 per year. In addition, it argued for the removal of direct public funding for arts, humanities, and social science degrees.

Much of the thinking behind the Browne Review centred on a desire to 'put students at the heart of the system' (Department for Business, Innovation & Skills, 2011), and that by linking funding directly to performance, universities would be incentivised into ensuring that their courses offered strong employment returns and value for money. The newly elected Conservative-Liberal Democrat Coalition Government accepted the recommendations to abolish direct funding for non-STEM subjects and alter the terms for graduate fee repayment, but it rejected the levy system in favour of increasing the current cap on fees to a maximum £9,000 per year for undergraduates commencing study in 2012/13.[5] The Government was able to quickly secure a parliamentary vote on the bill which, again, passed with a marginal majority – this time by 21 votes.

It was later revealed that research commissioned for the Browne Review (but excluded from the final report) found that most students and parents believed the state should pay at least half the cost of higher education because 'the personal benefits were seen by many to match the benefits of society' (THES, quoted in McGettigan, 2013: 21). As it turned out, Government funding cuts amounted to £3 billion, with the University and College Union (UCU) predicting that universities with a strong humanities profile could lose as much as 96 per cent of their current teaching budget (*The Guardian*, 20 October 2010). These reforms were not necessarily unforeseen – after all, the Browne Review had been commissioned in 2009 – but shock was felt in the speed which legislation was passed. In using secondary legislation from the 2004 bill, the Government was able to hold a 'snap vote' in Parliament without publishing a White Paper beforehand. This gave little time for the vagaries of the proposals to be teased out and debated in public, leaving staff and students unsure 'just what had been won and lost' (McGettigan, 2013: 21).

As an overall issue of grievance, the 2010 reforms represented for many people a violation of their *moral* principles (Klandermans, 1997; Ibrahim, 2011). This related to the role and responsibility of the state as funders of higher education, with NUS president Aaron Porter arguing that its reforms amounted to it 'effectively pulling out of higher education altogether' (NUS, 2010b). This centred especially on the notion of *fairness*: whereas Government policymakers had received their own university education for free, English graduates from 2015 onwards would incur debts of up to £27,000 from fees alone (plus maintenance loan repayments and interest). Moreover, higher education campaigners once again feared that long-term student debt would put people from poorer backgrounds off choosing seemingly devalued degrees in the arts, humanities, and social sciences, or even studying at university altogether.[6]

Creating Identity: Students, First-Time Voters, and the 'Jilted Generation'

To convert these grievances into collective action, it is necessary for some sense of *identity* to develop among its affected population. As we saw in the last chapter, identity is a contested concept in social movement studies, though for collective action frames it need only refer to the transformation of grievances into a collective sense of 'them' and 'us' (Klandermans, 1997: 41). Students already possess the foundations of a collective identity by virtue of their shared status as students and their political representation via unions, but this is restricted by constant cohort turnover and the growing heterogeneity of students' social and study lives. In more practical terms, governments invariably post-date higher education reform to take effect after the current cohort has graduated, thereby limiting the extent to which activists can appeal to specific personal or material grievances.

Of course, large numbers of students *did* protest in 2010/11. Ibrahim (2011: 415–416) argues that this is because a sufficient number of students considered the Government's reforms 'morally out of alignment with what is fair'. As students, most would have felt well placed to judge whether £9,000 represented an acceptable amount to charge, as well as debate questions of 'value' in higher education more generally. While this falls under Gamson's definition of a moral grievance, its mobilising power was limited by the fact that students' own education costs were not directly affected. Despite this, however, many students in 2010 were motivated into protesting because of a separate-but-related grievance of their own. As junior coalition partners co-responsible for translating the Browne Review's recommendations into policy, Nick Clegg's Liberal Democrats found themselves in an invidious position of their own making: in the run-up to the 2010 general election, the party had taken the bold step of publically opposing any increase in university tuition fees, and even pledging in their manifesto to abolish fees altogether if elected to government.

With university fees and funding polling consistently high among young people's concerns (Henn and Foard, 2012), the Liberal Democrats hoped taking a free education position would build a strong electoral base for the party among first-time voters (Furlong and Cartmel, 2012; Sanderson-Nash, 2011). Consequently, the party's election broadcasts drew attention to Labour's 'broken promises' over tuition fee increases, and Clegg made regular visits to university campuses to generate support. Along with 400 Liberal Democrat candidates, Clegg also signed the NUS's pledge to vote against any rise in tuition fees in the next Parliament (NUS, 2010a). When the 2010 election result produced no majority victory, the subsequent formation of a coalition government between the Liberal Democrats and David Cameron's Conservatives suddenly placed the Liberal Democrats' pledge in a new light. Clegg's decision to reverse his party's original policy on fees consequently represented a 'suddenly-imposed grievance' (Klandermans, 1997: 38) for the first-time voters who had only recently been swayed by the party's youth-friendly electoral campaign.[7] For the NUS and higher education campaign groups, students' sense of anger and betrayal became a resource for mobilisation, evidenced in the number of protests taking place outside Liberal Democrat party offices in autumn 2010 and activists' subversion of the party's 'broken promises' electoral rhetoric in their campaigns (see Channel 4, 2010).

If higher fees and cuts appealed to many students' sense of 'moral economy' (Ibrahim, 2011) and the Liberal Democrats' policy U-turn to their sense of betrayal, it proved easy to find connections between the two. Key to the Government's rhetoric surrounding education reforms was the perceived necessity of widespread public sector cuts to help reduce the state's structural deficit following the global financial crisis. For many students, it was hard not to feel that the Government's austerity programme was making them pay for a crisis that they had not caused, thereby lending credibility to the construction of 'them' and 'us' in generational terms. Howker and Malik's (2010) polemic 'Jilted Generation' placed student funding into a broader narrative in which the baby boomers had benefitted from the post-war expansion of the welfare state, whereas today's young people were left with escalating welfare costs, a housing shortage, and high unemployment. Similar arguments were also put forward by journalist Paul Mason (2012), who claimed that the graduates of 2012 were unique for being the first in the post-war era to expect to grow up poorer than their parents.

Protest and Making History: The Possibility of Agency

It should be clear that students drew on a number of grievances to assist constructions of a collective sense of 'us' (as students, Liberal Democrat voters, young people, left wingers) in opposition to 'them' (the Liberal Democrats, the political establishment, the baby boomers, neo-liberals), even if the extent to which this could be aggregated into a single pan-student 'collective identity' is open to debate. Mason's (2011b) characterisation of the London demonstrators as a 'dubstep rebellion' carried clear generational properties, as did Laurie Penny's (2011) describing of students as the 'generation that was sold out'. Others, however, saw this as a media-friendly narrative that ignored the fact that austerity politics had not only transcended generational divides, but also affected students in different ways: Gilbert (Gilbert and Aitchison, 2012), for instance, argued that activists' focus on fees reflected a loss of 'middle-class privilege' that did not resonate with poorer students already faced with a reality of long-term debt repayment.[8]

What is undeniable, however, is that collective grievance was converted into collective action, as between 2010 and 2011 students protested in large numbers using a range of different repertoires. According to Klandermans (1997: 18), it is through collective action that individuals may experience a sense of *agency*, which equips them with a belief that their actions have the power to transform social and political conditions. Of course, getting individuals to convert grievance into participation can be difficult: while many might accept the importance (even the duty) of collective action, this does not necessarily translate into a sense of efficacy. Mobilisations are more easily built around specific grievances or structural opportunities, which may include changes in policy and the political environment, evidence of sympathy and support from certain elite political figures, or the uncovering of divisions and instabilities at state level. Each is capable of giving groups and individuals the necessary 'cognitive liberation' that a successful outcome might be possible (McAdam, 1982).

For the past 20 years, UK student activists from successive cohorts have sought to generate a sense of agency by building and sustaining a strong and knowledgeable movement to fight higher education reforms. Its mobilising capabilities were largely dependent on the grievance cycle provided by each new funding proposal, the organisational resources available to activists at this time, and the level of political unity within the activism community. This was especially problematic in the 1990s, as the NUS was accused of failing to build an effective movement against tuition fees because of its historical ties to the very party – Labour – responsible for introducing them (Boren, 2001; Swain, 2011; Solomon, 2011). This reticence precipitated the formation of the independent Campaign For Free Education (CFE) in 1995, which in its efforts to push NUS into taking a free education position, entered into long-standing struggles to build a 'unity slate' of leftist groups for annual NUS elections.

CFE succeeded in pressurising NUS to become more active on fees campaigning in the early 2000s, and consequently NUS organised national demonstrations in 2000, 2002, and 2003 that each attracted around 20,000 people. Following Parliament's vote to increase fees in January 2004, February 25th saw up to two million staff and students walk out of lectures in protest, along with local rallies taking place across the UK (*The Guardian*, 25 February 2004). The subsequent election of CFE candidate Kat Fletcher as NUS president suggested the beginnings of a more radicalised student movement, but higher education campaigning instead fell back into decline in the late 2000s. CFE dissolved and was succeeded by 'Education Not For Sale' (ENS), which continued to put candidates forward for NUS election. Nevertheless, after holding two poorly attended national demonstrations in 2004 and 2006, NUS dropped its free education doctrine in 2008, citing a need not to 'revert to dogma' of militant left groups in order to debate effectively with government (*The Guardian*, 2 April 2008).

Student campaigning on higher education returned to prominence in 2009, as the commissioning of the Browne Review led to Government announcements that the higher education budget would likely face cuts of more than £500 million after the next election. This caused some universities to make pre-emptive cuts to degree programmes and departments, triggering a number of protest campaigns and campus occupations (Swain, 2011). Early 2010 saw the formation of three new campaign networks: the UCL-based NCAFC, the SWP-affiliated Education Activist Network (EAN), and the Leeds-based Really Open University (ROU), all of which shared information about higher education funding and posted reports on their websites of university teachings and occupations. These groups also helped pressurise NUS into calling a national demonstration for 10 November 2010.

Following the Browne Review's publication in October, student demonstrations and occupations started to appear across the UK. However, it was not until the NUS demonstration – and the attack on Conservative offices at Millbank – that students sensed a moment of true agency (see chapter 1). From this point until the parliamentary vote on 9 December, protests were widespread and frequent in number. Seeking to distance itself from the more radical aspects of the November demonstration, NUS played little part in subsequent actions other than to arrange a 'candlelit vigil' on the eve of the parliamentary vote. In its absence, NCAFC's 'National Walkout and Day of Action' on 24 November saw the participation of 130,000 college and university students across the UK (Solomon, 2011: 15). While some universities were keen to stress the 'peaceful' nature of their chosen activities, others used the day as a springboard for staging campus occupations. By the end of 2010, Palmieri and Solomon (2011: 60) calculated that at least 51 occupations had taken place across the UK, some lasting for more than two weeks.

The overall aim of the protests was to build and sustain enough coverage to pressurise MPs (particularly rebel Liberal Democrats) into voting against the fees bill. Occupations made extensive use of Twitter, Facebook, and Skype to establish online networks through which news and information could be shared and distributed publicly (Theocharis, 2012; Hensby, 2016a), though many soon broadened their political discussions to include critiques of neo-liberal capitalism (Ibrahim, 2011; Salter and Kay, 2011; Hopkins et al., 2011). The protests climaxed with Parliament's vote on the Government's bill on 9 December: an NCAFC and ULU-organised demonstration in London attracted 30,000 participants and featured violent confrontations between protesters and police – especially once news spread that the bill had been passed by Parliament. With the academic term drawing to a close, most campus occupations ended soon after.

By early 2011, the majority of student protest networks had stopped updating their websites, Facebook pages, and Twitter feeds, though activism remained strong at universities threatened with 'local' grievances, such as staff redundancies and course closures. The publication in June of a Government White Paper proposing further marketisation measures to the sector (McGettigan, 2013; Wolfreys, 2011) prompted NCAFC into calling a national demonstration for the autumn. While this demonstration – and the 15 or so occupations which soon followed – struggled to attract the same mass participation and media interest of the year before, student activists were at least able to declare victory when the White Paper was shelved in early 2012 (THES, 24 January 2012). Despite this, activists have continued to campaign against higher education marketisation in the intervening years. As well as reflecting an enduring dissatisfaction with the status quo, they also recognise that the White Paper's shelving represents only a temporary success before the next cycle of higher education funding reform gets under way.

The UK Student Protests in Context: Anti-Austerity Activism and the 'Movement of the Squares'

The student protests may represent the principal case study for this book's analysis, but it is important to place them in a wider context of contemporaneous campaigns and movements, both in the UK and internationally. The years between 2010 and 2013 saw a significant upsurge in protest across the globe, with the Arab Spring revolutions, the Indignados movement in Spain and Greece, and the global Occupy movement coalescing as a distinct 'movement of the squares' contention cycle (Gerbaudo, 2013; Biekart and Fowler, 2013; Kavada, 2015). While implying causal relations between these events and the UK student protests risks overstating the latter's influence, the mediation of the autumn 2010 demonstrations and occupations nevertheless reflected and contributed to a growing sense of agency for many students and citizens in other countries.

Certainly, UK students showed agency in their opposition to austerity politics. The alter-globalisation movement of the 1990s and 2000s had for many years highlighted the damaging effects of capitalist marketisation, but it was the 2007/8 global financial crisis that brought to the fore concerns over neoliberalism and the under-regulated global economy (Gamble, 2009; O'Byrne and Hensby, 2011). With states providing rescue packages and bailouts to keep the global economy afloat, resultant public sector cuts brought the crisis home for most citizens. Although protests had taken place in the UK prior to autumn 2010 (most notably in April 2009 when London hosted the G20 summit), the fees increase represented the first major test of the new Coalition Government and its austerity agenda. The scale and speed in which students mobilised drew the praise of trade union leaders, precipitating a number of public sector strikes and demonstrations throughout 2011. Students played a prominent part in these actions – in particular, the Trades Union Congress (TUC) demonstration in March – as well as sit-ins by anti-tax avoidance network UK Uncut.

The UK protests, together with the Arab Spring and emerging anti-austerity movements in Spain and Greece, also provided added motivation for students in other countries to take action. In Chile, students had grown frustrated with the lack of regulation for its private sector college loans market, and in combination with concerns over the lack of access and democracy, the Confederation of Chilean Students (CONFECH) organised mass demonstrations against the Government in May 2011. The lack of a response triggered Chile's largest protests in 20 years, as students were joined by labour unions, schools, and public sector workers in forcing nationwide strikes and demonstrations (Guzman-Concha, 2012). This was followed in spring 2012 by student protests in Quebec, which achieved mass mobilisation on an even more remarkable scale. With the provincial government proposing a 73 per cent increase in tuition fees over five years, the lack of consultation with students provoked 'the longest and largest student strike in the history of North America' (Hallward, 2012). Whereas in the UK the NUS had distanced itself from protests once they turned radical, the leadership of the Coalition large de l'Association pour une Solidarité Syndicale Étudiante (CLASSE) helped mobilise half of Quebec's student population into participating in the strike, with an estimated 200,000 taking part in the March 22 demonstration. The protests in Quebec ultimately succeeded in forcing a freeze in tuition fees, though the use of radical tactics contributed to students' extending their political critique to include the pernicious effects of neo-liberalism on contemporary youth (Giroux, 2013).

One can identify certain commonalities between the UK student protests and their international counterparts, with the former arguably helping promote certain repertoires of contention to the latter. As we have already seen, occupation camps have their own long history in student activism but UK students' interconnected network of simultaneous occupations arguably helped visualise its power and appeal for a mass audience. They were also notable exponents of social media technologies as a tool for facilitating spontaneous mobilisations, multisite communication networks, and generating 'informational exuberance' (Chadwick, 2012; Theocharis, 2012; Hensby, 2016a). The Arab Spring and Occupy movement were both built around a mediation of public occupation spaces, with the Occupy camps similarly eschewing formal organisational structures in favour of more transparent and consensus-based forms of decision-making (Gerbaudo, 2013; Biekart and Fowler, 2013; Juris, 2012).

In sum, while UK students are rarely cited as contributors to the 'movement of the squares' contention cycle, they were arguably forerunners in recognising the contemporary power of mediating occupation spaces to a national and international audience. Although it is difficult to identify direct causal relations, one can nevertheless claim that they contributed importantly to the cross-national diffusion of the mediated occupation tactic during this cycle. Of course, its initial adoption by students owed a great deal to the spatial properties of the university campus, as well as the dense networks operating within. This is the focus for the chapter's final section.

THE CAMPUS AS A FIELD FOR STUDENT ACTIVISM

Studying *how* students create protest events, build political dispositions and identities, and sustain activism networks requires an understanding of the campus as a field. 'Field' is applied loosely in the Bourdieusian sense to describe a setting in which specific social relations, shared practices, and resources are located. This is both enabling and constraining for student activism, as the campus represents something of a unique social environment. Despite the diversification of the student body in recent years, it remains the case that most undergraduates are at the same point in their life cycle, and live either on or close to the university site. Crossley (2008: 32) also notes that entering university structurally liberates young people from the controlling influence of parental/family ties. While this provides significant opportunities for political mobilisation, the confines of the campus field also restrict the campaigns, tactics, and identities student activism can typically create. Recalling the work of McAdam (1986) and Crossley (2008) from the previous chapter, taking this further requires an understanding how students form social networks on campus.

Nodes, Networks, and Repertoires

Political networks at universities can operate formally and informally. Campuses feature identifiable foci for politically engaged students to find one another, including party branches, campaign groups, as well as the student union. For already-politicised freshers, these foci will often represent a first port of call for meeting like-minded people and furthering his or her political interests (Crossley, 2008; Sherkat and Blocker, 1994). Alternatively, political networks may develop more organically through everyday interactions. Students regularly come into contact with each other through the core collective aspects of university life, be it attending lectures, using study facilities, sharing accommodation, or attending student social events, and this network density drives the formation of countless social, intellectual, and emotional relationships. In this context, the desire among freshers especially to make friends, or try new experiences, may serve as an initial 'selective incentive' for attending protest events.

The scope of participatory opportunities varies by university. Larger campuses are more likely to attract sufficient numbers with minority interests, enabling them to 'form the networks necessary for whatever forms of collective action inspire them' (Crossley and Ibrahim, 2012: 610). As a result, these campuses tend to feature a wider range of political societies, as well as a student union with the resources to fund full-time union sabbatical officers. Van Dyke (1998) claims that this can be self-reproducing, having found that American universities with a history of past activism were four times more likely to host student protest in the 1960s. This, she argued, was attributable to social networks maintained by a critical mass of students, a university's historical reputation for liberal values, the presence of politically active faculty members, and a sufficient number of elite students whose greater self-confidence enabled them to take positions of leadership in student groups. Nor are these trends limited to left-wing activists: Binder and Wood (2012) found that American universities were also inclined to foster the development of particular 'styles' of conservative activism depending on their intake and the groups and societies they typically hosted.

Although the university campus provides unique opportunities for student activism, it also provides unique constraints. The campus's population is in a permanent state of flux, with undergraduates expected to graduate after three or four years, and a new cohort of undergraduates arriving annually. This creates obstacles for political groups and societies wishing to build and sustain skills, resources, and knowledge across cohorts. Biddix and Park (2008) claim that the recent proliferation of online technologies such as websites and mailing lists makes it easier for activism groups and campaigns to overcome 'generational mortality', yet they nevertheless require a steady flow of students willing to take on leadership and organisational roles from those about to graduate.

As this suggests, the agencies responsible for sustaining campaigns across cohorts are a campus's political groups and societies, and its student union. These agencies tend to draw on an established portfolio of repertoires historically associated with student activism, ranging from low-cost/risk activities such as petitioning and leafleting, to more contentious tactics such as sit-ins and pickets. As illustrated by the NUS's role in the UK fees protests, student unions' status as representative and accountable bodies means they tend to favour so-called 'peaceful' actions, often organised in consultation with university management and the police. In contrast, radical repertoires such as occupations, acts of vandalism, and speech disruptions are more likely to be the work of independent groups and networks.

Despite this range of activities, evidence suggests that only a very low proportion of students can ever be mobilised to participate. According to Hoefferle (2013: 204–205), opinion polls carried out in the 1960s and 1970s found that committed activists consisted only of around 1 or 2 per cent of a university's population. Clarke and Egan's (1972: 507–508) study of students at Florida State University found activism to be more widespread, albeit divisible into distinct layers. At its core were student demonstrators who amounted to 22 per cent of the student population (less than a fifth of whom had participated in 'illegal' demonstrations). Outside of this was a layer of 'conventional activists' (19 per cent) engaged in relatively low-cost forms of participation. The majority of students, however, were those categorised as 'politically passive'. Participants also conform to certain demographic trends, with Altbach (1989) and Blackstone and Hadley (1971) finding that committed activists in Britain and the United States were more likely to have a non-religious background, study social science, and have left-leaning parents.

These committed activists form distinct social networks and identities on campus. In their research into activism worlds at the University of Manchester, Crossley and Ibrahim (2012) found that they typically coalesce around certain identifiable foci such as the student union and political societies. While these foci provide the resources for campaigning and protest, the overall surrounding *network* is afforded the greater significance as it operates as a tightly integrated political world where 'information, rumours, resources and directives are likely to pass very quickly around' (Crossley and Ibrahim, 2012: 603). Recalling McAdam's (1986) study, Crossley and Ibrahim (2012: 606) also find that *denser* networks afford greater potential for 'solidarity, support and participation incentives to emerge'. Once established, these networks can become self-sustaining, as they 'facilitate actions, and actions (qua foci) generate networks'. Examples include student activists living together, forming relationships, or co-running societies, all of which helps them keep one another 'in the frame' (Ibid.: 607).

Although densely bonded, these activism networks can also draw in students who are connected in non-political ways – such as housemates, coursemates, friends, and partners. Given the interconnectedness of the wider student population, Crossley (2008: 18) argues that this can create a 'self-perpetuating dynamic of politicisation', where 'new recruits go on to become recruiters'. On the other hand, Crossley and Ibrahim (2012: 608) also concede that networks can sometimes 'become too cohesive for purposes of collective action' and appear inaccessible to newcomers. Research by Hirsch (1990) links network density among activists on campus with the development of a shared ideological commitment, the practising of high-cost/risk protest repertoires, and the collective eschewing of self-interest. Moreover, he finds that the network's collective identity is reinforced by members' social polarisation from the rest of the student population. This suggests that student activism networks are capable of developing subcultural properties comparable to those identified by Saunders (2008), as well as the work of Goffman (1971) and Becker (1991) more generally.

In this context, 'collective identity' refers not to an overarching student movement but rather the shared values of these specific groups and networks. For issues where there is common ground, temporary or long-term coalitions might be formed, enabling activists to pool their collective skills and resources and create large protest events in and around campus. Although strong and productive identities can be forged across a seemingly heterogeneous range of groups, fault lines emerge when members perceive insurmountable philosophical, ethical, or tactical contradictions. This can also entwine with personal conflicts and rivalries, particularly among ideological factions on the left. A good example can be found in Crouch's (1970: 78) reflections on student activism at the LSE in the 1960s. He identifies clear political distinctions between activist 'moderates', who favoured working with the student union to campaign on more manageable goals, and New Left activists who advocated a more radical and spontaneous politics. This resulted in the university's activism network frequently splitting along ideological lines, despite their clear mutuality on many other aspects. Although coalitions could be established for common grievances such as the Vietnam War, conflicts would soon arise over activists' choice of protest tactics (see also Van Dyke, 2003).

Goals and Outcomes

Despite its undoubted mobilising opportunities, the campus field places constraints on the goals and outcomes student activists can realistically pursue. Co-ordinated class walkouts are an important part of their armoury, yet students lack the same capability of unionised workers to withdraw their labour. The politics of their campaigns also affects to whom activists communicate their aims. For campus-based issues such as improving facilities or seeking greater democratic representation, students usually seek to establish channels of communication with their university's senior management. This tends to produce fairly targeted campaigns, with petitions, marches, and occupations promoting a series of specific demands. For protests related to grievances bigger than the campus, however, students recognise the limited agency of individual universities and look to link with students from other universities and appeal to government or the wider public. Be it anti-war or anti-state, the intention here is usually to kick-start or join up with a wider national or international movement.

Due to the aforementioned constraints of cross-cohort campaigns, activist groups are under a certain amount of pressure to cast aside their grander political ideals in favour of goals that might be more achievable in the short term. In many ways, this is a classic social movement dilemma, in which either decision is likely to alienate at least one activist coterie. At the LSE, Crouch (1970) observed that the existentialist maxim that *action should be true to one's ultimate values* resulted in some activists attaching greater value to radical and uncompromising protests which brought disastrous failure than protests with more achievable aims that were partially successful. According to Tarrow (1998: 157), a similar dichotomy precipitated the collapse of the 1960s student movement in the United States. For many activists, the limited efficacy of radical protest tactics (not to mention their participatory costs and risks) hastened a move towards more institutional forms of activism via parties and unions. For the more radical minority, however, the desire to avoid compromising their ultimate values led to the favouring of more violent actions.[9]

In some cases, however, a middle ground can be more immediately sought, as smaller and more achievable goals might serve as a useful conduit for pursing greater outcomes. Recent protests seeking to pressurise universities into banning invited speakers or remove contentious statues (as with the Rhodes Must Fall campaign) may appear tokenistic or even trivial in isolation, yet through the resultant media coverage campaigners hope that such actions will trigger public debates about wider structural issues, be it institutional sexism or the legacy of colonialism. These intended outcomes also exude a symbolic power, as through protesting activists are also seeking to reclaim the campus space as belonging to *students* rather than senior management.

Given the historically low percentage of committed activists on campus, a key objective for most campaigns is to gain the approval of the overall student body. This can provide important leverage when dealing with university management, and so activists will seek evidence of wider support through petitions, lecture boycotts, and motions of support at the student union. This is because in the absence of mass turnout or a union mandate, university management will often challenge the assertion that activists are speaking on behalf of the wider student community and thereby discount their grievances. For issues bigger than the campus – such as anti-war demonstrations – building student support presents slightly different challenges. Crouch (1970) recounts the difficulties activists faced in mobilising against the Vietnam War because many ordinary students struggled to see the relationship between the protests' anti-war goals and the university as a site for protest and recruitment.

Perhaps an even greater challenge, however, is winning over the wider *public* to its views. Rootes's (1980) characterisation of students as an 'incipient intelligentsia' denotes activists' efforts to position themselves as society's de facto *vanguards*, tasked with drawing to public attention hitherto-underappreciated moral grievances. Achieving this depends heavily on protests gaining traction through national and international media coverage. When successful, this can undoubtedly inflate a student campaign's voice far beyond what it is typically capable, thereby providing it with a platform to shape political debate and influence public opinion. Indeed, media discourses around the 'spirit of '68' implies recognition of students' historical capacity to gatecrash the wider political process through provocative and eye-catching campaigns and events. When these provide a new slant on already-prominent news stories, the resultant coverage can be seen to suit the media as well as activists.

Media-centric campaigns carry obvious risks, however. As Gitlin (1981) argues, the media can be a capricious and ephemeral platform for activists to express themselves, especially when it turns on or loses interest in them. Often at the core of this tempestuous relationship is their attraction to covering episodes of protest violence. This has its own long-standing history in social movement politics (Tilly, 1969; Giugni, 1998; Juris, 2005), and as a tactic is usually justified by activists as a form of symbolic resistance against existing forms of oppression. *Deliberate* tactical violence is generally rare in student protest and seldom extends beyond acts of property damage. Somewhat more common is violence as the *outcome* of clashes with police or the escalation of direct action tactics (such as the refusal to leave an occupation). Students in the late 1960s recognised particularly the power of violence as a means of generating media interest: having grown frustrated with the limited gains of peaceful tactics, the mediation of violence had the potential to quickly and directly give student grievances a public platform as well as inspire further protest actions elsewhere.

As a tactic, the use of violence usually requires the portrayal of students as defenceless victims in order to provoke the necessary outrage and sympathy from the wider public. This mediation is notoriously difficult to control, however, as activists can easily be miscast as aggressors, resulting in campaign goals being superseded by lurid characterisations of student hooliganism. The protests against the US invasion of Cambodia at Kent State University in 1970 provide one of the most extreme cases of this: following successive days of radical protest (including police clashes and arson attacks), the National Guard was called onto the campus to disperse crowds. With protesters' refusing to comply, the Guard opened fire, killing four students. The immediate aftermath saw protests on hundreds of campuses across the United States (including deaths under similar circumstances at Jackson State University), yet public opinion erred towards the view that the Guard had acted lawfully.

These episodes also feed into a more general media narrative that students routinely face, namely that their youthful naivety, profligacy, and privilege render them ill-qualified to comment on matters such as war, public policy, or the economy. Furthermore, it is assumed that once students leave the university bubble and become part of the 'real world', their radicalism or idealism will inevitably fade. Of course, former students are not averse to changing their politics later in life, or even recanting their activist youth entirely, but these *ad hominem* portrayals arguably rest on rational choice assumptions that the politics of youth-based movements are somehow a product of self-interest, be it material benefit, egoistic attention seeking, or Bakhtinesque counter-cultural performance. Despite the pervasiveness of this narrative, research by Fendrich and Lovoy (1988) and Sherkat and Blocker (1997) indicate a subtler and more enduring legacy to protest participation among graduates. Both studies found that even moderate, 'run-of-the-mill' student protesters in the 1960s and 1970s remained distinctive in their politics later in life: as well as being more engaged and active than other graduates, their participation appeared to have influenced career, family, and lifestyle choices.

The diffusive influence of politically active graduates in public life has fed into the political process both directly and indirectly. On the one hand, former activist leaders have gone on to become high-profile politicians, be it Peter Hain in the UK or Camila Vallejo in Chile. On the other hand, the more diffusive effects of protest participation identified by Sherkat and Blocker have arguably helped spread greater tolerance and support for many issues in wider society, particularly gender and identity politics. This may fall short of the demands laid out by more radically minded activists, but one can at least contend that the outcomes of student activism should not be limited to the realising of its immediate political goals.

CONCLUSION

This chapter has considered student activism from a range of different angles. It has traced its historical development in the UK and the rest of the world, as well as the legacy it leaves as a form of modern protest. It has also covered the politics and campaigns that make up student activism today, including its relationship to structural and financial transformations in the higher education sector. Finally, it has analysed student activism through the lens of social movement sociology. This involved applying network approaches to explain how students mobilise for protest activities, and also summarising the repertoires and tactics students typically employ in their campaigns.

The chapter has also introduced in detail the narrative and grievances of the 2010/11 UK protests case study. Through this exploration, it is hoped that the commonalities between the case study and broader issues and debates in student activism research have been established. Certainly, the case demonstrates the advantages and disadvantages of students' dual role as a self-representing interest group and society's de facto *vanguards* to wider political issues. For the former, activists appealed to citizens in highlighting the moral grievance of £9,000 fees in a time of austerity to a society where many had received their higher education for free, and asking them to help pressurise Parliament into voting down the fees bill and revise its position on higher education funding. But for more radically minded students, fees and cuts were merely symptomatic of a broader struggle against neo-liberal capitalism, and so were engaged in finding ways of kick-starting a wider movement against the Coalition Government's austerity programme. In this sense, students took the role of de facto *vanguards*.

Also a pervading theme in this chapter is students' general need for specific political opportunities and action frames to achieve mass mobilisation and public interest. In cases where their grievances dovetail with the wider socio-political context, student protest can occupy the forefront of the key political debates of the time. This was the case in the 1960s, with students assuming key roles in civil rights, anti-war, and anti-state protests, as well as more recently through wider anti-austerity movements. Achieving this prominence, however, is largely reliant on gaining media attention, which has sometimes led to students seeking to create provocative and sometimes violent protest events. While these events can give students a public platform, they are also forced into a struggle to control their own image. Often their desire to be seen as progressive provocateurs drawing public attention to hitherto-unnoticed grievances and injustices can be quickly usurped by tabloid characterisations of students as immature yobs or holier-than-thou moralists. With their causes and campaigns often extending beyond the confines of the campus, students are often locked into this catch-22 relationship with the media and public.

Finally, this chapter has provided some important pointers for understanding student activism participation. As with most movements, participation in student activism requires a social context in which moral emotions and identifications are framed and converted into action. In this respect, the dense social networks of the campus are ideal. A network approach can explain the worlds through which identities are shaped and sustained, while generating ways to engage and disrupt, though it may also explain non-participation too. We will take this further in the next chapters.

NOTES

1. During this time the NUS saw itself more as an intermediary between students and government than a campaigning organisation as such. That said, it was able to

take a 'moral' position against South African apartheid, as well as express solidarity with American student civil rights initiatives (see Hoefferle, 2013: 65–68).

2. By way of an illustration, Barker (2008: 45) recounts the story from the early 1960s at the University of Oxford, where a male and female student were disciplined for being found in bed with each other: 'He was suspended for a short period while she was expelled permanently'.

3. An example of this is the repeated no-platforming of feminist author Julie Bindel on UK campuses. Although a long-standing feminist campaigner, her controversial views on transgender rights was deemed by a number of student unions to violate its safer spaces policy.

4. Although the case study's principal grievance concerns higher education funding in England, the field of study concerns the UK as a whole. This is because campus protests in 2010/11 extended to Scotland, Wales, and Northern Ireland. Following state devolution in 1998, higher education reforms have applied differently to the rest of the UK: unaffected by the 2010 reforms, students from Northern Ireland continued to pay annual fees of around £3,500 and Scottish students remained exempt from paying fees altogether (although Scottish universities charge its students from the rest of the UK their own tuition rates). Since the Welsh Assembly holds only secondary legislative powers, universities in Wales were subjected to a 12 per cent cut in government funding, but the assembly agreed to subsidise the fees increase so that its students studying in the UK would not have to pay any higher amount from 2012/13.

5. As was the case in 2004, most universities in England immediately chose to charge the maximum amount.

6. In practice, evidence so far points to a mixed picture. Following an initial dip in university applications, UCAS (2015: 2) reported in 2015 that 18-year-olds from across the UK 'were more likely to apply for higher education than in any previous year'. This owes in part to the work of the Office For Fair Access (OFFA), which stipulates and monitors widening participation schemes and outreach programmes at English universities as a condition of charging the top tuition rate. Despite this, data from the Press Association indicates that the proportion of poorer students has fallen among many of the Russell Group universities in the past ten years (THES, 2016).

7. Nick Clegg would later claim that his party had been prime movers in ensuring that not all of the Browne Review's recommendations were written into the bill, and that it had insisted on a fees cap. In the wider context of the party's sudden and very public change of policy, however, these achievements counted for little.

8. Indeed, some have argued that the bursaries offered to students from low-income backgrounds as part of universities' OFFA agreement have been more successful in reducing university access inequalities than Scotland's free tuition policy, even if English students on average incur more debt overall (see Wigmore, 2015).

9. The most famous (and extreme) examples of this being revolutionary guerrilla organisation the Weather Underground in the United States and the Red Army Faction – also known as the Baader-Meinhof Gang – in West Germany.

Chapter 4

Who Participates?

Patterns of Student Political Engagement and Action

The previous two chapters have demonstrated university campuses' potential as spaces for student politicisation and protest participation. Not only do many boast their own activism history, their dense student networks allow for ideas, information, and activities to be spread throughout its populations. Despite this, recent studies have indicated that young people are becoming increasingly detached from electoral political processes, instead favouring more sporadic and impulsive forms of engagement. This has led some commentators to suggest a turn towards politics by 'alternative' means, but research on contemporary student activism hints at emerging challenges. As noted by Giroux (2013), Brooks et al. (2014), and others, the marketisation of higher education is chipping away at students' openness to the broader benefits of university life, including union involvement and participation in activism and protest.

This necessitates a closer inspection of the basic patterns of contemporary student engagement and participation. As a result, this chapter draws principally on the study's own survey to measure UK students' attitudes and participation in electoral, civic, and activism politics. First, it considers students' political participation in general, drawing comparisons between constructions of a 'participatory ideal' and their participatory practice. This addresses which forms of participation students consider the most efficacious, including their attitudes and experiences of democratic and protest politics. In so doing, one can test some of the claims made by Bang (2004) and Marsh et al. (2007) about young people as cause-driven 'everyday makers' of politics. It will also look in more detail at the relationship between engagement and participation, including how knowledge and discussion informs students' political choices and commitment.

The second aim of this chapter is to identify basic attitudinal and participatory trends related to the 2010/11 student protests against fees and cuts. In focusing on a campaign where students broadly shared the same opportunities to take part, one can highlight some of the key characteristics that separate participants from non-participants. This enables the measuring of the protests' popularity among the overall student population, as well as the activities and repertoires students undertook. These activities and repertoires are then measured according to cost and risk they typically incurred, enabling the creation of distinct participatory categories. These categories will frame analysis in the following chapters.

THE SURVEY DATASET

Before studying students' participatory patterns, it is important to introduce the student survey in more detail. The survey sought to measure student political engagement and participation, both in the protests against fees and cuts, and more generally. In seeking a representative sample of students studying in the UK in the 2011/12 academic year, its scale and scope is unusual compared with previous student surveys. As we saw in chapter 3, these tended to focus on students from one university, and in dating mostly from the late 1960s and 1970s, reflected a smaller population of mostly 'home' undergraduates as was common to the time (e.g. Blackstone and Hadley, 1971; Clarke and Egan, 1972).

The survey was conducted between February and June 2012, and drew on a sample of 22 universities designed to give a broadly representative spread of regions and campus types. The questionnaire was distributed online via university staff forwarding emails to students in their academic departments. These departments were subject to sampling quotas, so that the distribution of degree subjects was broadly in line with statistics for universities in the UK (for a full breakdown of universities and departments and colleges sampled, see Appendix A). Since the research was faced with the paradox of inviting students with little or no interest in politics to participate in a survey about political participation, efforts were made to counter potential selection bias: the email invitation downplayed the questionnaire's political content in favour of its more-inclusive questions about the 'student experience', and completion of the questionnaire was incentivised via a small prize draw.

Because of the nature of this distribution process, response rates were difficult to calculate, but where cohort numbers were available departmental response rates varied between 7 and 15 per cent. Despite these low numbers, the survey achieved 2,485 respondents in total. As shown in table 4.1, the dataset broadly matches overall demographical statistics for universities in

Table 4.1 Students survey demographics compared with UK student population in 2011/12

		% UK Population (N = 2,496,645)	% Survey (N = 2,485)
General	Students (all)	100.0	100.0
	Undergraduates	77.2	79.7
	Postgraduates	22.8	20.3
Sex	Male	43.6	29.9
	Female	56.4	69.4
Domicile	UK	83.0	84.7
	Other EU	5.3	7.8
	Non-EU	12.1	7.4
UK domiciles*	England	84.3	79.4
	Wales	5.8	5.1
	Scotland	7.8	14.0
	Northern Ireland	2.1	0.9
Degree subjects	Sciences	42.0	37.1
	Arts, humanities, and social sciences	58.0	62.9

Note: UK population statistics are taken from HESA (2012). *UK population statistics are taken from first-year enrolment only.

the UK, though one can identify a higher proportion of female students, students studying in Scotland, as well as students from the arts, humanities, and social sciences. As a robustness check, survey analysis was weighted to account for the gender bias, though results did not significantly affect the findings presented in this book. Unless stated otherwise, all cross-tabulations featured in this and the following three chapters were tested for statistical significance using the Pearson Chi-Square $p < 0.1$ threshold.

CIVIC ENGAGEMENT AND FORMS OF POLITICAL PARTICIPATION

The survey first sought to capture whether students' attitudes towards civic engagement and democracy indicated a 'participatory ideal' analogous with the conclusions of Bang (2004) and Marsh et al. (2007), or more critical depictions of 'apathetic youth'. Adapting questions from Pattie et al.'s (2004) survey, respondents displayed little evidence of apathy towards political participation in principle, with 65.8 per cent agreeing that 'if a person is dissatisfied with the policies of the government, he/she has a duty to do something about it' – more, in fact, than the overall UK population, according to Pattie et al. (2004: 159). In terms of what 'doing something about it' might entail, there was more confidence in collective rather than individual action: 52.2 per cent agreed that 'my participation can have an impact on government policy in this country', whereas 68.8 per cent agreed that 'organised groups of citizens can have a lot of impact on public policies in this country'.

Although these statements do not specify any particular form of action, they principally centre on influencing public policy and government. Questions directly related to formal politics elicited a decidedly mixed response: 79.8 per cent agreed that 'most politicians make a lot of promises but do not actually do anything' and 60.4 per cent claimed to distrust political parties in general. Only a third of respondents, however, extended this distrust to the electoral process, with 33.9 per cent agreeing that 'I don't see the use of voting; parties do whatever they want anyway'. The fact that 53.4 per cent disagreed with this statement suggests the majority still believed in the *principle* of voting, even if they remained dissatisfied with the quality of politicians and parties currently on offer. This is illustrated further in table 4.2, showing that voting is considered by some distance the most effective form of political participation of the available options.

Comparing results from table 4.2 with those of Hansard (2009: 68), it is noticeable that students are more positive about the effectiveness of voting (85.7 to 72 per cent) than the general UK population. Table 4.2 indicates that the efficacy of protest repertoires divides respondents: on the one hand, a higher proportion considers strikes and direct action 'very effective' compared with letters to MPs and civic associations. On the other hand, a higher

Table 4.2   Perceptions of effectiveness of different forms of political action

	Very effective (%)	Somewhat effective (%)	Not very effective (%)	Not at all effective (%)	Not sure (%)
Voting in elections	37.7	48.0	10.0	2.4	1.8
Petitions	10.2	59.1	23.4	4.0	3.3
Consumer boycotts of products and services	15.6	45.8	25.7	7.0	6.0
Contacting an MP	8.0	45.6	26.9	8.2	11.3
Joining/financially supporting an SMO	10.5	51.6	21.5	5.9	10.5
Joining or forming a civic association (e.g. Fathers 4 Justice)	6.1	45.1	24.3	6.0	18.6
Protest marches	8.4	45.4	30.2	11.0	5.0
Strike action	17.0	48.5	20.9	8.5	5.2
'Direct action' protest (e.g. occupations, sit-ins, blockades)	10.7	36.8	29.1	15.2	8.2

N = 2,485. *Note*: Percentages by row.
Question: How effective a form of political participation do you think are each of these activities?

proportion of respondents consider direct action, strikes, and protest marches to be *not at all* effective compared to all other presented options. Recalling categorisations made in table 2.1 (chapter 2), there appears to be no recognisable correlation between effectiveness and the costs and risks that the participation repertoires may typically incur, as petitions and SMO membership were considered no less efficacious than strike action.

With voting considered more effective than non-electoral forms of participation, it was important to test respondents' attitudes towards democracy. Focusing on UK-domiciled students, table 4.3 shows only 23 per cent agree that 'no problem exists with the current democratic system'. There is clear support for increasing referenda for major issues of public interest, as well as introducing proportional representation for UK elections (though it is noticeable that a third appear unsure about their position, despite electoral reform having been an issue of public debate in 2011). On the other hand, support for the abolition of Parliament in favour of a system of direct democracy – a fairly radical notion – received as much as 18.2 per cent support. These findings suggest students see voting as the most effective means of political participation, but that its current means of delivery is inadequate. This has seemingly left students open to alternative models of democracy, even if the true extent of their engagement on this debate is less clear.

Of course, in the absence of a fully functioning democracy students might consider protest as the best means of making their views heard. Table 4.4 shows that most respondents had a positive overall view of protest, with

Table 4.3 Perceptions of democracy (UK-domiciled students only)

	Agree (%)	Neither agree or disagree (%)	Disagree (%)
Democracy in the UK would be improved by having more referendums on major issues of public interest	66.7	20.3	13.0
Democracy in the UK would be improved if a system of proportional representation was introduced for general elections	51.2	32.5	16.3
True democracy in the UK is only possible through the abolition of parliament and the creation of a new system of direct democracy	18.2	35.4	46.4
I see no problem with the current democratic system in the UK	23.0	27.0	50.0
Democracy in the UK already gives people too much of a say on political issues	5.6	21.1	73.3

N = 2,104. *Note:* Percentages by row.
Question: It has sometimes been argued that democracy in the UK needs to be reformed to allow for greater voice from its citizens. What is your view of the following?

58.5 per cent seeing it as an 'essential' form of political engagement, and only 11.3 per cent considering it 'illegitimate'. Questions regarding the *uses* of protest, however, elicited more mixed feelings. Respondents saw virtually no difference between the capacity of protest to change the policies of government or corporations: in each case, around 45 per cent think they could, which is lower than the overall effectiveness attributed to voting in elections or contacting an MP. Furthermore, 34.1 per cent agreed that 'there are always better ways of making your views heard than by protesting', with 32.7 per cent disagreeing and 33.2 per cent unsure. In other words, students saw protest as a necessary form of political participation *in principle*, but in practice it was considered effective only under certain circumstances.

In exploring what effective protest might look like, table 4.4 indicates a preference for so-called 'peaceful' tactics: 72 per cent disagreed with the view that effective protest requires taking power by force, and 69.3 per cent agreed that 'protest suffers because the actions of a minority usually spoil it for the majority'. Again, it would seem that while students uphold the principle of protest, they are less certain of the messier practicalities of protest participation. This is borne out by the most popular statement in table 4.4 being, 'protest can increase the wider population's knowledge and awareness of an issue'. In many ways, this chimes with the legacy of 1960s and 1970s student activism discussed in chapter 3, where identity politics slowly gained broader acceptance in wider society after protest campaigns had brought

Table 4.4   Attitudes towards protest

	Agree (%)	Neither agree or disagree (%)	Disagree (%)
Protest can positively influence the views and interests of the wider population	71.2	16.5	12.3
Protest can increase the wider population's knowledge and awareness of an issue	90.6	6.8	2.6
Protest can help change UK Government policy	45.8	28.0	26.3
Protest can help change the policy of corporations	44.9	26.5	28.5
Protest is an essential form of political engagement	58.5	23.6	17.9
Protest is not a legitimate form of political participation	11.3	23.6	65.1
Protest can only be effective if it involves taking power by force	10.8	17.2	72.0
There are always better ways of making your views heard than by protesting	34.1	33.2	32.7
Protest suffers because the actions of a minority usually spoil it for the majority	69.3	18.1	12.5

N = 2,485. *Note*: Percentages by row.
Questions: People might choose to protest for a variety of different reasons. What sort of impact do you think protest can have? To what extent do you agree with the following statements about protest?

them to public attention (Altbach, 1989; Hoefferle, 2013). In other words, protest might achieve a diffusive effect over society, with its ideas and values gradually contributing to citizens' overall thought and behaviour, even if the actions themselves are more difficult to explain or defend at the time.

STUDENT POLITICAL ENGAGEMENT AND PARTICIPATION

So far, this chapter has probed students' *attitudes* towards the political process. While this is useful for ascertaining their views on democracy and citizenship, perceiving certain repertoires to be efficacious or just does not automatically imply a willingness to participate in them. As noted in chapter 2, the regular discussion of politics is an often-necessary conduit for increasing engagement, with network approaches positing that embeddedness in a social context that values politics is likely to provide greater access to participatory opportunities (Passy and Monsch, 2014; McAdam, 1986). Hansard's (2009: 20) audit identified a strong correlation between interest and participation, but it also found that only 30 per cent of young people have 'discussed politics or political news with someone else in the last two or three years' – lower than any age group apart from the over-75s.

In contrast, the student survey shows much higher levels of political engagement: only 3.6 per cent claimed to 'never' discuss politics, with 76.3 per cent claiming to do so at least 'sometimes'. Around a quarter of students claimed to discuss politics regularly, although some social groupings were more likely to discuss politics than others. According to Hansard's survey, the most significant variable was social class, with a 48 per cent gap between ABs and DEs' discussion of politics. For the student survey, the discrepancy between those and 'working class' is narrower: 49.1 per cent of those identifying as 'upper middle class'[1] claimed to discuss politics often, whereas for those identifying as 'working class' the figure was 43.9 per cent.[2] This may reflect fundamental differences in how class is measured, but it may also be the case that embeddedness in dense social networks and access to participatory opportunities via the campus has a levelling effect on students from different social backgrounds (Crossley and Ibrahim, 2012).

The tuition fees increase was not only an issue for discussion among students during this time; for many who voted Liberal Democrat in the 2010 general election, it was also a personal cause for grievance. As discussed in chapter 3, the party bucked recent trends by appealing directly to young voters in pledging to oppose any fees increase. This appeal was arguably borne out in UK voting behaviour; according to data from Ipsos-MORI (2010), turnout among 18–24-year-olds was higher in 2010 than in 2005 at 44 per cent (though overall turnout was also higher in 2010). The Liberal

Democrats were most popular party among this cohort, achieving 30 per cent of the vote. According to the student survey, their share of the student vote was even higher at 45.6 per cent (among those willing to reveal their choice). With turnout also exceeding the UK total (74.7 per cent, excluding ineligible respondents), it can be concluded that at least one in six of all students voted Liberal Democrat in the general election.[3]

As we shall see later, this critical mass of Liberal Democrat voters would go on to play an important role in personalising the fees increase as a grievance for protest participation. Curiously, however, this experience did not strongly affect students' attitudes towards voting itself – 86.6 per cent of 2010 voters considered it an effective form of political participation, a figure that only dropped to 81.2 per cent for Liberal Democrat voters. This again supports the view that students drew clear distinctions between the value of participation in principle and their experience of it in practice. It also hints at a prevailing faith in formal political processes which runs counter to recent depictions of young people's politics by Bang (2004) and Marsh et al. (2007).

Beyond voting, table 4.5 shows students to have engaged in a wide range of civic and activism practices over the past three years. Although the most popular activities tend to be those which are typically low-cost/risk

Table 4.5   Students' participation in forms of civic and protest activism

	Yes, more than once (%)	Yes, I did this once (%)	I have not done this (%)
Signed a petition	66.0	18.6	15.5
Boycotted certain products and services for political, ethical, or environmental reasons	38.5	12.5	49.0
Bought certain products and services for political, ethical, or environmental reasons	52.5	9.2	38.3
Worn or displayed a campaign badge or sticker	26.5	14.0	59.4
Presented my views to a local councillor or MP	15.7	13.0	71.2
Been a member of a social movement organisation (e.g. Amnesty, Greenpeace)	17.8	11.4	70.8
Worked or campaigned on behalf of a political party	6.5	9.0	84.5
Stood as a candidate for school/student/local elections	12.3	14.2	73.5
Distributed flyers for a political campaign	8.6	8.7	82.7
Taken part in a protest march	16.2	14.0	69.9
Taken part in strike action	6.7	9.3	84.1
Taken part in an occupation/sit-in	4.4	8.2	87.4
Taken part in the blockade of a building or meeting	2.5	7.4	90.1

N = 2,485. *Note:* Percentages by row.
Question: Please tick if you have done any of the following political activities in the last three years (select all that apply).

(e.g. signing petitions and ethical shopping), the table also shows uptake for more 'demanding' forms of participation. Comparing findings with those from Hansard's 2010 audit, it would appear that students are more active protesters than the UK average: they are ten times more likely to have attended a protest march, and more than twice as many have signed a petition in the past three years. Moreover, only 7 per cent of the survey population qualify as 'pure' non-participants, having not participated in *any* of the listed activities. Again, this reflects their greater access to multiple participatory opportunities through the campus, as well as students' greater biographical availability (Crossley, 2008; McAdam, 1986) when at university.

As with voting, the survey generally finds a strong correlation between students' activism participation and its perceived efficacy. For occupations, 63.7 per cent of occupants considered 'direct action' tactics effective compared to 45.2 per cent of non-occupants. Similarly, 67.6 per cent of marchers felt protest marches were effective compared to 47.9 per cent of non-marchers, and 71.7 per cent of petitioners thought petitions were effective compared to 56.1 per cent of non-petitioners. The disparity is narrower, however, in the case of strike action: 74.7 per cent of strikers saw strikes as effective, compared to 63.7 per cent of non-strikers. For most students (especially undergraduates), opportunities or invitations to strike in the past three years are likely to have been limited, aside from acting in solidarity with academic staff. Non-strikers might have also opposed strike action precisely *because* it is effective.

Although the survey question presented in table 4.5 recalls Hansard's (2010) measurements of participation, it differs in one crucial aspect by distinguishing between *repeated* and *one-off* activities. What becomes clear is that certain repertoires are likelier to be practised more than once, such as signing petitions, wearing campaign badges, ethical shopping, and joining SMOs. In contrast, taking part in blockades, distributing flyers, occupying, and working/campaigning for a political party are comparatively less likely to be practised more than once. To some extent, this reflects differences in the supply of, and access to, many of these activities: petitions are widely available via different campaigning organisations, whereas students may have had only limited opportunities to campaign for a political party. Nevertheless, there is evidence to suggest that one-off participants found their particular experience less meaningful and efficacious than those who repeated the same activity. For example, 78 per cent of repeated participants consider direct action effective compared with 56.1 per cent of one-off participants. Similarly, 73.9 per cent of repeated participants considered protest marches effective, compared with 60.2 per cent of one-off participants. This suggests that while one-off participants might have done enough to qualify as activists according to Hansard's (2009) calculation, not all will have found their experience positive enough to want to participate again.

Linking repeated participation directly to efficacy recalls the rational choice perspectives championed by Olson (1965) and others. However, a more contextual approach advocated by Passy and Monsch (2014) posits that these choices are shaped by an individuals' 'cognitive toolkit' of available resources, including accumulated knowledge and everyday discussion. For those interested in politics but lacking in conversation-facilitating social networks, opportunities for regular participation might be limited. In other words, it is important to think of the networks that frame an individuals' participatory decision-making. Table 4.6 finds significant patterns between students' activity and their discussion of politics. Generally, it indicates that

Table 4.6 Cross-tabulating political discussion and confidence with selected participatory activity

Activity	Frequency of participation	% Discusses politics regularly/often	% Agrees 'I often feel that I don't know enough about politics to fully engage in it'
Signed a petition	More than once	57.3	49.0
	Did this once	29.1	64.6
	Not done this	30.9	66.5
Boycotted certain products and services for political, ethical, or environmental reasons	More than once	63.5	45.4
	Did this once	50.2	54.0
	Not done this	35.2	62.0
Bought certain products and services for political, ethical, or environmental reasons	More than once	57.4	50.7
	Did this once	42.8	59.4
	Not done this	36.3	58.9
Worn or displayed a campaign badge or sticker	More than once	65.6	42.5
	Did this once	48.7	54.2
	Not done this	39.9	60.1
Worked or campaigned on behalf of a political party	More than once	82.1	24.7
	Did this once	61.9	42.2
	Not done this	43.9	58.2
Stood as a candidate for school/student/local elections	More than once	59.5	44.1
	Did this once	52.3	52.0
	Not done this	45.2	56.9
Taken part in a protest march	More than once	76.6	37.8
	Did this once	55.3	47.8
	Not done this	39.9	59.9
Taken part in an occupation/sit-in	More than once	70.6	35.8
	Did this once	66.3	36.6
	Not done this	45.1	57.3
Taken part in the blockade of a building or meeting	More than once	71.4	30.2
	Did this once	64.1	37.5
	Not done this	46.0	56.7

those who have participated in high-cost/risk activities (such as standing for election, taking part in an occupation, or joining a protest march) discuss politics more frequently than low-cost/risk participants (e.g. signing petitions, ethical shopping, wearing campaign badges). In fact, for one-off low-cost/risk participants, their level of discussion is sometimes closer to *non*-participants than repeated participants. For high-cost/risk activities, however, a clearer gap opens up between participants and non-participants, with one-off and repeated participants showing a comparably high regularity of discussion.

To some extent, these findings support arguments made by Morozov (2011) and Putnam (2000) that participation in low-cost/risk activities reflects a limited engagement in politics. Yet these interpretations also emphasise the determining power of resource mobilisation agencies, while implying that such activities are enough to satiate individuals' engagement. In seeking to measure students' confidence in their political knowledge, the second column of table 4.6 suggests something more complex. Whereas blockaders, occupiers, and party campaigners display high levels of confidence in their political knowledge, the percentage of low-cost/risk participants who admit to 'not knowing enough about politics to fully engage in it' frequently exceeds 50 per cent. Again, there are significant gaps between repeated and one-off participants – roughly two-thirds of students who signed one petition in the past three years reveal a lack of confidence in their political knowledge, a similar fraction to those who have not. In other words, infrequent, low-cost/risk participants not only discuss politics far less frequently, their corresponding lack of political *confidence* implies deeper uncertainties – uncertainties which may impede further participation.

SUMMARY: A CIVIC IDEAL?

The survey finds students to be more politically engaged than the UK population as a whole, as well as more dedicated to the principle of an active citizenship. This 'civic ideal' tends to prioritise electoral politics over protest politics, with the latter usually serving as an auxiliary for raising awareness of issues. Despite this, students are often dissatisfied with the practice of electoral politics – both in the conduct of politicians and parties and the extent of democracy on offer to ordinary citizens. In this respect, protest may represent politics by alternative means, albeit one that is not considered any more efficacious.

This overall portrayal of students chimes with Hay's (2007) depictions of a cynical, rather than disengaged, citizenry, though results do not indicate an outright rejection of formal political processes. Students are found generally to be more active than the UK population on a range of electoral, civic, and protest activities, but their participation does not necessarily reflect high levels of political knowledge or confidence. This varies according to activity: participants in more demanding activities – both electoral and protest – display relatively strong levels of political confidence and everyday political discussion, especially repeat participants. In other words, their dissatisfaction with the quality of politics on offer has led them to take action in order to change it. On the other hand, students who participate sporadically in low-cost/risk activities discuss politics less often and lack confidence in their political knowledge. In this respect, their actions reflect less an autonomous desire to do politics on their own terms than an uncertainty borne out of occasional, tentative forays into active participation – be it civic, protest, or electoral.

These results point to divergent political cultures within the university campus, but they also highlight potential problems in framing studies around a basic participation/non-participation binary. Exploring in more detail the significant intersections between the two will be a key consideration throughout the proceeding chapters.

STUDENTS' ATTITUDES TOWARDS UNIVERSITY AND HIGHER EDUCATION FUNDING

So far, this chapter has separated its analysis of participation from the specific political grievances they might relate to. While this helps identify overarching patterns between students' activity and engagement, it also risks flattening out differences between the issues, goals, and agencies from which they spawned. With results pointing to key variations in political knowledge and everyday discussion, the student protests case study enables one to consider students' response to a single grievance and the specific participatory opportunities it generated. As noted in chapter 3, Government proposals to treble the tuition fees cap did not materially affect students studying at university during the 2011/12 academic year, but it did centre on an issue about which students claimed first-hand knowledge and experience, namely the cost and value of higher education.

Focusing on students' personal attitudes towards higher education funding, table 4.7 finds that the cost of fees and subsistence was a factor for 73.4 per cent when deciding whether to apply for university. This experience, in combination with the subsequent fees increase, left students with strong views on the issue, with 83.2 per cent agreeing that 'access to an affordable university education is a right, not a privilege'. It is, of course, open to interpretation how much an 'affordable' university education should cost – some, such as NUS and the Labour Party, advocated a graduate tax instead of tuition fees at the time of the Browne Review's announcement, whereas student campaigning groups such as NCAFC felt that tuition fees should be abolished altogether. Survey findings at least indicate a strong consensus that the £9,000 annual fees introduced by the Coalition Government were too expensive: 84.3 per cent agreed to concerns that higher fees would 'put some strong candidates off applying for university altogether'.

Although strong in their opposition to the Government's policy, evidence that students' grievances reflected a 'generational consciousness' is harder to gauge. Table 4.7 shows 63.6 per cent of students agreed that 'politicians don't care about the interests of young people' – a clear majority, but some 20 per cent below other anti-fees statements. Admittedly, agreeing with this view does not necessarily imply possession of a generational consciousness, but it does at least suggest a belief that the fees increase is connected to other policy issues – be it housing, employability, or the cost of living. This hints at a wider political awareness, so it is arguably telling that this view is less popular that those solely concerning the fees increase. Moreover, the survey also shows comparable levels of agreement among 18–23-year-old students (63.8 per cent) and students above the age of 30 (55.5 per cent), indicating little evidence of a political consciousness among 18–23-year-old students that is distinguishable from mature or postgraduate students.

Certainly, there were generational properties in the Liberal Democrats' decision to take an anti-fees stance in the 2010 general election, and it is therefore unsurprising to see from table 4.7 that 72.9 per cent felt 'let down' by the party following its policy reversal. Table 4.8 explores this further by

Table 4.7   Student attitudes towards higher education funding and the 2010 UK general election

	Agree (%)	Neither agree or disagree (%)	Disagree (%)
Access to an affordable university education is a right, not a privilege	83.2	5.5	11.3
I am concerned that higher fees will put some strong candidates off applying for university altogether	84.3	6.0	9.7
I feel let down by the Liberal Democrats over their reversal of tuition fees policy	72.9	19.2	7.9
Politicians don't care about the interests of young people*	63.6	16.1	20.4
Parties should always be held accountable for their election pledges once they become part of government	85.5	9.6	4.9

N = 2,485 (*N = 977[†]). *Note*: Percentages by row.
Question: To what extent do you agree with the following statements about recent changes to the funding of higher education in the UK?
[†] This question was a late addition to the survey questionnaire, and so is drawn from a reduced sample.

comparing party voters' attitudes towards higher education funding. What quickly becomes clear is that Liberal Democrat voters were strong advocates of affordable higher education, with many sharing views with Labour voters on funding through taxation. This not only supports the view that student voters were swayed into voting Liberal Democrat by the party's pledge on tuition fees, but also indicates that the majority were closer in their politics to Labour than the Conservatives. Following their coalition with the latter party, it is perhaps inevitable that 88.7 per cent of Liberal Democrat voters felt let down by the party over its policy reversal, with 90.4 per cent also agreeing that 'parties should always be held accountable for their election pledges once they become part of government'. Evidence of antipathy was also found in students' precoded survey responses to which party they had voted for:

'Foolishly, Liberal Democrats'; 'Lib Dem (Wasted Vote)'; 'lib dem. ... i feel betrayed'; 'Lib Dems (BIG MISTAKE)'; 'Lib Dems (unfortunatley) [*sic*]'; 'Liberal Democrats ... tactically!'; Liberal Demofucks'; 'Liberal lying Democrats'

Table 4.8 Student attitudes towards higher education funding and the 2010 UK general election

	% Liberal Democrat voters agree	% Labour voters agree	% Conservative voters agree	% All students agree
Access to an affordable university education is a right, not a privilege	86.0	90.1	68.9	83.2
I feel let down by the Liberal Democrats over their reversal of tuition fees policy	88.7	85.6	43.3	72.9
Parties should always be held accountable for their election pledges once they become part of government	90.4	93.8	79.9	85.5
Maintaining higher education funding is not a priority when public service cuts have to be made	28.2	23.0	43.3	28.1
Higher education funding should be maintained through higher taxes	41.0	44.0	15.2	33.2
Taxpayers who did not go through higher education should not be expected to pay for the higher education of others	19.5	14.8	26.8	19.2

$N = 2,485$.
Question: To what extent do you agree with the following statements about recent changes to the funding of higher education in the UK?

The party's coalition role and tuition U-turn left a significant population of students suddenly feeling uncertain of their political allegiances. This is illustrated by findings from table 4.9, which cross-tabulates voting with current party identification. Whereas the Conservatives and Labour retained the support of around 73 per cent of their 2010 voters by spring 2012, the Liberal Democrats retained only 14.2 per cent. Although party identification typically atrophies between election cycles, this marks a significant contrast between the parties, with most Liberal Democrat voters either having jumped ship to Labour and the Scottish National Party (SNP), or declining to identify with any party. Support for the SNP arguably betrays the survey's bias towards Scotland-based students, but it may also reflect a migration towards a party that made free education a cornerstone of its identity – a point its leader Alex Salmond was unhesitant in exploiting during the protests themselves (see The Journal, 27 October 2010).

In sum, there is plenty of evidence to suggest that the majority of students felt strongly about the cost of university study, feelings that were partly drawn from their own ongoing experiences as 'consumers' of higher education. By appealing to this strength of feeling, the Liberal Democrats' electoral pledge on tuition fees served as a clear electoral incentive for many young people. The party's subsequent U-turn therefore added a crucially *personal* dimension for a large number of students otherwise unaffected by proposals at the time of their announcement. Moreover, the swiftness (not to mention publicness) of the U-turn made it easier for it to be framed as a specific grievance than other, more subtle generational issues detailed in chapter 2. In so doing, it also conforms to the sorts of 'cause-based' politics that Bang (2004) and others see as appealing particularly to young people.

THE PROTESTS AGAINST FEES AND CUTS: PARTICIPATION/NON-PARTICIPATION

Students might convert their grievances into action in a variety of ways. While those more accustomed to electoral politics may have felt unsure how to legitimately or effectively express their views, for others the answer was clear: not only did protest symbolise a rejection of ineffective electoral processes, it also arguably represented a more direct means of influencing governmental decision-making. This outlook was especially pertinent during the autumn term of 2010, as students were effectively given seven weeks to build a campaign and pressurise MPs into voting down the fees bill in Parliament.

In the survey, students were asked if they participated in the protests against fees and cuts before being invited to specify what they did. It should be noted that the initial question does not specify a timeframe for participation

Chapter 4

Table 4.9 Cross-tabulating current party identification with Conservative, Labour, and Liberal Democrat voters in the 2010 general election (UK domiciles only)

UK domiciles		Current party identification					
		Conservatives	Labour	Liberal Democrats	SNP	None
Party voted for in the 2010 general election	Conservatives	% of 2010 voters' current party identification	73.5	6.2	1.2	1.9	13.6
	Labour	% of 2010 voters' current party identification	1.2	72.7	0.4	7.9	10.7
	Liberal Democrats	% of 2010 voters' current party identification	4.4	30.1	14.2	18.1	26.2

N = 1,670. *Note:* Percentages by row.
Question: With which political party, if any, do you most closely identify with right now?

in the student protests, allowing respondents to base their answer on activities undertaken at any time they saw as relevant. Table 4.10 breaks down students' responses, finding that 22.3 per cent claimed to have taken part in the protests in some way. This figure might seem quite high for a single campaign – as a fraction of the total UK student population in 2011/12 this amounts to half a million people – yet the percentage is far below that of students believing an affordable higher education to be a right not a privilege, thereby opening up a potentially sizeable intersection of 'unconverted' non-participants.

Table 4.10 reveals variations within this fraction of participants. Given that they enrolled in autumn 2011 – some time after the bulk of protests had taken place – it is unsurprising that first-year undergraduates had a lower participation rate than second- and third-year undergraduates. However, the fact that this was as high as 19.4 per cent reflected the ongoing availability of participatory opportunities on most campuses in 2011/12 (including the NCAFC demonstration recounted in chapter 1), as well as possible mobilisation opportunities accessed via school/college the previous year. Indeed, with second- and third-year student participation levels hovering nearer 26 per cent, one can speculate that around 650,000 students studying in the 2010/11 academic year took part in the protests.

Among the less-active participants are postgraduates and international students. This likely reflects their looser connectedness to undergraduates and the student union, as well as latter's possible unfamiliarity with contemporary UK politics. Despite this, fees and the cost of study are also relevant causes for grievance among postgraduates and international students, and with both groups having played prominent leadership roles in the history of UK student activism since the 1960s (Hoefferle, 2013), their failure to be mobilised in larger numbers might be considered something of a missed opportunity for campaigners.

An alternative interpretation of this deficit is that it shows just how popular protest participation was among *undergraduates*, especially those at university in 2010/11. Table 4.10 further records that participation was at its highest for students studying social science (29.1 per cent), students self-identifying as 'working class' (29.8 per cent – challenging to some extent Gilbert's [Gilbert and Aitchison, 2012] allegation that the protests were middle-class dominated), and students who voted Labour (38.7 per cent). Although participation among Conservative-voting students was notably lower (13.4 per cent), it still represented a significant enough proportion to suggest that the fees grievance partly transcended party tribalism.

Returning to the theme of the Liberal Democrats, it is notable that around a third of the party's student voters took part in the protests. Among those participants, a third now claim to identify with Green or socialist parties (more so than those identifying with Labour), adding further evidence of their

Table 4.10 Participation in the student protests as percentage of demographics

		Participated in the student protests (%)
All students	All students (N = 2485)	22.3
Sex	Male (N = 742)	21.7*
	Female (N = 1,724)	22.4*
Domicile	UK (N = 2,104)	23.9
	Other EU (N = 193)	20.7
	Non-EU (N = 184)	6.0
Class identification	Upper-middle class (N = 701)	16.5
	Lower-middle class (N = 1,035)	23.7
	Working class (N = 503)	29.8
	No class identification (N = 227)	17.6
Party voted for in 2010 election	Conservatives (N = 164)	13.4
	Labour (N = 243)	36.2
	Liberal Democrats (N = 415)	31.6
	Did not vote (N = 416)	15.1
Degree subject	Art and design (N = 128)	20.3
	Humanities (N = 786)	24.3
	Social sciences (N = 650)	29.1
	Natural sciences (N = 642)	16.7
	Logic and technology (N = 279)	14.3
Degree type	Undergraduate (N = 1,981)	23.4
	Postgraduate (N = 504)	17.9
UG by domicile	UK (N = 1,762)	24.2
	Other EU (N = 122)	23.0
	Non-EU (N = 97)	9.3
UG by year of study	First year (N = 717)	19.4
	Second year (N = 590)	24.2
	Third year or more (N = 674)	26.9

$N = 2{,}485$. $*p > 0.05$.

voters' left-leaning instincts. Table 4.10 also finds that only 15.1 per cent of students who did not vote (when eligible to do so) participated in the student protests – a similar proportion to participants who had voted Conservative. This rather goes against some of the journalistic hyperbole that claimed the protests had woken up 'apathetic youth', even if voting should not necessarily be taken as a reflection of an active knowledge and engagement.

Of course, survey findings also show that 77.7 per cent of students did not participate. Although this stands in contrast to the groundswell of opposition to higher fees, it remains possible that these students made a rational choice *not* to take part. Table 4.11 compares the attitudes of participants and non-participants towards higher education funding, protest participation, and the legacy of the student protests themselves. In general, participants

Table 4.11 **Comparison of attitudes between participants and non-participants in the student protests**

	% Participants agree	*% Non-participants agree*	*Total respondents*
Access to an affordable university education is a right, not a privilege	92.9	80.4	83.2
I am concerned that higher fees will put some strong candidates off applying for university altogether	94.8	81.3	84.3
Higher education funding should be maintained through higher taxes	50.8	28.2	33.2
I see no problem with the current democratic system in the UK	12.7	26.0	23.0
Protest is an essential form of political engagement	79.9	52.4	58.6
Protest can help change UK Government policy	55.9	42.9	45.8
Protest is the last meaningful form of political engagement available in the UK	39.1	24.7	27.9

N = 2,485.

demonstrated moderately stronger opposition to higher tuition fees and cuts than non-participants, though this gap is notably wider on the subject of raising taxes to pay for higher education. This indicates that for at least half of participants their opposition came from a more politically developed left-wing perspective. Others, however, may have favoured alternative means of resolving the funding issue or had few thoughts beyond registering their basic opposition to it.

Perhaps of more significance are the differences between participants' and non-participants' attitudes towards protest. Certainly, a far higher proportion of participants considered it to be an 'essential' form of political engagement than non-participants. In contrast, non-participants demonstrated greater faith in formal democratic processes: twice the proportion claimed to see no problem with the current democratic system, and 15 per cent fewer agreed that protest represents the 'last meaningful form of political engagement available in the UK'. While this may partly reflect a post hoc analysis of the protests' failure to overturn the fees bill, one can argue that students opposing higher fees may not have converted this into participation because they lacked belief in the effectiveness of protest to influence government policy. As a general theme, this will be returned to in more detail in chapter 7.

STUDENTS' PROTEST PARTICIPATION:
WHAT DID THEY DO?

Analysing the student protests according to a basic participation/non-participation binary is useful for identifying some of the essential properties that distinguish each category, but it would be unwise to automatically assume a collective identity among the 22.3 per cent who took part. Taking things further, students who answered 'yes' to having participated were asked specific follow-up questions about the nature of their participation, and their experiences more generally. Table 4.12 lists students' participation in a range of activism activities put to them in the questionnaire. Once again, the most popular activities were predominantly low-cost/risk – 84.9 per cent of participants signed petitions, and 63.6 per cent 'liked' campaign Facebook pages – whereas high-cost/risk activities such as organising protests and participating in blockades were the least popular.

Somewhat bucking this trend, however, is the finding that nearly half of participants attended local, regional, and national marches and demonstrations – around 10 per cent of the student population as a whole. This is

Table 4.12   Student activity in the student protests against fees and cuts

	I did this more than once (% of participants)	I did this once (% of participants)	Participants as % of all students
Signing a petition	42.9	42.0	18.9
Wearing or displaying a campaign badge or sticker	17.5	20.3	8.4
Distributing flyers	8.9	9.4	4.1
Attending a national- or regional-level student march	15.6	25.1	9.1
Attending a student march in your own/ nearest town or city	15.6	31.3	10.4
Taking part in the blockade of a building or meeting	4.5	7.4	2.7
Taking part in an occupation/sit-in	6.5	11.8	4.1
Taking part in the organising of a protest event	6.1	6.3	2.8
Attending a student-led teach-in or activism workshop	6.1	8.7	3.3
Attending a university or union-arranged debate or meeting about student fees	10.5	17.5	6.2
Like/join a protest page/group on Facebook	26.9	36.7	14.2
Follow a protest group on Twitter	11.0	10.5	4.8
Other	3.6	2.5	1.4

$N = 553$.
Question: If you clicked 'YES' to the last question, please tick if your participation in the student protests involved any of the following activities.

illustrative of the density of local and national demonstrations that took place across 2010 and 2011, particularly in autumn 2010. The latter point is supported by a slightly higher attendance rate for second- and third-year undergraduates, though the narrow marginality of difference – 3.5 per cent[4] – suggests that first-year undergraduates' participation was not as affected by their absence from university in autumn 2010 as one might expect. This is even borne out in the data on repeat participants, with only 1.5 per cent[5] more undergraduates in their second year or above having attended multiple demonstrations than first-year undergraduates. It would therefore seem that first-year repeat demonstrators had attended a national or regional demonstration prior to coming to university, and had a sufficiently positive experience to join one again.

In terms of recorded case numbers, occupations in the autumn of 2010 were more widespread on UK campuses than they had ever been in the UK – including 1968 – but only 4.1 per cent of students took part in them. This seeming disparity is partly explained by the fact that unlike demonstrations, occupations do not depend on mass participation to be considered effective. Moreover, occupations took place in fewer than half of UK universities between 2010 and 2012, as well as being more frequent in 2010/11 than 2011/12. This is reflected in the fact that 19.4 per cent of undergraduates in their second year or more took part in occupations compared with 11.5 per cent of those in their first year.[6] Unlike marches and demonstrations, however, the vast majority of occupations took place on campus. Consequently, young people not yet at university may have felt insufficiently connected to occupiers to access what may have seemed a 'campus-only' protest event.[7]

The relatively low uptake also reflects the fact that occupying is often a demanding form of participation. Like national demonstrations, campus occupations in 2010/11 carried the threat of heavy sanction, with participants risking arrest, legal action, and suspension of their studies, as well as enduring multiple sleepless nights in cold rooms with little time for academic work. Comparing this to signing petitions or 'liking' Facebook pages raises obvious questions over the diversity of experiences among protest participants, and the extent to which participants shared a common purview or identity. To effectively unpack participation, one can recall classifications made in chapter 2 and employ McAdam's (1986) measurements of participation in terms of their cost and risk. Admittedly, such ordinal scaling can be easily misconstrued as a measurement of participatory *value*, with low-cost/risk activities perceived as lacking the efficacy and virtue of more high-cost/risk ones. Rather than simply reproducing this assumption, however, categorising participation in this way allows it to be tested by comparing categories with perceptions of efficacy and individuals' politicisation.

For the construction of this model, table 4.13 shows how each participation activity has been given a score of 1 (low-cost/risk), 3 (medium-cost/risk), or

6 (high-cost/risk), with scores doubled for repeated activity. Scores correlate to those set out in table 2.1 from chapter 2, which sought to broadly categorise participation by cost and risk in a western context. Categories of participation are then calculated based on the cumulative aggregate of each score type. This means that low-cost/risk participants are identified on the basis that they score between 1 and 10, with 10 being the highest an individual can score while only engaging in low-cost/risk forms of participation. Consequently, medium-cost/risk participants are those with scores between 11 and 32, and high-cost/risk participants are those who score between 33 and 92, 92 being the aggregation of every (repeated) activity on the list.

The categorising of activities by cost and risk has been specifically tailored to the case study. For this reason, 'local marches' are categorised as medium-cost/risk on the basis that these events were close to the students' university, and rarely attracted violence or disorder. 'National or regional marches', on the other hand, has been categorised as high-cost/risk. There are three reasons for this. First, these events mostly took place in non-campus locations, namely the city centres of London (six demonstrations between 2010 and 2011), Manchester (one in 2011), and Edinburgh (one each in 2010 and 2011). As a result, the majority of students had to travel some distance to attend these events. Second, whereas most student unions arranged coach travel to the NUS-organised march in November 2010, students often had to make their own arrangements for attending the four 'unofficial' national demonstrations that followed. Third, following Millbank, London demonstrations in particular became associated with direct action tactics, as well as controversial forms of public order policing (notably kettling). Given the amount

Table 4.13   Scoring participation repertoires in the student protests by cost and risk to participants

Participation type	'Did this once' score	'Did this more than once' score
Signed a petition	1	2
Wore or displayed a campaign badge or sticker	1	2
Liked/joined a protest page/group on Facebook	1	2
Followed a protest group on Twitter	1	2
Distributed flyers	3	6
Attended a local student march	3	6
Attended a student-led teach-in or activism workshop	3	6
Attended a debate or meeting about student fees	3	6
Attended a national or regional student march	6	12
Took part in the blockade of a building or meeting	6	12
Took part in an occupation or sit-in	6	12
Took part in the organising of a protest event	6	12

Question: If you clicked 'YES' to the last question, please tick if your participation in the student protests involved any of the following activities.

of media coverage this attracted, one can reasonably argue that national and regional demonstrations were a more high-cost/risk activity in 2010/11 than had been the case in previous years.

Applying this measurement to all participants, figure 4.1 shows the overall mode score is 2 – equivalent to having signed more than one petition. From this point on, there is a sharp and consistent downward curve the higher the participation score, with six students achieving an overall top score of 76 points. Table 4.14 divides these scores into three separate participatory bands using the low-, medium-, and high-cost/risk score aggregates.[8] This banding reveals that half of participants reside in the low-cost/risk category, making up 11.3 per cent of students overall. The 2.6 per cent of students who qualify as high-cost/risk participants is slightly higher than Hoefferle's (2013) estimate of radical activists at British universities in the 1960s. In other words, students are not only more politically active than the current UK population, the proportion who participated in the 2010/11 protests against fees and cuts is at least comparable to student activism's supposed 1960s heyday.

Table 4.15 compares the social demographics of each participatory category. Findings suggest no statistically significant difference in the level of participation between undergraduates and postgraduates, as well as degree subject categories. What *is* significant is that a higher proportion of male

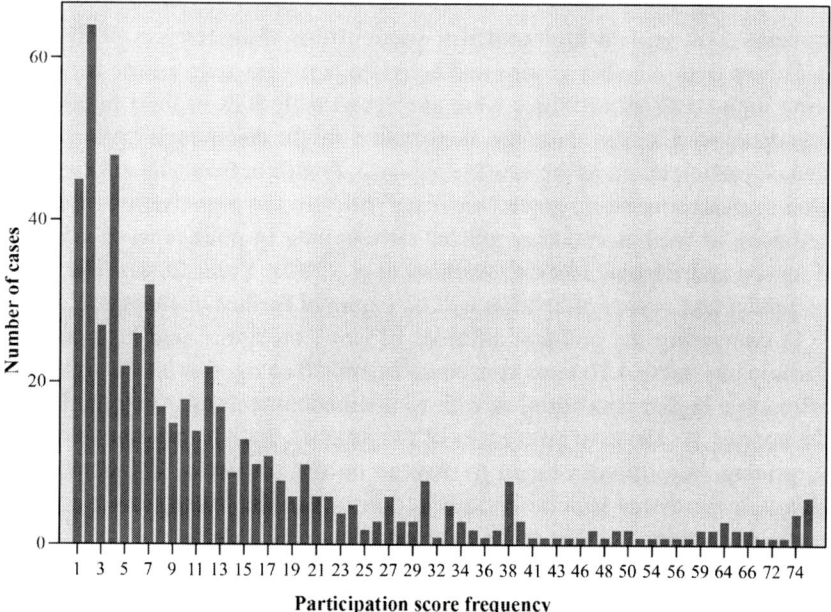

Figure 4.1 Range of scores for student participation measured by cost and risk.
Source: Courtesy of the author.

Table 4.14 Participation in the student protests against fees and cuts measured by cost and risk

	Score range	Frequency	Per cent (%)	% of all students
No specified participation	0	7	1.3	0.3
Low-cost/risk participant	1–8	281	50.8	11.3
Medium-cost/risk participant	9–32	200	36.2	8.0
High-cost/risk participant	33–80	65	11.8	2.6
Total		553	100.0	22.3

N = 553.

Table 4.15 Student protest participation categories as percentage of demographics

		Low-cost/risk participant (%)	Medium-cost/ risk participant (%)	High-cost/risk participant (%)
Sex	Male	42.9**	38.5**	15.5**
	Female	54.4**	35.2**	9.8**
Subject	Sciences	56.5*	34.7*	6.8*
	Arts, humanities, and social sciences	48.8*	36.7*	13.5*
Degree	Undergraduate	51.4*	36.5*	10.6*
	Postgraduate	47.8*	34.4*	17.8*

N = 553. *$p > 0.05$; **$p < 0.05$.

students took part in high-cost/risk participation than females. This raises questions over whether groups and activism networks responsible for organising high-cost/risk activities were subject to male bias in their politics and organisation. Clearly, there are factors that might discourage high-cost/risk female participation: as we saw in chapter 3, female activists have long struggled to overcome being given 'auxiliary' roles in the organisation of student activism, as well as enduring gender stereotyping in politics more generally (Lawson and Barton, 1980; Einwohner et al., 2000; Yulia, 2010). The theme of gender and non-participation will be explored further in chapter 7.

In comparing the political attitudes of low-, medium-, and high-cost/risk participants, table 4.16 finds consensus across all categories on the right to an affordable higher education, as well as disillusionment regarding the Liberal Democrats. As the core grievances of the protests, such a consensus is hardly surprising, but attitudes begin to diverge on the subject of UK democracy: although there was general dissatisfaction across the board, lower-cost/risk participants were notably more cautious about direct democracy and protest as participatory alternatives. In contrast, more than half of high-cost/risk participants were supportive of a system of direct democracy. This suggests a certain ideological divide between high-cost/risk participants and the other participants. This is also noticeable in students' response to the proposal

Table 4.16 Political attitudes by participation in the student protests

	% Low-cost/risk participants agree	% Medium-cost/risk participants agree	% High-cost/risk participants agree	% All students agree
Access to an affordable university education is a right, not a privilege	92.5*	92.0*	100.0*	83.2
I feel let down by the Liberal Democrats over their reversal of tuition fees policy	90.0*	91.0*	96.9*	72.9
Higher education funding should be maintained through higher taxes	44.8	51.5	80.0	33.2
I see no problem with the current democratic system in the UK	17.1	7.5	7.7	23.0
True democracy in the UK is only possible through the abolition of parliament and the creation of a new system of direct democracy	26.3	30.5	53.8	18.2

$N = 553$. *$p > 0.05$.

that 'higher education funding should be maintained through higher taxes': 80 per cent of high-cost/risk participants agreed with this view, compared to less than half of low-cost/risk participants. In other words, participants were united in their opposition to higher fees and cuts, but the more radical politics of high-cost/risk participants – typified in the free education, 'tax the rich' policies of many occupation groups – found only limited support among most other protesters.

Recalling earlier findings from table 4.6, these differences in participants' political attitudes may reflect the sort of information and everyday conversation they had access to. The social network properties of these conversations will be explored in more detail in the following two chapters, but table 4.17 considers students' information access via political news media. Perhaps unsurprisingly, results indicate that medium- and high-cost/risk participants consume news media more regularly than low-cost/risk participants (as well as non-participants). Exploring the sources of students' consumption, low-cost/risk participants are found to be fairly traditional in their choices, with 68.7 per cent regularly/fairly often accessing news and political information from the television – more than any other participatory category. High-cost/risk participants, on the other hand, are more 'omnivorous' in their consumption – alongside mainstream sources, they also make regular use of independent media outlets, blogs, and social networking sites. In this context, their interest in alternative models of democracy is understandable as such debates are less likely to appear via the mainstream channels favoured by low-cost/risk participants.[9]

It is also notable that despite young people's widespread usage of social networking sites such as Twitter and Facebook (Dutton and Blank, 2011), comparatively few non-participants and low-cost/risk participants use such forums to access political information. This perhaps reflects the reciprocal nature of social networking and how this shapes personal interests: students with little interest in politics are less likely to have politically active Facebook friends or follow political Twitter feeds, and students with few politically active Facebook friends and political Twitter feeds are consequently less likely to receive political information and foster an interest in politics. In contrast, high-cost/risk participants not only have more politically engaged friends online, but their social networks may also facilitate the sharing of more niche forms of news media. The fact that these forms often require greater knowledge and navigational skills to access online (Anduiza et al., 2009) suggests a clear correlation between students' political views and the sources of information they typically have access to.

Given the differences in their chosen policy alternatives, information access, and level of participation, it is perhaps inevitable that students had differing attitudes towards the legacy of the 2010/11 protests. Table 4.18 finds a consistent correlation between the cost/risk of students' participation and the protests' impact on their wider political engagement. Again, this hints at divergent participatory experiences, with only half of low-cost/risk participants feeling more engaged by the protests compared to 83 per cent of high-cost/risk participants. This is certainly reflected in students' attitudes towards violence in the protests, with low-cost/risk participants appearing to take a more critical view of this than high-cost/risk participants. Whereas many of the latter will have experienced or witnessed police responses to

Table 4.17 Students' news media consumption – 'Regularly/fairly often'

	% Non-participant	% Low-cost/risk participant	% Medium-cost/risk participant	% High-cost/risk participant
Television	57.7*	68.7*	59.5*	55.4*
Newspapers	66.6	75.1	82.0	89.2
Alternative news sites	43.1	49.1	63.5	83.1
Independent blogs	14.9	21.4	36.0	61.5
Social networking sites	44.6	49.8	62.0	81.5
Emails and newsletters	20.5	31.3	46.5	67.7

$N = 2,485$. *Note:* Percentage by column. $*p = 0.05$.
Question: Do you use any of the following to access news and information about political issues?

Table 4.18 **Participant and non-participants' attitudes towards the student protests' legacy**

	% Non-participants students agree	% Low-cost /risk participants agree	% Medium-cost/risk participants agree	% High-cost/risk participants agree
The tuition fees issue has made me more politically engaged	35.2	64.1	75.0	86.2
The student protests have made me more politically engaged	23.6	51.2	70.0	83.1
The student protests will be remembered more for violence than politics	59.0	63.3	52.5	35.4
The student protests have made me more prepared to protest on issues important to me in the future	20.4	46.3	72.5	75.4
The Government and police force have made protest appear an illegitimate and deviant act	50.6*	70.1*	79.5*	81.5*

$N = 2,485$. $*p = 0.05$.

protesters' direct action tactics, table 4.17 provides a reminder that low-cost/risk participants and non-participants were more likely to have viewed these events via (often-critical) television or newspaper reports.

Despite differences over the role of violence in the protests' legacy, participants were broadly united in their hostility to the Government and the police's treatment of protesters during this time. Although mass arrests, draconian sentencing, and the condemnation of students' actions by many ministers were widely reported in the UK press, it is nevertheless surprising that 70.1 per cent of low-cost/risk participants agreed that these actions had made protest appear as an 'illegitimate and deviant act'. This implies a wider solidarity among participants than their political views and actions otherwise suggests – a solidarity that even incorporates half of *non*-participants. However, these actions appear to have had a lasting impact on a large number of participants: only 59.1 per cent felt more prepared to protest in the future – a figure that drops below 50 per cent for low-cost/risk participants. These attitudes appear to be shaped by students' varying experiences of participation, experiences which will be the focus of the following two chapters.

CONCLUSION

It is clear that the politics of higher education funding is of interest and concern to the vast majority of students, most of whom have given the affordabil-
ity of their own education some serious thought. In view of their inclination
towards sporadic, cause-based forms of engagement – albeit with a greater
interest in electoral politics than young people more generally – students'
widespread engagement in, and position taking on, the Government's plans
to treble the fees cap and cut university funding should come as no surprise.
In addition to this 'moral grievance' (Ibrahim, 2014), students' engagement
was clearly bolstered by the unexpected ascent of the Liberal Democrats as
partners in the Coalition Government. Many had been attracted by the party's
election pledge to abolish fees and vote against any increase in Parliament,
and following their U-turn deserted them in large numbers. With at least one
in six students having voted Liberal Democrat, this auxiliary grievance was
a significant factor in building a critical mass of anti-£9,000 fees sentiment
on UK campuses.

Converting this sentiment into mass action, however, was a different matter. While the percentage of students who claimed to have participated in
the protests – 22.3 per cent – is not inconsiderable, it is significantly lower
than the percentage of students who opposed the Government's proposals.
To some extent, non-participation reflected certain demographic patterns
(including subject studied, domicile, and party voted for), though it is difficult
to generalise their attitudes on the evidence presented here. Plenty were at
least *following* the protests, with around a quarter claiming to have become
more politically engaged as a result. That said, a sizeable number may have
been put off participating by episodes of 'violence' as mediated and reported
by the mainstream media, though others showed signs of sympathy and
solidarity with protesters. Non-participant attitudes and demographics will be
explored in greater detail in chapter 7.

For students who *did* participate, the majority took part in lower-cost/risk
activities such as signing petitions, wearing badges, and 'liking' groups on
Facebook. As with student activism in the 1960s, only a very small minority
engaged regularly in 'high-cost/risk' activities, though as protest organisers they were also responsible for facilitating participatory opportunities
for the wider student population. Indeed, that attendances for marches and
demonstrations amounted to 10 per cent of the total student population was a
testament to the density of local-, regional-, and national-level marches they
organised in 2010 and 2011. Beyond a shared opposition to cuts and higher
tuition fees, however, high-cost/risk participants notably differed from the
rest when it came to their views on funding higher education, improving
democracy, and the legacy of the protests themselves. Their omnivorous

consumption of media, too, hints at different information and ideas being shared and debated in comparison to the vast majority of students.

Overall, it would seem that students' knowledge and discussion of politics played a significant part in their decision to participate – both in the student protests and in politics more generally. Among participants in the protests, these differences may have restricted opportunities for building a strong cross-repertoire collective identity – an issue that will be analysed further in chapter 6. Findings also indicate students' uncertainty with their own responsibilities as engaged and active citizens. Most were dissatisfied with the delivery of politics by parties and politicians, but were hesitant about supplanting formal politics for activism, ultimately considering the latter to be less effective than voting. While this did not preclude 93 per cent from having participated in some sort of political activity in the past three years, students were more politically engaged and confident the higher the cost/risk of activities they were typically involved in.

The emphasis on knowledge, conversation, and confidence arguably points to the importance of specific participation cultures which surround certain groups and activities. It is therefore necessary to explore in greater detail *how* students mobilise, including the social paths (and barriers) to their participation in protest and politics more generally. This forms the focus of the next chapter.

NOTES

1. Since only 19 respondents (0.8 per cent of the sample) identified as 'upper class', this category has been excluded from comparative analysis in this study.

2. $p = 0.05$.

3. Given that most of the survey's first-year undergraduates were ineligible to vote in the 2010 election, the fraction is likely to have been higher still for the 2010/11 academic year.

4. 7.3 per cent of first-year undergraduates took part in national/regional demonstrations, compared with 10.8 per cent of undergraduates in their second year or more ($p = 0.01$).

5. 2.4 per cent of first-year undergraduates took part in more than one national/regional demonstration, compared with 3.9 per cent of undergraduates in their second year or more ($p = 0.01$).

6. $p = 0.03$.

7. The UCL occupation in autumn 2010 was notable for attracting participants from the local Camden School for Girls (who had staged an occupation of their own), but this appeared to be atypical of campus occupations overall. Regrettably, school or college activism against fees and cuts was beyond the scope of this research.

8. Aggregating these scores reveals the anomaly that seven respondents participated without appearing to specify any particular activity. Four had ticked the 'other'

category, for which respondents were invited to state their activity in a free-text box. These results are not included in the participation index due to the problem of adding post hoc categories to the scoring, as well as the low yield of responses ($N = 34$).

9. The media preferences of low-cost/risk participants are also broadly comparable with the UK population as a whole (see Ofcom, 2013).

Chapter 5

Becoming a Participant

Activism Mobilisation and the University Campus

This chapter traces students' pathways to participation in activism, and how they are mobilised for action. Mobilisation has long been a subject of interest in social movement studies, with researchers seeking to expound on what lies between grievance and action. Given the importance of the campus for facilitating participatory opportunities, this book advocates a field and network approach for studying student mobilisation. This necessitates focusing on two key drivers: students' pre-university socialisation and their social networks on campus. The former is important considering the previous chapter's emphasis on accumulated knowledge, as students already equipped with a political background via family or school are well placed to quickly make the most of activism opportunities at university. In the case of the latter, authors such as Snow et al. (1980) and Oegema and Klandermans (1994) have argued that an individual's mobilisation is largely dependent on prior contact with recruitment agents, either formally (via an organisation's recruitment strategy) or informally (e.g. friends or other personal contacts). Through its density of social networks *and* its range of political agencies, the campus provides access to activism opportunities on a scale that most students will not have experienced before.

This chapter is divided into two sections. The first focuses on students' pathways to becoming politically active at university. Using survey and interview data, it considers the importance of family background and political upbringing on students' expectations of university and getting involved in activism. The second section considers paths and barriers to mobilisation in the fees and cuts protests – specifically concerning the sequence of events between October and November 2010. This studies how student campaigners generated protest events and activism opportunities on their respective campuses. In particular, it looks at mobilisation for two notable protest events:

the NUS national demonstration on 10 November 2010 and the NCAFC-facilitated 'National Walkout and Day of Action' two weeks later. Since chapter 4 identified a significant deficit between the percentages of students opposed to higher fees and those taking part in the protests, attention is also paid to the lesser-studied social *barriers* to participation. This includes the inhibitive effects of a students' apolitical socialisation and the neutering effects of campus 'counter-networks'.

STUDENT INTERVIEWS

In addition to survey data, chapters 5–7 draw extensively on the personal accounts of students interviewed for this book. Interviewees were based at six universities selected from the survey's overall sample: University of Cambridge, University College London (UCL), University of Edinburgh, University of Leeds, University of Roehampton, and University of Warwick. These were chosen on the basis that they represented relatively active campuses during the 2010/11 protests, enabling participants and non-participants who broadly shared the same mobilising opportunities to be studied side by side. Survey respondents were invited at the end of the questionnaire to be interviewed for the research, with prospective interviewees selected in order to ensure a sample of different participatory levels, including non-participants. Given their smaller fraction in the survey population, the recruitment of high-cost/risk participants was supplemented by forms of purposive sampling, with activism organisers contacted directly via social media or occupation blog sites, as well as through snowball sampling.

This process yielded a total of 56 interviewees from six universities. These took place between March and October 2012, principally in cafés located on each interviewee's campus. Analysis of participatory and non-participatory trends weaves survey data with interview quotations from all six universities, though the narrative of the protests traced in chapters 5 and 6 draws principally on the accounts of interviewees at Cambridge, Edinburgh, UCL, and Warwick. This is mainly because their respective accounts bore strong commonalities: all had sent large numbers of students to the NUS and NCAFC demonstrations, as well as hosting occupations in 2010 and 2011. This narrative coalescence made it easier to identify and analyse key variables which separated participants from non-participants, as students were often reacting to similar events, disputes, and mobilisation opportunities.

Of course, prioritising these four universities arguably comes at the cost of overall representativeness: as large, high-status Russell Group institutions with well-funded student unions, their student demographics and available resources should not be taken as typical of UK universities overall.

Nevertheless, these accounts are placed within the more representative trends of the survey dataset, while also allowing for more detailed comparisons of participants and non-participants who broadly shared the same opportunities to convert their sympathies into action.

POLITICISATION, FAMILY, AND SCHOOLING

In *Distinction*, Bourdieu (1984: 440) argues that 'political education ... is always partly received from the family, from the earliest days of life'. This emphasises the *process* of politicisation, including the accumulation of knowledge and the normalising of certain values and activities. Given how its repertoires have often resided outside traditional modes of citizenship, these processes are particularly relevant for activism socialisation. For example, Braungart and Braungart's (1990) life-course study of 1960s youth activist leaders found that most participants had in some way followed the direction of their parents: some cited the influence of their early exposure to activism through being taken picketing, whereas others took their inspiration from activism in their family history. This socialisation is partly dependent on accessibility to activism worlds and specific participatory opportunities, but it is nevertheless worth considering the effect of family background and pre-university activism on students' protest participation at university.

Table 5.1 considers the impact of students' upbringing on their activism participation prior to university. Survey respondents who recorded having participated in any of the issues listed in the questionnaire – including those specified as 'other' – are aggregated as having been engaged in activism before they became a student. There are admittedly limitations in how accurately this variable measures activism involvement: not only are definitions left unspecified, the listed choices show bias towards what might be considered 'left-wing' campaigning issues (even if a wider range were represented via the 'other' category, such as Help For Heroes and the Countryside Alliance). Nevertheless, results show 37.5 per cent of students were involved in some form of activism prior to university. There is correlation between this and family background: 53.3 per cent of students involved before university had grown up in a household where politics was discussed regularly or fairly often, whereas the corresponding figure for those not involved is 32.9 per cent. A similar pattern can be found with regard to the political participation of students' parents/guardians: 45.4 per cent of those with pre-university involvement had parents/guardians who were very/fairly active, whereas for those not involved the figure is 28.9 per cent.

The political socialisation of students with a pre-university activism background was explored in further detail in interviews. In line with findings from

Table 5.1   Comparing students' political background with their pre-university participation

		% Involved in activism prior to university (N = 931; 37.5%)	% Not involved in activism prior to university (N = 1,554; 62.5%)
At the time when you were growing up, how often was politics discussed at home?	Regularly	28.0	14.2
	Fairly often	25.3	18.7
	Sometimes	23.1	32.4
	Rarely	19.0	27.5
	Never/don't know	4.5	7.3
How politically active were your parents/ guardians when you were growing up?	Very active	8.9	3.9
	Fairly active	36.5	25.0
	Not very active	38.6	46.5
	Not at all active	13.7	21.4
	Don't know	2.3	3.3

N = 2,485. *Note*: Percentages by column.
Question: Please tick if you have been involved in any campaigns and protests relating to the following issues before you became a student (select all that apply): human rights/global justice; the environment; anti-racism/ethnic discrimination; gender rights and sexual politics; anti-war campaigns; anti-capitalism/ neo-liberalism; campaigns against cuts to the public sector in the UK; other (please specify).

table 5.1, the majority spoke of growing up in a household where political knowledge and media were readily accessible, and as teenagers they were encouraged to 'discuss politics around the dinner table'. Certain formative experiences were described with some significance: Andrew (Cambridge), for example, recalled finding a copy of Bertrand Russell's *History of Western Philosophy* in the family bookcase, whereas Lindsey (Edinburgh) spoke of learning about climate change via copies of *New Scientist* left 'by the loo at home'. For both, these interests led to reading contemporary writers such as Noam Chomsky and George Monbiot ('the slightly clichéd anti-establishment thinkers', according to Andrew). While neither claimed their respective parents qualified as activists, others were able to speak knowledgably about their family's political history and affiliations:

> I've been, like, left-wing all my life really – my family is political. My grandfather was very involved in the miners and stuff like that; my aunt was a full-time student organiser for a number of years. (Peter, Edinburgh)

> My parents met in the International Marxist group, and then joined the Labour Party on the Bennite wing. They both resigned their memberships in 1994 when Blair abolished Clause IV. So yeah, I was always brought up to be left-wing and sceptical of parties. (Damon, UCL)

Although many spoke admiringly of their political heritage, few claimed that this had determined their current activist identity. Parallels can be drawn here to research by Binder and Wood (2012), whose study of Conservative activists in the United States found that students were usually reluctant to present their politics as somehow unreflexively inherited from their parents, preferring instead to emphasise the development of their own political agency. Though this is hardly surprising given broader trends towards individualisation since the 1960s (see chapter 2), and it may be true that the political *content* of their upbringing differs from their current identity, this socialisation nevertheless provided students with a platform from which to embark or their *own* political journey. This includes the acquisition of skills (such as the ability to debate and defend political positions) and experiences of participation. UCL student Brett, for example, casually recalled 'being dragged along to the odd march by my parents', yet within these formative experiences he gained the legitimation of protest as an activity, as well as an ability to perform in this role accordingly.

Not all students involved in activism prior to university could draw on comparable formative experiences, however. Table 5.1 shows that 54.6 per cent did not consider their parents/guardians to have been active during this time, and 23.5 per cent claimed that politics was discussed rarely or never. For many of these students, their initial politicisation instead came from school. As illustrated in the case of Gaz, this typically developed out of studying history or politics, joining debating societies, or meeting already-politicised pupils:

> There was this guy at school and he must have been a socialist, and I remember starting to question the Iraq War and he was like, 'look, quite clearly this is about oil' and explained it. And at that point lots of things started to make sense. ... I was frequently involved in the debating society, and the more I did research for these debates the more I started to think this was *definitely* really bad. (Gaz, UCL)

The global protests against the Iraq War coincided with most 2010/11 undergraduates' early teenage years, and so represented for many their first major political issue of interest. Brett recalls 'spend[ing] hours and hours discussing Afghanistan, Iraq, and the War on Terror' when he was in sixth form, whereas Damon – having already been taken on London's 'million march' by his parents – helped organise walkouts in his school. For Andrew, commuting to a larger city for his sixth-form studies enabled him to befriend pupils from different social and ethnic backgrounds. With socialist parties also canvassing regularly outside his college, he soon felt motivated to start organising protests himself:

> The first real form of activism I took was when I mobilised a group of students from my sixth-form to go down to the Unite Against Fascism demo. It was quite

a terrifying experience because it was the first time I'd ever actually done something with my politics apart from read about it. (Andrew, Cambridge)

At a practical level, these formative experiences were an invaluable part
of developing a 'radical habitus' (Crossley, 2003) – Andrew, for example,
claimed that his demonstration-organising skills came in useful for his later
involvement in protest campaigns at university. At a more symbolic level, it is
also interesting how he and others identified particular biographical moments
from which they began to self-identify as an 'activist' or 'radicalised'. As
evidenced in Ronnie's experience of an anti-fascist protest against the British
National Party, and Gaz's participation in the 2008/9 Gaza protests in London, these moments involved witnessing or experiencing injustice, and then
seeing protest provides an effective and empowering response:

> I'd say that I've always been aware of [political] problems, but it wasn't until
> about 5 or 6 years ago that I ever thought it would be possible to act in a way
> where you could effect change. ... I think the fact that the first demonstration
> I went on was so effective – that was in Derbyshire, you know the BNP confer-
> ence? That was considered to be a very successful action – it pretty much shut
> down their conference. (Ronnie, Warwick)

> With Gaza there was the first big protest, and there were thousands who started
> to gather at the embassy. The police ... I just couldn't understand it, they were
> being just so violent, so physical. ... I just couldn't understand what they were
> doing, and it made me really fucking angry. (Gaz, UCL)

For others, their development of a political identity was predicated on the
absence of participatory opportunities. Table 5.1 identifies a third of students
who were not involved in activism prior to university who grew up in a
household where politics was discussed regularly/fairly often. Although some
may have instead participated in forms of electoral or civic politics, interview
accounts point to limited opportunities as instilling feelings of 'otherness':

> I'm from a village where nothing much really happens, so there isn't much dis-
> cussion of politics. ... I'd read a couple of books by Chomsky and stuff, but never
> sort of clicked applying this to day-to-day life so much. (Jeremy, Edinburgh)

> I moved from a school which had a big mix of people to a school that was in
> the middle of the countryside that was full of, like, racists and sexists and just
> Tory bastards really. And that made me think a lot about what my own politics
> were. (Bekka, Edinburgh)

> We do talk about politics a lot at home, and when I was at school that was
> something that marked me out a lot from my peers because they just weren't
> interested in politics and they didn't know anything about it. I didn't know any-
> one who would want to go to protests. (Angie, Cambridge)

These accounts point to common environmental factors that delayed Jeremy, Bekka, and Angie's entry into activism politics. Jeremy's frustrations came from the absence of participatory opportunities in his local environment, whereas Angie and Bekka lacked kindred spirits willing to battle against the seemingly apolitical (or right-wing) consensus at school. This contrasts with Damon and Andrew's schooling in culturally diverse urban centres, which gave them access to local events and grievances and a critical mass of potential co-conspirators. For Jeremy, Bekka, and Angie, accessing comparable opportunities would have to wait until university.

Of course, a significant proportion of students with no pre-university activism involvement did not grow up in politically active households either: more than a third recalled politics being discussed rarely or never, and two-thirds claimed that their parents/guardians were not very/at all politically active (more than 40 per cent of the total survey population). Student interviewees in this category recounted a pre-university socialisation that was at times antithetical to accounts presented so far. For example, when asked if they knew who their parents voted for, many were unable to provide a definite answer:

> We don't discuss [politics] at all. I have no idea what any of my family's political opinions are. I know my dad is not Conservative, but I don't know what he actually is. (Heather, Leeds)

> My parents never really discuss politics. I think my parents are probably Lib Dem supporters if I had to [guess]. Maybe that's why I'm not particularly politically strong. (Louise, UCL)

The opaqueness of their parents' political self-identification is indicative of a family socialisation in which political thought and action was afforded little social value. As a result, certain key tools of active engagement – listening to and critiquing arguments, reading up on an issue, defending one's own views – were not passed onto these students at this stage. For Cambridge student Cynthia, the legacy of this apolitical socialisation was felt very strongly. She claimed that her parents avoided politics as a point of conversation on the grounds that to talk about it would be invasive and impolite, leaving her feeling ill-equipped as an adult to even discuss politics with close friends. Recalling the work of Eliasoph (1998), it would seem that an 'apolitical' habitus can be inherited in much the same way as a 'radical' habitus. But whereas this was a source of frustration to Cynthia, Sharon felt comfortable with her family's attitude towards political participation:

> The main reason people vote the way they do is because that's what their parents voted, and I make no pretence that I'm not active because I'm just copying

them. ... We're political in that we complain a lot, but there's never been any
kind of 'let's go and make a difference, let's go and protest'. We wouldn't write
a letter to our MP or anything like that. (Sharon, Warwick)

In some ways, Sharon's explanations for her limited engagement recall
findings from chapter 4 about the *delivery* of politics being the problem.
Her experience is shared, albeit more benignly, by Julian (Leeds) and Rick
(Edinburgh), both of whom recalled growing up in a household where politics
was discussed more as a subject for satire than debate and action:

We were big fans of satirical news programmes, so we used to watch *Have
I Got News For You* and so on. We did talk a lot about politics, and generally it
was quite negative towards whoever was in power at the time! ... I think maybe
because politics is something that we openly discuss, that diffuses the need to
go out and do something active. (Rick, Edinburgh)

It was a very liberal household, so there was always some scathing comment
about something New Labour were doing, or whatever. But we never really
talked extensively about it – we'd see it through things like *Have I Got News
For You* – that's where the political discussions would come out – [but] I never
spoke politics that much with my parents. (Julian, Leeds)

This 'sideways' view of politics also seemingly played a part in Julian and
Rick's decision to study politics at university. Of course, studying politics
does not discourage participation – several self-defined activists had also
taken the subject – but in Rick's case especially it may have reinforced his
characterisation of political discussion and political participation as somehow
incompatible. Moreover, when asked about his reluctance to participate, he
recounted his parents' experience of accidentally getting caught up in an anti-
Iraq War demonstration in Edinburgh. This incident had seemingly given him
a lasting impression of protest as a volatile activity:

One time they were going down Princes Street and ended up being kettled
because they were too close to some people protesting. That sort of idea puts
me off wanting to be anywhere near active protests, because even if you're not
taking part you can end up getting caught up in it. (Rick, Edinburgh)

Rick's positionality (via his parents) as a cautious spectator stands in stark
contrast to those of Ronnie, Gaz, and Andrew, all of whom found being in
the thick of such volatility a trigger for feelings of empowerment. As well
as providing many of the emotional responses to protest that Jasper (1997)
and others consider as exhilarating for participants, these experiences would
give them a clear head start when later provided with activism opportunities
on campus.

ARRIVING AT UNIVERSITY

It is clear that students' formative experiences of protest and activism played a significant part in shaping their political engagement once at university. Table 5.2 shows a strong relationship between access to political discussion growing up and discussion of politics once at university: three-quarters of those whose family home saw politics being discussed regularly/fairly often have continued this since arriving at university. However, the percentage of students who grew up with politics being discussed rarely/never and who have continued this at university stands at only 53 per cent. This suggests that the campus has had a politicising effect on many of these students, with nearly a quarter now claiming to discuss politics regularly or fairly often. This owes a great deal to the resources provided by the campus field, both socially and institutionally. For most first-year undergraduates, entry into university involves a relative or temporary disconnection from home ties, necessitating the establishing of new ones. Those living in campus-managed accommodation are especially advantaged for this task, due to their close proximity to fellow residential students. The intimacy of this 'instant social network' (Sims, 2007) is therefore likely to encourage conversation and debate around students' differing backgrounds, as well as their expectations of university.

In more practical terms, the need to build social networks also gives motivation for trying out new activities and experiences. This may include politics and activism: as discussed in chapter 3, most large campuses feature a range of different student-run political groups and societies and a corresponding social network of activists who run them. According to Crossley and Ibrahim (2012), this overarching 'political world' generates most activism opportunities on campus, even if its network density of mutual affinities and loyalties can be difficult for newcomers to penetrate. Accessing this network is notably easier for freshers already equipped with prior involvement in activism: not only will they have acquired valuable knowledge and skills that may be

Table 5.2 Comparing students' pre-university activism with current discussion of politics

		Discussion of politics		
		Regularly/ fairly often (%)	Sometimes (%)	Rarely/never (%)
At the time when you were growing up, how often was politics discussed at home?	Regularly/fairly often	75.9	19.6	4.6
	Sometimes	34.5	46.1	19.4
	Rarely/never/ don't know	23.7	23.3	53.0

N = 553. *Note*: Percentages by row.
Questions: At the time when you were growing up, how often was politics discussed at home? How often do you discuss politics?

useful to groups and societies, but they also are more likely to possess a social *confidence* when it comes to establishing bonds with other activists. For students such as Andrew (an undergraduate) and Graham (a postgraduate), their possession of a 'radical habitus' even extended to having connections with activists and groups on campus prior to their arrival:

> I'd been talking to various people who'd found that I was going to Cambridge and contacted me and said 'oh yeah, there's this great anti-cuts group, since you're really political'. (Andrew, Cambridge)

> I started at UCL and the very first thing I did on campus was a London Living Wage protest. I recognised a couple of faces from the old political landscape, and on the back of that I got some space on a [fresher's fair] stall to promote a mass-action to shut down the oil refinery in Kent. By doing that stall, I met a couple of the old-hat union activists. ... So very quickly I got to know the limits of the amount of people that were doing stuff here. (Graham, UCL)

Graham and Damon's experiences recall Tilly's (2004) concept of the 'social movement entrepreneur' insofar as both came to university intent on bringing specific campaign issues to the campus. For Damon, this issue was higher education policy:

> I came into university knowing that I was going to be political so I was elected a delegate to the NUS conference in my first year. Most of the activism I started doing was UCL Students for Free Education because NUS had ditched free education as a policy and started backing a graduate tax, and we felt that we had to do something or it would just fall entirely off the agenda. (Damon, UCL)

For students from political backgrounds who had *not* been active prior to university, arriving on campus represented an opportunity to make up for lost time. Raphael and Angie were proactive in their efforts to situate themselves firmly in the sorts of groups and networks they had lacked at school:

> I researched exactly what I wanted to do before I even came here. I found this little group and looked at different groups on campus, so I made contact with them, probably in the first week of being here, and then joined in at that point. (Raphael, Warwick)

> Something that I found really nice about coming to university is that I could get involved a bit more. Part of the reason why I chose King's as my college was because I knew it had a reputation for left-wing politics. (Angie, Cambridge)

Angie's choice of college recalls Van Dyke's (1998) argument that an institution's past reputation can generate its own self-sustaining activism culture through the new recruits it attracts. Not all campuses necessarily

boast such prominent histories, however, nor might freshers have the autonomy to position themselves in certifiably 'political' residencies: Peter and
Bekka, for example, both arrived at Edinburgh with comparable political
ambitions, but cited their respective halls of residence as creating network
cross-pressures:

> My first year was basically a write-off – I came expecting to do lots of politics
> and activism and so on, [but] it just never really happened. I was in catered
> halls and it was quite an inward-looking community there, and I ended up doing
> very dull things like drinking Carlsberg. In my second year I got much more
> involved. (Peter, Edinburgh)

> I remember in first year getting a bit involved in Socialist Worker, and a lot of
> my friends I made in halls – who aren't my friends anymore – were kind of con-
> demning me for that, and didn't really, like, understand the reasons for wanting
> to get involved more in politics. ... I think as well when you're first starting to
> engage in politics and going on demos and stuff, especially if you don't know
> people, like, your friends aren't doing it, it can be kind of alien[ating]. (Bekka,
> Edinburgh)

Both accounts speak of environmental factors as having a demotivating
effect on students' access to participatory opportunities. This may reflect the
fragile confidence and social malleability of some students when first entering a new and unfamiliar social setting, but it also adds a further dimension
to Crossley and Ibrahim's (2012) findings – namely, that belonging to the
wrong networks can delay or preclude participation. Bekka's experience in
particular recalls Oegema and Klandermans's (1994) concept of 'erosion':
in cases where participating threatens to cause *too much* social pressure and
antagonism – especially among friends – non-participation becomes the
easier option. For Bekka, this network positioning appeared to erode – or
rather, *corrode* – her confidence as a budding activist, leaving her effectively
trapped in a 'counter-network' of disapproving non-participants.

If some students found themselves in the wrong networks to realise their
political ambitions, others unsuspectedly found themselves in the *right* networks for such opportunities. In Marianne's case, the collegiate network
at Cambridge provided a pathway to her participation in union politics. In
contrast to Bekka, this environment helped her develop a social confidence,
resulting in her later becoming president of her college union:

> I had done a bit of committee stuff previously, but never been the person who
> stood at the front of things. I came to university and realised I could do things
> I probably didn't think I could do earlier on. I think it's a social confidence, but
> also realising that other people were perhaps not any better at things than I was!
> (Marianne, Cambridge)

In sum, it would seem that students' initial network positioning plays a significant role in how they develop personal interests and affinities, political or otherwise. To some extent, this is governable, with the more confident students proactively seeking out the groups and networks they wish to join. Students with a political family background or prior involvement in activism are likely to find this process easier, as they already possess the skills, knowledge, and confidence to self-identify as activists and perform accordingly. For those lacking in these resources, however, their involvement is more dependent on the luck of the draw: some may find themselves in a social context that encourages participation (even if they did not initially seek it), whereas others will find their ambitions dampened by a context where activism is either undervalued or actively discouraged. After all, finding friends and acclimatising to university life represents a fundamental priority for most freshers, and without the external prompting of major grievances, this process may not necessarily stimulate their interests in politics and activism.

There has been little discussion so far of the mobilising appeal of such grievances. It might be the case that collective action frames which attract widespread media attention have the potential to get these networks talking about politics, and even inspire self-generated paths to participation. In such contexts, explaining *non*-participation – especially in the case of a 'popular' grievance such as the 2010/11 protests – necessitates the introduction of new variables.

THE 2010/11 STUDENT PROTESTS: COORDINATING NETWORKS AND RESOURCES

As detailed in chapter 3, the 2010/11 student protests against fees and cuts has its roots in the commissioning of the Browne Review in November 2009. With sector leaders anticipating its recommendation of an increase to the cap on tuition fees for students in England, free education campaigners across the UK were braced for the arrival of a new grievance requiring mass mobilisation. For activists based at universities such as Cambridge, Edinburgh, UCL, and Warwick, these grievances were at least partly directed at their own management: as members of the elite Russell Group, they had effectively spent the past decade lobbying for the tuition fees cap to be abolished altogether. Those at Warwick and UCL further bemoaned their university's 'right-wing' reputation, with students from the latter having run no-confidence campaigns against their vice-chancellor for his advisory role in recent NHS restructuring reforms.

What activists at each of these universities – along with many others in the Russell Group – had in their favour was an access to considerable campaign resources. Much like Crossley and Ibrahim's (2012) study of the University of Manchester, each university boasted a large, interconnected network of left-wing political groups and societies. For new students interested in getting involved in activism, this density of groups offered multiple entry points, especially at Edinburgh:

> There was everything you can imagine – so, in terms of political parties there were Tories, Labour, SNP, Lib Dems, Greens, and Socialists. In terms of campaign groups People & Planet was probably the biggest, but there was Stop Aids, Amnesty, Students Act for Refugees, Students For a Free Tibet, others I've probably forgotten. I don't know of any other university that has all those different groups. (Lindsey, Edinburgh)

In aggregation, this network offered great organisational and mobilising potential, though interviewees' depictions of the relationships between left-leaning activism groups prior to the protests tended to vary. There was usually a strong personnel overlap, which created a productive relationship when it came to mobilising for each group's respective campaigns. This also reflected a broad underlying consensus between these groups on left-leaning issues and causes, from anti-fascism and nuclear disarmament, to LGBT activism and the environment. Recalling historical patterns of fractional disputes discussed in chapter 3, however, fault lines frequently emerged between Labour Party affiliates and the more radical left-wing groups such as the Socialist Workers Party (SWP) and Alliance for Workers Liberty (AWL). Activists also recalled disagreements within the radical left milieu itself, and while these differences usually had ideological roots – anarchism versus socialism, reform versus revolution, hierarchy versus network – they also took on a *social* character due to the fusing of political groups with affinity networks. This point is well described by Ronnie:

> In the social circles that I'm in, people's friends tend to be quite ideologically close, so one exacerbates the other, which is that you don't like it when somebody challenges your political beliefs, but you don't like it when somebody challenges your friends, and if that's both, then I think it makes the factionalism worse. … I think that group-herd mentality leads to people drawing boundaries that often aren't really there between yourself and other people with whom you share 90–95 per cent of the same beliefs. (Ronnie, Warwick)

These factional tensions sometimes reflected how the overall network's 'core' would periodically shift between different groups and societies. This would usually depend on which group was the natural focal point for the most prominent leftist campaign issue of the time, and/or boasted the network's largest membership overlap. In other words, the network core could be found wherever the largest number of members met the most frequently. When Eric arrived at university in 2008, the group in question at Cambridge was ENS:

> Before I came to Cambridge I looked up on the website of societies and picked a load that looked quite interesting. I very quickly found that ENS was quite active, and lots of people from other societies were using ENS as an umbrella group. So it was quite a good coordinating hub. (Eric, Cambridge)

Considering the relative lull in free education campaigns during this time, the network centrality of this particular group owed in part to ENS's status as a national campaign and de facto pressure group to the NUS. At Edinburgh and Warwick, however, activism in the late 2000s was dominated by the work of SJP. Israel's military assaults on Gaza in late 2008 presented a collective action frame for students to mobilise in solidarity with Palestine, as well as promote its grievances to a largely impervious wider population. Given its added symbolic appeal, students revived the campus occupation as their key repertoire, with approximately 20 taking place across the UK in early 2009. Not only did these occupations herald the return of simultaneous, high-cost/risk student protest on UK campuses, interviewees from Cambridge, Edinburgh, and Warwick recalled that they also had a significant coordinating effect on their respective activism networks. Aided by the adoption of consensus decision-making processes via recent Climate Camps, each brought together activists from across the network into an open, discussion-based environment. This also had long-term benefits, as at least five or six participants would later help establish similarly organised occupations for the tuition fees protests in autumn 2010:

> What [the occupation] did was get a lot of the student left together in a room for a long enough time that they got to make friends and learn from each other, which was very useful preparation for what happened two years later – I think that happened nationally. (Lindsey, Edinburgh)

For students only semi-connected to activism networks, the Gaza occupations represented an opportunity to meet a wider range of activists on campus. They also provided a forum to challenge some of their own political preconceptions, while learning new organisational skills and campaign tactics. The experience was undoubtedly valuable for John and Marianne, both of whom would later participate in campus occupations in 2010 and 2011:

> That was the first time I met lots of the people who were involved in the left on campus. … I went to the Gaza occupation originally thinking 'I agree with

everything they're saying but I just don't like their tactics', but actually when I got there I had a conversation with a couple of people and decided to stay. (John, Edinburgh)

On the one hand I felt like I *should* be there, and on the other hand I felt 'this is so out of my comfort zone'. ... But I came along a couple of times and spent one or two nights there. It was a sort of gentle entry to methods that I had never been involved with previously. (Marianne, Cambridge)

Despite this skills transfer, activists remained conscious of the problems in maintaining groups and campaigns across successive cohorts. Communications technologies had made it easier to pass groups' online architecture of mailing lists, campaign content, and websites onto new members, but interviewees nevertheless highlighted difficulties associated with losing influential personnel once they graduated. Of particular value were activism 'advocates', whose social connectedness and mobilising skills were extremely valuable for organising protest events. Advocates differ from political 'leaders' in the Weberian sense insofar as they do not necessarily hold any formal position of authority. Rather, they are highly networked individuals who can harness their connectedness – both inside and outside of activism worlds – to promote events and help ensure strong turnouts (see also Raine and Wellman, 2012). This also reflected the general shift in popularity from traditional group hierarchies (headed by either elected leaders or self-appointed committees) to more horizontal and consensus-based organisation processes. Although 'leaderless' in principle, the latter nevertheless required skilled and knowledgeable participants to ensure their effective running. The role of organisational structures and their impact on participation will be a key theme for chapter 6.

BUILDING FOR THE NUS DEMONSTRATION

It was noted earlier in this chapter that the late-2000s represented a relative fallow period for higher education funding activism at UK universities. On the campuses studied, this was further hindered by the fact that certain free education campaigners had graduated without being replaced, while other activists had shifted their energies to Climate Camp and pro-Palestine movements. Anticipating the Browne Review's likely recommendations, Raphael, Damon, Eric, and Peter all recognised the need to resurrect free education as a campaign issue. This necessitated building new groups and coalitions with fresh identities in order to attract new members:

We used to run a magazine called Dissident Warwick, which published two or three times a term ... but those were the Blair and Brown years so it was a much smaller group. Most of them left after my first year, because they were all in their final year. (Raphael, Warwick)

In April 2009, all of the left at UCL went off on a year abroad so I'm left running Stop the War society, Friends of Palestine society, the Free Education campaign, the Living Wage campaign. Over the summer we start talking about a national convention against fees, the idea being at the time that free education is falling off the political map because NUS isn't backing it. (Damon, UCL)

So 2009/10, post-ENS, there wasn't very much going on at all. Lots of people went out and did Climate Camp stuff. There wasn't any broad forum so the task for activists in the next academic year was setting up something called the Cambridge Left Group. (Eric, Cambridge)

Towards the end of my second year, I was like, 'okay, there's all these different groups on campus doing things – why are all these people not co-ordinating?' ... There was some appetite for it, and then what actually happened is a separate, simultaneous initiative from the SWP *did* start, and that was the Anti-Cuts Coalition. (Peter, Edinburgh)

'Austerity politics' soon became the key issue of scrutiny following the formation of the Conservative-Liberal Democrat Coalition Government. Their programme of mass cuts to the public sector provided a UK-wide context to higher education funding, making it the pre-eminent collective action frame for students by autumn 2010. Consequently, these new groups and coalitions were important for reframing left-leaning activists' political focus on campus away from other campaigns and interests, and providing the central forum for debate and discussion within the wider activism network:

[I organised] the UCL Education Forum, which was every Wednesday at 5pm, with free food and drink. And I branded it in quite a lefty way, and we got quite a lot of random people coming to it, so it was 30–40 people and we would sit in a big circle and we'd talk. (Damon, UCL)

By the second meeting there were suddenly 80 people there. That was the day after the Browne Report, and we realised that we were entering a different period now. So it became a kind of anti-Browne Review meeting, and it happened every Wednesday and eventually we had to book bigger rooms. ... [We] got a whole wave of new people who had maybe done a bit of activism here and there, now brought into educational activism for the first time. (Eric, Cambridge)

The upsurge in attendance reflected that, in Eric's words, student activism was 'entering a different period'. With mainstream and alternative media providing regular commentaries of the new Coalition Government's policy programme, austerity politics was now the political conversation of the day. The NUS's position, however, remained cautious. Due to its historical links to the Labour Party, it had grown unaccustomed to organising major collective action drives against government during the 2000s. Labour's general election defeat, however, enabled NCAFC and EAN to pressurise the NUS into calling a national demonstration for 10 November 2010 in London – two weeks after the Browne Review's publication, and the first of its kind since 2006.

Following the Browne Review's publication in October, and the Coalition Government's resultant proposal to treble the cap on fees to £9,000 per year, the Liberal Democrats' earlier electoral pledge to oppose any increase in Parliament was attracting considerable media scrutiny. This left the newly formed campaign groups confident in their ability to mobilise resources for the NUS demonstration. According to Andrew, Cambridge Defend Education (CDE) succeeded in pressurising Cambridge University Students' Union (CUSU) into organising multiple coaches to London, resulting in 362 students attending the march (*The Guardian*, 10 November 2010). The same paper also reported 150 attendees coming from Warwick and 1,000 from UCL (aided, of course, by its central London location). Landed with the steeper task of mobilising students for an 800-mile round trip, activists at Edinburgh were especially keen to ensure a strong turnout:

> I was one of the very few people who was heavily involved in the Anti-Cuts Coalition whilst still being very involved in EUSA [Edinburgh University Students' Association]. ... We didn't even charge them, which from what I can tell is quite rare in student union politics. So people would give a five pound deposit: that got them the journey there and back, and a packed-lunch for the day – like a school trip (*laughs*). We spent almost £10,000 on it. (Peter, Edinburgh)

EUSA later reported that five coaches containing a total of 250 students travelled to London for the demonstration (EUSA, 2010). Given the critical mass of disgruntled Liberal Democrat voters highlighted in chapter 4, there was seemingly no shortage of potential participants. Jeremy, Rhiannon, and Danny – all undergraduates with nascent interests in politics but no prior activism experience – were attracted by the twin advantages of low entry costs to participation, and the availability of friends with whom they could attend:

> I was going to go on the demo because a friend – a new friend at uni – said, you know, 'Let's go on this, it looks like fun'. And so I thought, 'Yeah, this is what you do at uni: yeah, what a great opportunity – £5 bus to London and back.' (Jeremy, Edinburgh)

I was with a group of friends from first year – about six of us. Of those six, four are now really involved. (Rhiannon, Edinburgh)

I found out that my flatmate was going. I decided I would go down, but a big concern with going on this trip was not knowing anyone on it – that was a *terrifying* concern, so it helped that I knew she was going. (Danny, Edinburgh)

As Danny's initial worries attest, first-time demonstrators commonly cited the importance of attending in the company of friends. Nobody wanted to go alone. This highlights the fact that for most people, attending a demonstration is a fundamentally *social* activity, and for first-timers especially, the presence of friends would help them share and make sense of the experience. However, participation was not necessarily dependent on the possession of ties to experienced activist advocates who could act as 'brokers'. Rather, the public prominence of the fees grievance – amplified by its extensive media coverage – encouraged a 'pull up' effect, whereby micro-networks of students with little or no prior activism experience would encourage each other into taking part. This recalls McAdam's (1986) emphasis on recruitment networks as generating mutual expectations between prospective participants, yet this desire not to be 'left out' arguably also reflected students' anticipation of participating in an event that was likely to be of national significance. Given students' high newspaper consumption identified in chapter 4, this point is well captured by Damon:

Students believe that a movement is worth fighting in when they see it reflected by an alternate reality. When the mainstream media is writing the same kind of articles that appear in their student paper, they go 'ah, wait – this one matters'. (Damon, UCL)

The magnifying impact of this 'alternate reality' also contributed to Donna's mobilisation: as a UCL student, she was not faced with high participatory costs for attending the London-based demonstration, yet felt similar barriers of inexperience and social hesitancy to those travelling from Edinburgh. These reservations were clearly outweighed by the social pressures created by the fact that her whole friendship group attended:

I was interested in [politics], but I wasn't an activist. … I had a boyfriend at Oxford who was incredibly political and as soon as the Browne Review came out, all my friends at different universities were talking about it, and he got involved immediately in organising something. So I was hearing about that a lot, and I was talking about it with my friends, and some of my friends were quite political – not activists – they were keen Labour supporters. But I wasn't. So we were all talking about it, and we decided to go on the first demo which was on 10th November. My whole friendship group went on that march. (Donna, UCL)

Network pressures were felt differently by more experienced activists: some felt a sense of duty or obligation to attend, but this was not matched by any social hesitancy. As well as being seasoned marchers, they could also participate in the confidence that, like Brett, they would likely 'bump into' various activist friends along the way. For lacking this network connectedness, or the 'pull up' effects of Jeremy, Rhiannon, Danny, and Donna's friendship groups, we may again consider the role of counter-networks. Not only do these networks remove a key social motivation to participation, they may normalise or even legitimise non-participation. This was arguably true for Bekka, whose initial enthusiasm for activism had been knocked back by the corroding effects of her friendship group:

> I had my opinions about [the fees increase]. I thought – and still think – that it's absolutely disgusting and it's elitist. But I wasn't really as engaged as I should have been – I didn't go to any of the things in London, and I don't feel guilty about that but I kind of feel that I should have stopped being so lazy and done it. Me and my flatmate were just like, 'oh yeah, we should really go to that, yeah, we should really go … oh whoops, we haven't gone'. (Bekka, Edinburgh)

As an Edinburgh student, Bekka was subjected the same travel incentives for the NUS demonstration as Jeremy, Danny and Rhiannon, but lacked the surrounding network links to make participation appear desirable or expected. Much like Bourdieu's habitus, however, counter-networks should be seen as *constraining* rather than determining. By her final year of study, Bekka recognised that she would have to be more proactive in order to convert her dormant interests into action. Consequently, she extracted herself from her counter-network, joined groups and societies, made new friends, and ultimately reinvented herself as a student activist. However, most students in her position may not possess the self-awareness and wherewithal to break out of the latent constraints imposed by their network position. To do so requires subverting the norms and values of one's environment and seeking out new and unfamiliar situations – a process Bekka described as akin to 'going to a party where you don't know anybody'.

DIGESTING MILLBANK: STUDENT NETWORKS OF DELIBERATION

As recounted in chapter 1, the NUS demonstration on 11 November 2010 provided the fees and cuts campaign its dramatic scale shift. Although a smattering of local marches and occupations had taken place in the immediate aftermath of the Browne Review's publication, this was the event that focused the attentions of students, the media, and the general public on what was at stake. The scale and mobilising reach of the march engendered a sense of awe, pride, and solidarity among most participants, but it was the attack on Conservative HQ that suddenly transformed expectations of students' collective agency. Certainly, for those activists who had drifted towards Climate Camp and other high-cost/risk campaigns, Millbank opened up the possibilities of what sort of mass movement could be achieved:

> I knew there was a protest, but I hadn't really paid much attention to it. I was expecting it to be fairly washed out, few thousand, like what happened with the last one. (Gaz, UCL)

> To be honest, I was very defeatist about the entire thing, thinking it would just be this stupid march where you walk around for a bit, and Tony Benn speaks, and just … the usual. And I didn't realise how big of a struggle and how big of an issue it was. (Raphael, Warwick)

> I was thinking 'oh, it's going to be another march, we'll sing a few chants and we'll march along' … but I was amazed by how many people were there. … Just seeing sixth-form kids smashing up Tory HQ and dancing around to dubstep was fucking brilliant – they're only kids, I'm a bit older than them, but they fucking know instinctively that the Tories are fucking scum (*laughs*). (Brett, UCL)

Given that the previous student march against fees in 2006 had drawn around 5,000 people, such low expectations were not entirely without reason. Organisationally, the turnout of 52,000 students owed not only to NUS's significant resource outlay, but also to the work of numerous activism groups across the UK which, like CDE at Cambridge and Edinburgh's Anti-Cuts Coalition, had successfully lobbied their student unions into providing travel arrangements. The demonstration's relevance to the contemporary news story of the as-yet-untested Coalition Government's new austerity agenda was expected to attract the attentions of the UK press, but its scale and unfolding disorder saw Millbank dominate the news for that week. However, the mediation of violence divided students, leaving many in a quandary as to its value:

> We were all absolutely terrified, like, 'I can't believe that they've done that, they've ruined our protest and they're just going to think we're all really violent'. So we left and went to a pub, and the pub had the TV on showing the student protests with all the footage from Millbank! So were all sitting there, going, 'ah, we wouldn't have really got this coverage otherwise, would've we?' and we had this awkward moment of being, like, 'it's great! We're on the news … but that was really awful'. (Rhiannon, Edinburgh)

Arguably a key component of Millbank's power was the *uncertainty* caused by the protesters' actions, recalling Alinsky's (1971: 129) maxim that 'the threat is usually more terrifying than the thing itself'. For certain activists experienced in anarchist tactics – and, indeed, first-time participants with a strong appreciation of media spectacles – Millbank succeeded in disrupting the now-normalised conventions of student protest and, in so doing, forced its way onto the media agenda. Both on the ground and on television, this occupation of space had generated its own form of counter-power, instilling feelings of empowerment that far outweighed in significance the physical actions themselves:

> I was very much seeing it from a tactical perspective, of suddenly going 'wow, this caused a massive media storm', looking at it from the media side of things. (Jeremy, Edinburgh)

> I think the feeling on that day – especially speaking to some of my friends who wouldn't have defined themselves as 'activists' before that, they really felt empowered, they felt that for the first time in their lives they had the power to make the people *with* power pay attention to them. (Ronnie, Warwick)

> I remember going home feeling that it was a significant thing that had occurred, and that the political landscape in the UK ... you know, things weren't going to be quite the same afterwards. (Graham, UCL)

For other participants, however, Millbank was considered self-defeating – both in the fear and uncertainty *they* had felt on the day, and in the way it depicted students to the wider public. The latter was especially a concern for Roehampton students Laura and Hayley:

> We ended up in a pub because everywhere was not letting students in. And we were sitting there and this woman was like, 'has this got anything to do with you?' and she was pointing to the TV. And as we were watching it, people [were] throwing things off the top of Millbank. I felt quite disgusted because ... I mean, I don't always agree with the police and their approaches to things, but to drop something off of a building is absolutely disgusting – you cannot justify it. (Laura, Roehampton)

> [Millbank] upset me because a lot of people – friends, people in passing – know that you're a student directly after that. ... 'Oh, you're a student, oh don't start a riot!' ... Every student is now sort of in a box, and because I live off campus I was incredibly offended to be associated with it. (Hayley, Roehampton)

It is interesting how Laura and Hayley both recalled anger at being made to feel somehow *accountable* for Millbank. There may have been a network aspect to this: as mature students, neither was strongly embedded in undergraduate student life since both worked part-time and lived away from campus. Hayley was mother to a young child and spoke of the reaction other parents had to the event on her school run. Given their range of surrounding social networks, it is perhaps unsurprising that both placed greater emphasis on how events such as Millbank – especially the fire extinguisher incident – would be perceived by non-students. Despite their strong opposition to the fees increase, both would play a more limited role in the rest of the campaign.

For many of the demonstrators who *did* participate in follow-up protests, Millbank was received with a mixture of excitement and caution. Although appreciative of how it had broken the shackles of ineffectual 'polite protest' (a notion many linked with the 2003 Iraq War demonstration), they were also concerned that the media coverage would alienate the wider public and deter ordinary students from participating in future actions. Again, students' network position was important to how this was resolved. In the week following the NUS demonstration, debates took place formally via student unions and informally among networks and affinity groups. It was through these debates that high-cost/risk activists developed a shared consensus on how Millbank should be framed:

> I think I stood by Millbank being very bad up until there was a motion taken to Student Council – by this point I recognised the people who I thought were the people who were clever and who got it and who I wanted to be friends with. And that was the first time I heard someone say that violence is very different if it's towards an inanimate object. ... I guess hearing people talk about that changed my mind a huge amount. (Rhiannon, Edinburgh)

> My immediate reaction to Millbank was kind of 'ah, this is crazy', and now I've revised my opinions of it. ... I spent a lot of time thinking about it myself, and then I started talking to other people about it, bouncing ideas off people – political friends whose opinions I trusted ... and I realised that I'd been thinking about it in a kind of reactionary way. (Andrew, Cambridge)

Both Rhiannon and Andrew's reflections capture the importance of social networks as a resource for developing shared narratives. Through listening to activists whom they respected and trusted, both gained confidence in articulating a political defence of Millbank. Moreover, this process brought with it a growing sense of their activist identity – especially for Rhiannon, who as a fresher in her first term of study was still seeking out friendship networks that matched her interests. For each campus's activism network, reaching consensus over the 'Millbank defence' enabled activists to more effectively counteract mainstream media discourses that the protests had been 'violent', 'thuggish', and 'infantile'.[1] With the 'fire extinguisher incident' sidestepped as an unfortunate anomaly,[2] this involved distinguishing between 'symbolic' and 'actual' violence (see DeLuca and Peeples, 2002). Most activists at least agreed that Millbank had created a political *event* out of the fees and cuts campaign, to the extent that students' grievances were now being amplified by the mainstream media on a scale far beyond what they could typically achieve by themselves. With the fees vote still four weeks away, and the NUS reluctant to organise further events within this time,[3] activists recognised the need to bring this sense of agency back to the campus. NCAFC's 'National Walkout and Day of Action', scheduled for 24 November, was therefore perfect:

> Millbank gave us coverage in terms of all of a sudden every newspaper in the country would be calling you, going 'when is the next big mobilisation?' … So activists on the student left felt confident, and they had a date two weeks away, which is a decent amount of time to build for an action. (Damon, UCL)

This sense of agency became all the more palpable in the week following the NUS demonstration, with interviewees recalling a surge in attendance for anti-fees and cuts campaign meetings. Meetings often involved debates on the ethics of Millbank – with many students voicing criticisms – but given the broad underlying opposition to the fees and cuts, this was not considered a problem for campaigners. As Damon recalled, 'It was "job done" – they were in the room!'

BRINGING MILLBANK TO THE CAMPUS: THE NCAFC DAY OF ACTION, AND THE UNIVERSITY OCCUPATIONS

Key to the appeal of the 'Day of Action' was its merging of local-and UK-level activism, and the openness of its brief. In addition to announcing its own demonstration in central London, NCAFC's press release encouraged 'students of all ages and backgrounds to take peaceful and creative forms of political protest and direct action' (NCAFC, 2010). This provided a focal point for student groups to mobilise simultaneously en masse across the UK, thereby coordinating a single spectacle out of multiple local events. Moreover, its flexibility enabled students to organise events on their own terms: activists at University of East Anglia, for example, stressed the peaceful nature of their march *in opposition* to the radicalism of Millbank (Norwich Evening News, 2010). Those at Cambridge, Edinburgh, UCL, and Warwick, however, all planned a similar sequence of events to those of the previous fortnight, namely a union-arranged march that could be diverted into occupying university property. This had the dual benefit of maintaining the campaign's radical narrative post-Millbank, while also encouraging the participation of students who had not attended the NUS demonstration. With invitations sent out via Facebook, banners put up across campuses, and the UK press eagerly anticipating the 'next big mobilisation', news of the Day of Action was able

to reach students in halls of residences and shared houses who had hitherto
been impervious to activism. This was certainly true for UCL student Justine,
who, like Donna before, was persuaded to take part via friendly peer pressure:

> [My housemates] were friends I made on my course – I never even knew that they
> were political! ... They went to a couple of meetings and then were like, 'There's
> going to be this thing called an occupation ...' and I was like, 'I don't care about
> the fee rise, what's it got to do with me?' And so my friend was like, 'Do you
> think I would have even been able to start doing any of this if the fee rise had come
> into play before we started our degree?' And so I got really emotional – because
> I'd had a bottle of wine, obviously – and was like, 'Oh, that's *so* true ... okay,
> actually no to fee rises'. So I texted my dad saying okay, I'm doing this [occupa-
> tion] tomorrow, and I think that everything you said ever is wrong. (Justine, UCL)

Some campuses had already gone into occupation at this point – notably
Manchester and Sussex – but at least a third of the 51 that took place in
autumn 2010 were initiated on the 24 November Day of Action. To avoid
alerting university management of their intentions, planning relied strongly
on existing networks of experienced activists, particularly those with prior
involvement in the 2009 Gaza occupations. Also crucial was attracting a critical mass of participants that could outnumber security staff and successfully
'hold the room'. To achieve this, activists at Edinburgh and Warwick would
wait until their respective marches were well under way before disseminat-
ing plans for occupation through the crowd. Although not all participants
followed this tactical switch, both occupations were successful in attracting
upwards of 200 students to their intended locations. UCL activists took an
even more daring approach. Aware that no Gaza occupation had occurred on
campus in 2009, activists advertised and then staged a 'mock' rally, promising to lead its students to the main demonstration in central London. Instead,
they exited UCL only to march back onto campus and occupy the Jeremy
Bentham Room. While some immediately opted to leave for their original
destination, this trick helped draw a number of students who had not expected
to find themselves engaged in direct action, but decided to stay on.

Activists at Cambridge had initially planned their occupation in much the
same way as Edinburgh and Warwick, but found that their intended location –
the Old Schools Combination Room – had been locked up by the university's
facilities staff. Consequently, a group of students planned to stage an occupation a few days later. This was akin to a military operation, with a group
of 20 students occupying the Combination Room at 10:00 am, followed by
another 20 students who locked the doors. Again, this drew strongly on existing activism networks, and the experience of former Gaza occupants:

> I rang the Labour Club. I texted lots of people who weren't there and everybody
> rang their mates and soon that 40 became 50, 60, 70, 80 – it was established in

the first afternoon, so it happened quite quickly. But we knew there was a large milieu of people who had maybe been to one or two meetings that we could rely on to be involved. (Eric, Cambridge)

I was with someone who was much more experienced, and basically used their legal knowledge for why we couldn't be chucked out. (Andrew, Cambridge)

Despite the relative openness in their mobilisation strategy, the planning of occupations drew heavily on pre-existing networks and affinities. All occupants interviewed were able to identify at least two prior friendships with other attendees, but occupations were not the sum of an already-established student network. In addition to experienced activists, interview accounts indicated that they had also attracted students with weak ties to its organisers, as well as 'unattached' groups and pairs with little or no activism experience. For students in the latter two categories, their comparative lack of knowledge and expertise left them initially unsure of their role and purpose as occupants:

I remember getting a text from a friend one day saying 'we're in Old Schools – come down, bring food'. I was like 'What? Okay!' … But it was kind of like 'What do we do now?' I wasn't sure! (Angie, Cambridge)

There were people there – third and fourth years – who knew each other from past causes and things that they all did together. … I think I was just intellectually a bit out of my depth, but I stayed because I wanted to learn and hear all the stuff and decide what I thought about it. (Rhiannon, Edinburgh)

For more established activists, the inexperience of some participants did not really matter as – to paraphrase Damon's earlier comment – *they were already in the room*. Recalling McAdam's (1986) model of recruitment to the Freedom Summer campaign, putting individuals in a position of *opportunity* was enough of a mobilisation victory on the part of the organisers, as from this point on the students were experiencing high-cost/risk participation. Although some did not stay for long, others – such as Angie and Rhiannon – soon became more involved. The political and social factors involved in participants' growing commitment to occupations are explored further in chapter 6.

MEASURING NETWORKS OF RECRUITMENT

Earlier in this chapter, it was suggested that network paths to activism participation may become more productive and dynamic during collective action frames. At a basic level, this is hardly surprising: their combining of grievance, collective identification, and sense of agency typically provides activists with all the elements they desire for stimulating mass mobilisation. Less clear is the extent to which collective action frames can galvanise these networks to attract individuals with little or no prior activism involvement. Of course, networks were not the only mobilising agents during the 2010/11 protests: as we have seen, student unions committed considerable organisational resources for the NUS demonstration. While it is difficult to disentangle the efficacies of different formal and informal recruitment agents, it still bears thinking how far and wide across the campus students were *invited* to participate, and who was most likely to respond.

It has been argued throughout this chapter that students' political backgrounds are important for quipping them with knowledge and experience of protest, as well as an appreciation of its social benefits. Table 5.3 appears to support this view, finding a much higher uptake among those with pre-university activism involvement – 36.7 per cent, compared to the overall figure of 22.3 per cent. Conversely, only 13.6 per cent of those without pre-university activism involvement were mobilised for the protests. In other words, despite students' widely shared grievance regarding fees, students with the 'head start' of pre-university activism experience were generally better placed to convert their grievances into action. This is not to say that the less-active lacked representation among participants. Although the 'pre-university activism' variable does not account for students' participation *between* arriving at university and the commencing of the 2010/11 protests, one can at least claim that more than a third of participants had no pre-university activism experience.

This head start also impacted on students' level of participation. Table 5.4 shows that the vast majority of high-cost/risk participants had been active before university, suggesting that university generally builds on whatever level of prior involvement students first arrive on campus with. Certainly, participants without pre-university involvement engaged predominantly in low-cost/risk activities, with only 4.8 per cent venturing into high-cost/risk

Table 5.3   Participation in the student protests and pre-university activism

		Participated in the student protests (N = 553)	Did not participate in the student protests (N = 1,932)
Involved in activism before coming to university (N = 931)	% by row	36.7	63.3
	% by column	61.8	30.5
Not involved in activism before coming to university (N = 1,554)	% by row	13.6	86.4
	% by column	38.2	69.5

N = 2,485.

Table 5.4 Comparing students' pre-university activism with participation in the 2010/11 protests

		Involved in activism prior to arriving at university (N = 931)	*Not involved in activism prior to arriving at university (N = 1,554)*
High-cost/risk	% by row	84.6	15.4
participant (N = 65)	% by column	16.3	4.8
Medium-cost/risk	% by row	69.0	31.0
participant (N = 200)	% by column	40.8	29.8
Low-cost/risk participant	% by row	51.6	48.4
(N = 281)	% by column	42.9	65.4

N = 553.

activities. This appears to place the high-cost/risk recruitment of hitherto-inactive students such as Justine and Donna in a distinct minority.[4]

Of course, the likelihood of converting political interests into action depends to a large extent on whether a student has been *asked* to participate or not. The modes of invitation may differ, but this is as true for 'liking' Facebook pages as it is for joining occupations. Although a central tenet of Verba and Nie's (1972) resource mobilisation theory, this applies to social networks as well as institutional recruitment strategies. To measure this, survey respondents were asked to state whether they had been invited to participate in the student protests by a range of different recruitment agents and channels, results of which are presented in table 5.4. 'Participation' is again subjectively defined to include any action the respondent considers relevant, but it is clear that the protests achieved a wide invitational reach, with 70.9 per cent recalling being invited via at least one of the available options. Despite this, the percentage of those who *acted* upon this invitation is not especially higher than the overall participation rate, at 29.1 per cent.

This necessitates a comparative analysis of the different recruitment channels. Perhaps inevitably, table 5.5 shows that the student union had the widest invitational reach. This reflects the fact that unions typically have access to email lists for their university's entire student population, though its largely impersonal mass-communication method may also account for its low conversion rate: only 30.1 per cent of invited students took part in the protests. In contrast, 'network' invitations via university friends and course colleagues achieved a much higher conversion rate. Although they account for a smaller yield of students overall, they do again point to the value of the *social context* of activism participation, as evidenced in the interview accounts of Danny, Rhiannon, Jeremy, Justine, and Donna. It is possible that their friendship groups would not have known about the NUS demonstration without the

Table 5.5 Invitations from networks and mobilising agencies to participate in the student protests, and their rate of conversion

	% Were invited in this way	% Participated in the protests
Student union	53.7	30.1
Course colleagues	26.3	42.1
Friends from your university	36.8	40.8
Friends from other universities	23.4	46.8
Facebook group/event invitation	49.0	32.4
Any of the above	70.9	29.1

$N = 2,485$.
Question: Have you been invited to participate in the student protests against fees by any of the following? Have you participated in any way in the student protests against fees?

publicity provided by their student union, but it was arguably the network that ensured that their initial interest did not go unconverted.

Given the large amounts of press attention paid to the new social networking technologies at students' disposal (Mason, 2011b; Penny, 2011), it is perhaps unsurprising that 'Facebook group/event invitations' achieved the second-highest reach of invitations to students. Unlike mass emails, there is a reciprocity to Facebook event invitations as users are encouraged to RSVP. Moreover, users will receive them through groups/pages they have joined/liked, or via individual friends. Recalling discussions from chapter 2, student interviewees recognised Facebook as a key site for promoting activism events and activities, both online and offline:

> If you're gonna organise a protest you put it on Facebook – that's how I find out about protests. So I think definitely that's how you spread the word – yeah, it's primarily through Facebook. (Angie, Cambridge)

Despite this added personalisation, Facebook's conversion rate is only marginally higher than for student unions and around 10 per cent lower than offline social network routes. What might not be captured in the data is the supplementary role online social networking played in tandem with offline social networking. In the case of demonstrations especially, sharing information about the event online may trigger concurrent face-to-face discussions. Facebook event invitations also allow tentative attendees to see *who else is going*, enabling students to arrange to attend with friends. However, such deliberations were still largely determined by the strength of 'offline' social ties, as interviewees often drew distinctions between invitations from 'real friends', and invitations from 'Facebook friends'. To help ensure a good turnout, activists would typically invite their entire friend list, yet invitees with weaker and more distant social ties were less likely to consider this as subject to any social pressure or sanction. A good example of this distinction can be found in non-participant Rick's invitation to join the 2010 NUS demonstration.

> Most people who were going invited people just through massive Facebook events, and I think for most of those I clicked 'no' or 'maybe' – because 'maybe' is just a polite way of saying 'no' – but I never really had to explain myself for not going ... because the people who I know who went on those demos are people who I don't tend to interact with too much directly – it's mostly online. (Rick, Edinburgh)

For these less-connected users, Facebook nevertheless remained useful for participating within the platform itself – be it signing a linked petition or 'liking' a group page. This provided opportunities to increase engagement, which in turn, could improve students' confidence and stimulate action offline. One such student was Danny, who was connected enough to attend the NUS demonstration but lacked the necessary offline links to broker his integration into his university's autumn occupation. Despite this, his 'online' links proved useful for monitoring debates and developing his own knowledge of the issue:

> I remember reading about [the tuition fees increase] online, probably through Facebook – so someone would link a blog and I would read it. I do remember reading and just thinking in my head, and speaking to my friends who were more politically engaged than I was at the time. (Danny, Edinburgh)

Returning to table 5.5, it is notable that 'course colleagues' possessed the second-highest conversion rate of participants among the available categories.[5] Taking this further, table 5.6 compares this invitational reach by students' degree subject type. It is clear that the arts, humanities, and social science subjects function more effectively as recruitment networks than the science subjects. This arguably reflects their more 'political' subject content, the

Table 5.6 **Invitations to participate in the student protests via course colleagues: conversion rate per subject type**

Degree subject type	% Invited to participate by course colleagues
Art and design (N = 128)	29.7
Humanities (N = 786)	28.8
Logic and technology (N = 279)	15.4
Natural sciences (N = 642)	19.0
Social sciences (N = 650)	34.0

N = 2,485.

specific threats issued to non-STEM subjects in the Browne Review, as well
as the greater political engagement among its students and staff. In the case
of the latter, interviewees from the humanities and social sciences reported
that academic staff would sometimes discuss the campaign in class, or even
relocate their classes to the occupation venue.

A further means of measuring students' network positioning is through
their personal connections to *other* participants. Table 5.7 measures the participation rate of students by their social connectedness to other participants.
Admittedly, the act of participating by its very nature increases the likelihood
of meeting other participants, though it is noticeable that around half of students with five or more personal connections also participated themselves. In
contrast, among students with only one personal connection, one in ten participated. This further suggests the importance of network density as a path
and barrier to participation. Whereas Donna's attending of the NUS demonstration reflected her social circle of interested, prospective participants, Rick
and Bekka's concurrent non-participation highlights the stymieing effects of
being outnumbered in a counter-network of sceptical or uninterested actors.

Table 5.7 Participation measured by social network connectedness to protest participants

	% Participated
Nobody (N = 1,032)	8.2
One person (N = 201)	12.4
Two to four people (N = 612)	21.9
Five people or more (N = 640)	48.3

N = 2,485.
Question: How many people (other than yourself) do you know personally who have participated in the student protests against fees at your university?

Table 5.8 Student protests participation type measured by social network connectedness to protest participants

	Nobody (N = 1,032) (%)	One person (N = 201) (%)	2–4 people (N = 612) (%)	5 people or more (N = 640) (%)
Non-participant (N = 1,932)	49.0	9.1	24.7	17.1
Low-cost/risk participant (N = 281)	21.4	6.0	30.2	42.3
Medium-cost/risk participant (N = 200)	10.0	3.0	21.5	65.5
High-cost/risk participant (N = 65)	1.5	1.5	6.2	90.8

N = 2,485. *Note*: Percentage by row.
Question: How many people (other than yourself) do you know personally who have participated in the student protests against fees at your university?

This returns the discussion for the costs and risks of participation, and the importance of network connectedness for mobilisation. Table 5.8 finds that 90.8 per cent of high-cost/risk participants personally knew five or more participants, compared to 42.3 per cent of low-cost/risk participants. This partly reflects the fact that activities included under the former are inherently more social than many included under the latter: for example, one may not need multiple personal connections to be motivated into signing a petition, but it might be considered more important to attending a protest march. This was certainly evidenced in Donna, Jeremy, and Danny's mobilisation for the NUS demonstration, as the costs and risks involved in the activity (and social enjoyment) could be collectively shared.

CONCLUSION

A recurring point made throughout this chapter is just how *social* paths and barriers to protest participation are. Although to claim that mobilisation does not take place within a vacuum borders on sociological cliché, students' political backgrounds and network position nevertheless play significant roles in shaping their participation and non-participation. The majority of students who participated in the 2010/11 protests – particularly high-cost/risk participants – were politically engaged and active prior to university. This prior involvement was typically shaped by their family socialisation, giving them a head start for actively pursuing participatory opportunities later in life. For others, however, family socialisation provided significant *barriers* to political engagement, as their lack of knowledge and confidence left them less inclined to pursue future activism opportunities.

To some extent, the effects of family and schooling are consolidated once students arrive at university, though network factors provide additional paths and barriers. Students already equipped with an activism background possess the knowledge, skills, and confidence to actively seek participatory opportunities on campus, with many soon finding themselves ensconced within the sorts of activism networks identified by Crossley and Ibrahim (2012). Among less-experienced freshers, their new friendship groups on campus might provide social pathways to convert their nascent political interests into action, or they might instead hold them back even further. The latter 'counter-networks' add further layers of social interaction and conflict to the recruitment networks analysed by McAdam (1986) and others.

These conclusions broadly explain paths and barriers to protest participation in general, but within certain collective action frames individuals can be more easily 'fast-tracked' to participation. This was clearly the case during autumn 2010, with students mobilised in great numbers via multiple participatory opportunities on campus. The creation of these opportunities at Cambridge, Edinburgh, UCL, and Warwick was aided by the coordination of each university's activism network. These new groups and coalitions pressurised student unions into building for the NUS demonstration, as well as plan the sorts of actions that unions would never be able to officially sanction – notably, campus occupations.

Paths to mobilisation were also aided by online social networks. Facebook functioned as a platform for sharing e-petitions and mobilising for demonstrations, even if the latter still drew principally on friendships and affinity links already developed offline. Nevertheless, social media sites served as a crucial junction where information, debate, and mobilisation opportunities coexisted. Helping synthesise all three, however, was the extensive news coverage provided by the *mainstream* media: having identified the fees vote as the first major test of the Coalition Government, its resultant mass coverage of the protests (particularly Millbank) provided the campaign with an 'alternate reality' so that it came to represent a national event. This helped fuel discussions among students hitherto lacking in activism experience, and among friendship groups with a critical mass of interested students members spurred each other on into participating.

Yet while these micro-mobilisation networks generated a 'pull-up' effect for students who may have otherwise not participated, students in counter-networks found their enthusiasm for participation corroded by their peers' lack of interest and enthusiasm, resulting in their non-participation. Counter-networks are similar to van Stekelenburg's (2013: 229–230) 'disapproving networks', which 'nourish beliefs, values, norms, and identities that may … *discourage* participation'. The counter-networks described so far are shown only to have a nullifying effect on an individual's interest in participating, but they can also strengthen their own norms and values by asserting their *distance* from participant networks. Chapters 6 and 7 will explore in more detail how counter-networks may promote a 'non-participant identity' among their members – especially in response to the strong collective identities developed by participants.

NOTES

1. See, for example, 'Student demo thugs' Tory HQ riot' (*The Sun*, 11 November 2010).

2. The perpetuator, 18-year-old sixth-form student Edward Woollard, came forward to the police and was later sentenced to two years and eight months imprisonment. Although activists would routinely include Woollard in their support for protesters subjected to 'draconian' sentencing, his actions were usually depicted

as an impulsive, regrettable 'moment of madness' (see https://support4edwoollard. wordpress.com/about-2/).

3. Under pressure from occupation groups, President Aaron Porter twice changed his mind on whether to condemn or condone Millbank. This hesitancy ultimately created a leadership vacuum for alternative activist voices – including most notably, NCAFC – to define the campaign for themselves (Hensby, 2016b).

4. This is indicative from interview accounts only, given that neither student was recruited via the survey.

5. 'Friends from other universities' achieved the highest conversion rate, but also the lowest percentage of invitees. This was highest among campuses in the south of England, potentially indicating a 'London pull' effect in which London-based students encouraged nearby friends to visit for national demonstrations. Further analysis, however, was hindered by the lack of data on cross-university friendship or activism networks.

Chapter 6

Being a Participant

Commitment, Radicalisation, and the Building of Collective Identities

So far, this book has identified the political attitudes, social backgrounds, and recruitment networks that separate participants from non-participants. It is also necessary to consider the experience of protest itself. Protesting can spawn unique, personal feelings of empowerment and catharsis, and engender strong affinities with others. These affinities not only encourage continued participation, but they also promote collective identifications that further distinguish participants socially from non-participants. The construction, maintaining, and perception of these collective identifications are the key focus of this chapter.

As we saw in chapter 2, applications of collective identity to social movements tend to fall under one of two broad definitions: identity as a constructed 'product' and identity as an 'outcome' of participants' sustained interactions. This chapter analyses the impact of both on recruitment for the autumn 2010 protests and activists' efforts to build a wider student movement thereafter. Most were understandably keen to promote the image of 'students' as a united group defending their interests against the Government in the run-up to the fees vote. Although this was represented most publicly by the network of campus occupations across the UK, their organisers sought to construct a multi-repertoire campaign that would appeal to all students. Yet while this campaign was bonded by a shared commitment to pressurising Parliament into voting down the Government's bill, it belied underlying ideological and tactical tensions. These tensions deepened as distinct 'outcome' identities developed out of activists' shared high-cost/risk experiences, especially within the increasingly radical occupation spaces.

In exploring students' collective identity formation, this chapter resumes the narrative of the campus occupations at Cambridge, Edinburgh, UCL, and Warwick in autumn 2010, focusing on how the creation of liminal political

spaces helped establish strong solidarity ties among participants. It also analyses network relations between occupations and the wider campus, paying
particular attention to the *dis*-identifications triggered by activists' efforts to
politicise the whole campus. Finally, it highlights how the strength of activists' collective identity – intensified by the costs and risks endured during the
previous autumn – contributed to a growing social and political polarisation
from the rest of the student body.

INSIDE THE OCCUPATIONS

Melucci's (1988) definition of an 'outcome' collective identity posits that
it is most likely to emerge in environments where affective ties are given
the time and space to develop. Conversely, Snow's more 'product'-based
definition emphasises the collective sharing of discernible interests, goals,
and attributes. In autumn 2010, the students' multi-campus network of occupations arguably produced both. Palmieri and Solomon (2011: 60) estimate
51 occupations took place during that term, and while some lasted only
24 hours, others – notably at University of Kent – lasted for nearly a month.
With the NUS's leadership compromised by the events of Millbank, this
network represented the campaign's unofficial nexus in the weeks leading
up to the Parliamentary vote. Not only were the spaces regularly mediated
nationally and internationally via television, newspapers, and social media,
they also became the focal point on campus for students to meet each other,
discuss politics, and mobilise for actions.

The longevity of the occupations at Cambridge (which spanned 10 con-
secutive days), Edinburgh (8 days), and UCL (16 days) owed much to the
choice of location and the organising structures put into place within the first
24 hours. UCL's Jeremy Bentham Room, Cambridge's Old Schools Combination Room, and Edinburgh's Appleton Tower were all large, relatively
comfortable spaces in central locations – UCL and Cambridge's featured
kitchen areas, and Edinburgh's even had showers. Although occupying these
spaces was disruptive to the university timetable, they were arguably not
disruptive *enough* for university management to quickly and aggressively
force evictions. In contrast, Warwick's choice of the commercially licensed
Warwick Arts Centre represented a more direct attack on the university's
finances. Subjected to greater ostracism from management, this more ambitious occupation could not be sustained beyond one night – a cause for regret
for participant Ronnie:

> [The occupation] achieved very little, outside of a few column inches in a few
> papers. The university clamped down very heavily, and because the movement

didn't have the strength to respond, it lasted 12–14 hours or something – so I think calling it an occupation is quite generous! ... I think the longer occupations go on, and go on successfully, the more places go into occupation – that's how the Gaza thing worked – people go 'Well, if they can do it we can do it'. And I think *failing* almost undermines confidence in others, not just yourself, so what I took away from that was that sometimes you need to compromise if ultimately it's gonna benefit your movement. (Ronnie, Warwick)

Ronnie's admission that 'the movement didn't have the strength to respond' to external pressures is instructive: as will become more apparent throughout this chapter, the building of collective affinity and trust in large numbers was vital to occupations' durability at Cambridge, Edinburgh, and UCL. Comparatively undisturbed in their respective locations, these occupations were able to quickly transform the space to suit their needs. All three established an organising structure of working groups, daily assemblies, consensus decision-making, and a 'safer spaces' policy.[1] This model had been a feature of camps associated with the alter-globalisation movement since the 1990s (Graeber, 2009), and had been employed both in recent Climate Camps and the 2009 student Gaza occupations (and later in Occupy movement camps). Working groups focused on one aspect of the occupation's overall running, be it kitchen, media, security, or negotiating demands.[2] The groups were a key foundation for fostering a sense of belonging within the occupation, as they instilled a purpose and responsibility for each participant. This was especially valuable for students with little or no prior activism experience, including Justine:

I know so many people like me that came in on the first day of the occupation and kind of got involved because there was this massive spirit of 'Yeah, we're doing something amazing here'. Within a couple of hours they realised that they didn't really have a place to fit in. ... But luckily I had this tiny little thing with Twitter which meant that I had a *role* [otherwise] I would have felt really, really obsolete. (Justine, UCL)

A key advantage to this occupying structure are the liminal conditions it helps create: by sleeping and working in the space, participants were encouraged to separate themselves from normal structural constraints and build their own 'autonomous geographies' (Pickerill and Chatterton, 2006; Yang, 2000). Consequently, the campus occupations initiated an ontological shift where politics became *practised* as well as discussed on a daily basis. These effects were clearly felt by Donna:

I guess because if you do consensus meetings and you start to arrange your daily life in a different way – and it happens really fast – you start thinking about the world in a different way. Because those are the only conversations we were having ... you learn a lot, and it's all you are thinking about for two and a half weeks. (Donna, UCL)

Occupations' use of consensus decision-making was also important for creating this liminality. The model requires participants to employ a language of different hand signals, and a trained facilitator so that consensus on a given proposal can be reached. Its anti-hierarchical structure emphasises the individual autonomy of all participants, so that group decisions can be made openly and organically without leaders or representatives speaking on others' behalf. Although the majority of interviewees spoke positively about the system overall, many were conscious of its obvious flaws – most notably, the tendency to produce very long meetings after which consensus was not always even reached. More problematic still was the long-standing argument that the system creates a 'tyranny of the structureless' (Freeman, 1970), as participants with greater activism knowledge and expertise can become accidental or implicit leaders (Purkis, 2001). This has some overlap with the concept of 'advocates' discussed in chapter 5, as network connectedness can sometimes operate as an instrument of power and influence. Eric, for example, recalled seeing this in action during the Cambridge occupation:

> I remember somebody had a proposal to do something and said 'Oh, shall I run it past X?' who they thought was in charge. And they went over to this guy and said 'Can we do this?' and the guy's like, 'Well I'm not in charge!' But the *impression* that certain activists give off is that they actually are in charge, and unless they agree with something it doesn't really happen. But because they're not *formally* in a position of authority they're actually not accountable. (Eric, Cambridge)

Consensus advocates were usually conscious of this problem and therefore keen to train up more participants as facilitators, though the less-experienced occupiers often admitted to finding the process overwhelming: Rhiannon recalled hardly speaking in meetings, feeling that some of the political discussions were going 'so over my head', whereas Justine admitted to often copying the hand signals of someone she liked. Donna noted how infrequent visitors to the UCL occupation struggled to pick up the system well enough to take part, though it is unclear if the system itself was a direct impediment to their more active participation. For Donna, Justine, and Rhiannon, however, their stronger occupation ties provided motivation (and expectation) to persevere with the system, enabling them to become more confident participants over time.

As noted in chapter 5, the student protests at Cambridge, Edinburgh, and UCL were as much a victory for coordinating pre-existing activism networks on campus under a single issue as they were for mobilising large numbers of students. This was felt particularly at UCL, where there had been no Gaza occupation in 2009. Not only did its occupation bring together union officers, Labour members, anarchists, socialists, Liberal Democrat voters, and even reportedly one or two Conservatives, it also became a hub for attracting London-based activists who were not tied to occupations elsewhere in the city. This produced an unusually broad and diverse network of occupants. Their productive synthesis of different backgrounds and skills is well illustrated in Justine's initial encounter with Noel, an experienced activist:

> On the first day of the occupation, I was, like, 'What do you do?' 'I occupy'. That's what he said he does. [Noel's] one of those people who just *terrify* you when you're new to everything. ...When I first met him he had an instant dislike to me because he hated the internet [and] the thought that he couldn't trust every single person through knowing them from endless meetings and protests. And as much as I learned that people like him aren't necessarily scary – they're just *entrenched* – he had to learn that people like me might actually be a little bit useful to the cause, and maybe they wouldn't have got, like, half as many people out on the protest if we hadn't just been like. ... 'We're gonna tweet about it babes, okay? I know you don't want us to'. (Justine, UCL)

Despite the initial wariness of some activists, social media quickly became a valuable tool for the occupations – both as an organising network for the occupiers, and as a platform for engaging with UK press and the wider student body. This was arguably helped by the fact that the media working groups at UCL and Edinburgh were run by less-experienced activists, who, like Justine, were keen to utilise Twitter and Facebook's capacity to 'expand the room'. This had a significant effect on the occupation's collective identity 'product' in an aesthetic as well as political sense: keen to avoid some of the intensity, dogmatism, and earnestness traditionally associated with political activism, occupiers sought to make the space appear socially and aesthetically appealing to visitors:

> I mean, we didn't sit there thinking [advertising exec voice] 'How can we be new, how can we be exciting, how can we synergise?' – but I remember being quite keen to work on its image, which is why I did a lot of the graphic design [on the occupation website] because I wanted it to appear quite modern and not fall into a sort of outdated, irrelevant thing like the SWP. (Gaz, UCL)

> [We were] trying to present this image of being savvy, something exciting, a bit cool. (Jeremy, Edinburgh)

Through their sharing of articles, videos, press releases, and blog entries, activists recognised implicitly the value of generating informational exuberance through their social media output (Hensby, 2016a: 6; see also Chadwick,

2012). Although most of this related to higher education funding and critiques of austerity politics, certain content – notably a YouTube 'dance-off' between UCL and Oxford occupations, which became viral video[3] – were intended to convey the fun and camaraderie occupiers were also experiencing. To the surprise of many of the more experienced activists, this strategy succeeded in attracting regular mainstream media interest to the occupation spaces, especially at UCL:

> We had journalists coming in all the time – they'd be like, 'do you want to do an interview for Sky News?' 'Do you want to do Radio 5?' The moment where you have any kind of political agency where the media is *coming to you*, that's really rare – most of the time if you're involved in any kind of political activism, you're chasing the most minute bit of coverage. (Brett, UCL)

The occupations' mediation reflected back through the regular stream of supportive wall posts, hashtags, and retweets further strengthened participants' commitment to the space. This helped visualise their wider impact and equip occupants with a sense of collective agency:

> I got Twitter that week, and if you're following it online and realising how big it was … I'd never been in something that felt that big, this national thing where all these people were feeling similar things and it might've gone somewhere and, you know, achieve something. (Rhiannon, Edinburgh)

As well as helping to promote the fees grievance, this media traction was also used by occupants as a form of leverage against university management: although occupations were routinely threatened with forced eviction, senior staff were nevertheless mindful of the negative publicity such an action would cause. The shared weight of these costs and risks, underpinned by the shared cause of the fees vote, and intensified by the effects of living and sleeping in a shared physical space, resulted in occupants quickly developing strong social ties to each other:

> It's so ridiculous how you bond with people so quickly, because you suddenly realise that there *is* this one thing you can have in common with someone which you never would have even considered talking about with them before, but you're all in this same space – it kind of takes away that awkward small talk at the beginning of any conversation, and then friendships are built and it's wonderful. (Justine, UCL)

> That was the best thing – it didn't really matter where you stood. … As a Marxist-socialist, that was the only point I think where I've been involved in the left where I've never had any political arguments with anyone else! (*laughs*) Like, 'Against fees and cuts? Good! That's it'. (Andrew, Cambridge)

In some cases, these ties extended across different occupation spaces. Interviewees recalled occupations regularly Skyping each other to exchange messages of solidarity and support. This connectedness would also prove useful tactically when occupation spaces were faced with evictions:

> It was really nice actually, when you're tired and then Manchester or Edinburgh tweet or Skype and be like 'Hi! What's up?' and you're like, 'Oh hey, a room very similar to ours with lots of posters up and loads of crazy lefties too! This is great' – it showed that we were actually physically not alone at that stage. (Justine, UCL)

> There was a Twitter hash-tag involved, and there were messages of solidarity coming from across the country – UCL in particular, I remember. And there was a movement across the country where if [an occupation] ended up getting kicked out, we would basically jam the phones to the whole university, so you'd get people from across the whole country calling up the university! (John, Edinburgh)

In sum, the occupations' strong campaign and tactical consensus, along with its emerging social and emotional bonds, contributed to the development of 'product' *and* 'outcome' collective identities. This dual process is arguably true of social movements more generally, though the application to direct action tactics warrants further clarification. Given its historical roots in Marxist class politics, collective identity has been rejected by authors such as McDonald (2002) for assuming group uniformity while ignoring its anarchism-inspired emphasis on individual autonomy. In this case study, however, the term aptly describes the affinities and relations of trust which emerged from the shared practice of occupying, together with the shared goal of defeating the fees bill. In this sense, political or philosophical differences – at least in 2010 – did not act as barriers to the emergence of a collective identity. Moreover, a reflexive sense of 'we, the students' was also produced through the UK-wide network of simultaneous occupations. This helped reinforce and legitimise activism at a local level, as participants spoke positively about feeling part of something bigger and more powerful than the room itself.

BUILDING AN INCLUSIVE CAMPAIGN

Of course, occupiers were not contented with simply building a network of occupations – at their core was a desire to pressurise Parliament into voting down the HE bill. Recognising that the numbers of students opposed to higher fees extended far beyond those currently sleeping in campus buildings across the UK, occupiers set about using the spaces as organisational hubs from which an inclusive, multi-repertoire campaign could be built. This involved using social media platforms to promote low-cost/risk forms of participation – including following Twitter accounts, 'liking' Facebook pages, and sharing YouTube videos – as well as encouraging users to debate with each other. Campus petitions supporting the occupation also proved useful: as well as enabling the more distantly connected or biographically unavailable to register their solidarity, the scale of student – and staff – signatories could also be used as a form of leverage against university management eviction threats. Occupations also generated forms of medium-cost/risk forms of participation, including local marches and flash mobs. These sometimes had a clear campaign objective – such as targeting the local MP into voting against the fees bill – though others were arranged with the specific intention of keeping students' grievances on the front pages:

> We had two of our own demos whilst we were in occupation, a week apart. So each time we were getting maybe 400 people or so, not doing any real publicity – just putting it online, tweeting it and saying 'Let's meet here'. … Once you get the core people and different political groups that are already established, and just having them send out messages, get[ting] their friends along, it makes a big difference. (Jeremy, Edinburgh)

> We could get demos weekly by demand – just call a demo, make a Facebook page and a couple of hundred people show up. It was simple … those were the times we were in. (Eric, Cambridge)

The organisational capacities of Facebook ensured that these events were easy to plan and promote at short notice, though the platform's mobilising power was arguably dependent on two factors. First, chapter 5 noted how the protests were inextricably linked to the pervading media narrative of the Coalition Government's new austerity agenda, resulting in the amplification of students' grievances far beyond their own organisational capacities. Given Facebook's invitational reach, marches could be organised quickly and easily, with the fees grievance virtually selling itself. Second, Jeremy's above comment again indicates the power of social networks to promoting and normalising protest as an activity. As with the NUS demonstration, mobilisation proved especially fruitful when both processes operated in tandem, with activists able to point to the 'alternate reality' of the fees grievance in the media to aid the transformation of friendship networks into recruitment networks.

The occupations themselves also served as participatory spaces for non-residents. During the day, they hosted talks and debates related to the fees and cuts grievance,[4] whereas evenings were filled with social events such as film screenings, open mic nights, and ceilidhs. Events were usually geared towards politicising the student body and recruiting new participants, but their uptake arguably reveals vagaries in how one might go about defining 'occupation participation'. Certainly, interviews pointed to the existence of implicit cores and peripheries. Students who slept over most nights and participated in daily assemblies were more likely to absorb the political ethos and gain a sense of shared solidarity which, as per McAdam's (1986) recruitment model, encouraged students to keep participating. Beyond this operating core, occupations' outer layers are neatly described by Angie:

> Obviously there was the hardcore group who'd been there from the start and stayed there to the end. Then there were people, like me, who went there every day and might have stayed there a few nights, but weren't there permanently. And then there were quite a lot of people just dropping in and out to show their support, or because they'd heard something good was happening there. (Angie, Cambridge)

At UCL and Cambridge especially, these outer layers tended to draw on college and degree course networks, giving occupation events a distinct social character. This also helped attract students who were connected to participants in non-political ways:

> It was like a beacon. So for instance, my girlfriend had never done anything political ever, and her friend got involved in it and a guy that she knew – a PhD student who was working at the coffee shop she went to – gave her a leaflet, and she looked at it and saw that her mate was going along and decided to go with him. And now that's opened her up to a whole new group of people and a whole new set of ideas. (Eric, Cambridge)

> It was really sociable. ... People invited their friends to come, like, my brother came to visit, people from other universities when their occupations ended, they came down. (Donna, UCL)

> It was mostly King's [College] people there – partly because it was next door to King's – so people from other colleges who came in were like, 'Oh, it's always all King's people'. So I guess you're drawing from a slightly different pool of people, because it was people who weren't necessarily even that interested in politics, who were vaguely onside, but they were coming up because that's where people were hanging out on an evening. The student bar was empty all of that week. (Angie, Cambridge)

Despite the power of these mobilisation networks, occupiers at Cambridge sometimes expressed frustrations over the extent to which visitors were willing to engage with the occupation's political content, or actively contribute to the running of the space:

I think we even had a couple of hundred there one night, after a particularly fun evening. Maybe they weren't convinced of all the ideas, and I've actually had people tell me subsequently that they didn't actually believe in free education – it shocked me a little bit. I think I was glad that lots of people were there, but I was a bit concerned that it was becoming an extension of the English Faculty poetry scene ... which was pleasant and nice, but it begs the question of what the occupation is for, really. (Eric, Cambridge)

[It] does irritate me when people are just like, 'I'm going to turn up and educate myself but I'm not going to take *any* time out of my day to actually help build this thing'. (Marianne, Cambridge)

This highlights the different layers of occupation participation, and, by proxy, the different levels of collective identification it produced. For those on the periphery, it was not always clear whether they even recognised their 'partici-pation' as such: Leeds student Heather, for example, revealed in her interview that she had brought soup for the occupiers, yet did not include this in the survey as part of her 'participation'. Conversely, another survey respondent specified 'providing food for occupiers' as one of their 'other' participa-tory activities. It is therefore questionable whether infrequent visitors to the occupation *felt* that they were participants, especially when comparing them-selves to individuals more heavily involved in its day-to-day running (see Bobel, 2007). Justine and Rhiannon also identified accidental hierarchies as a potential barrier to recruitment: not only did long-term participants develop a stronger sense of ownership over the space, this potentially compromised the occupation's apparent 'openness' to more peripheral participants:

I think that a lot of the time people might not have enjoyed that sense of coming into a space where clearly people have been sleeping, eating, living, breathing, existing – not everyone is as comfortable with that. (Justine, UCL)

[The occupation] *did* draw people in, so obviously it was effective. But it is a small number of people who will go down because it takes two days for 30 people to hang out together and all get to know each other and then it's a clique. (Rhiannon, Edinburgh)

Generally speaking, students who spent most nights sleeping at the occupation were most likely to access its liminal powers. Over time, this created signifi-cant perspectival differences between core and peripheral participants – espe-cially as the former began to collectively develop a more radical politics than the latter. This was partly contextual, as core occupiers grew frustrated with university managements' eviction threats and unwillingness to meet any of their demands, though it also bore the growing influence of the space's more experienced activists. Although cores were typically comprised of students with a range of political backgrounds, the regularity of conversation in an environment free from the constraints of day-to-day life created opportunities for discussions around ideas such as anarchism, communism, and other utopian ideals. This process of deliberative radicalisation (see Aitchison, 2011: 435–436; Sunstein, 2009) resulted in occupations extending their politics beyond a basic opposition to £9,000 fees, and towards a broader critique of capitalist marketisation. For students with little prior political knowledge or activism experience, occupation participation thus served as a gateway for a deeper engagement with leftist politics – one in which the fees grievance was found to be only the tip of the iceberg.

Occupation radicalisation was tactical as well as ideological. With the effects of Millbank still fresh in the memory, some activists saw a need to maintain this spirit through multiple direct action 'escalations'. Examples included chalking political slogans on campus buildings, blockading senior management from accessing their offices, and shutting down corporate events on campus. For some participants outside of the core, this sometimes generated personal tensions. Angie – who tellingly began her interview by stating that she 'wasn't one of the hardcore people who stayed there the whole time' – recalled two of her occupying friends instructing her to come to the occupation one evening and partake in a 'secret' direct action protest which they would only reveal once she arrived. When she expressed hesitation, her friends angrily questioned her commitment to the cause. Although they would later apologise for their behaviour, for Angie the episode reflected the growing divide between 'hardcore' and peripheral participants. Such tactics were invariably nonviolent, but their disruptiveness – especially when occurring on campus – sometimes compromised others' efforts to create an inclusive campaign. While such differences within occupations could at least be debated in their general assemblies, students unconnected to the occupation and unaffected by its liminal powers looked upon such escalations rather differently.

BEYOND THE OCCUPATIONS: LATENT SUPPORTERS AND COUNTER-NETWORKS

Despite the power of surrounding social networks, mobilising for campus occupations was still constrained by its high participatory costs and risks. Not only were they deviant and disruptive in nature, they also required a sufficient number of participants sleeping at the space each night (during what was a particularly cold winter). In this context, it is perhaps unsurprising that mobilisation drew strongly on pre-existing social networks, as an individual's fear or hesitancy could be alleviated by group loyalties or personal relations of trust. For students lacking in these social ties, however, occupation participation lacked appeal or feasibility. For example, Anoushka, Yvonne, and Danny had all participated in other marches that autumn, but had neither strong social connections to the occupiers or friends interested in joining. Without a social context to counter its higher costs and risks, none ultimately felt that occupation participation was an option personally open to them:

> If I knew more people who were going I would have gone. I mean, I *knew* people, as in a couple of people involved because of Facebook, but I was never formally invited. (Anoushka, Cambridge)

> I wasn't involved in the occupation – I remember thinking it was a bit ridiculous. I didn't even know it was happening, to be honest. I walked through there a couple of times, saw people, didn't know any of them, and didn't want to approach them! (Danny, Edinburgh)

> It's the same people involved again and again. I know – not personally too much – some of the people, but they are all older than me, so I guess there were no freshers involved. (Yvonne, Warwick)[5]

Despite this reluctance to participate, it is interesting that all three interviewees admitted to some personal connection with occupation participants. In theory, 'weak ties' have the potential to function as a form of bridging social capital, but in these instances they could not be activated as a pathway to participation. This arguably reflects an imbalance between the cost/risk of the activity and the strength of the tie, with the latter ultimately unable to support the former. This points to certain limitations in Crossley's (2008: 18) 'self-perpetuating dynamic of politicisation' for campus recruitment: although a student body can be viewed as an interconnected network, many of its internal ties are arguably too weak to facilitate participation. This, too, may be replicated in students' social media ties: Anoushka's above-mentioned reference to Facebook chimes with Rick's distinction from chapter 5 between 'real' and 'Facebook' friends, with the latter far less likely to facilitate offline mobilisation than the former.

Occupiers were generally conscious of these limits to network recruitment: Damon, for example, admitted that in an ideal world 'the networks never stop', but in reality the occupation's magnetic pull would weaken by the time it reached students '14 layers of connection' away. Despite this, their visibility on campus (as well as in the press) ensured that they attracted a regular flow of curious passers-by. To capitalise on this, occupiers ran daily 'information desks' to inform and discuss with visitors higher education funding grievances, and what they could do about it. The latter, of course, played into a secondary purpose, which was to explain and defend the occupation itself, as occupiers at Edinburgh soon found out:

In the lobby we had tables where people would be sat all day, talking to students. People were unsure what to make of it, because this is very much something new. People weren't saying 'Oh no, we disagree with this' or anything, there were just lots of people saying, 'yeah, it's quite right that you're doing this'. (Jeremy, Edinburgh)

Hardly anyone came in and disagreed with us completely – everyone was like 'Well, yeah, I get that, but how is this going to change that?' That kind of attitude was difficult. (John, Edinburgh)

Visitors' confusion over the relationship between activists' political goals and the occupation space is arguably indicative of the more general challenges in conveying direct action tactics to a wider audience – a challenge that Occupy movement activists would experience on a much wider scale 12 months later. While activists could at least invoke the occupation's list of demands, the space's more liminal and transformative effects remained invisible to most visitors:

I didn't really understand why they were occupying the university when it had nothing to do with fees, especially in Scotland. (Danny, Edinburgh)

Seeing the occupy thing here saying that they were against student fees was like, 'No one is seeing this banner that you put up; no one that can actually change this is aware that you're doing this!' So I think in a policy sense I think they're generally pretty useless. (Lawrence, Warwick)[6]

This recalls survey findings from chapter 4 indicating that the majority of respondents recognised protest as a legitimate form of political participation, but were unsure of its overall effectiveness. Not all non-participating visitors were necessarily sceptical of the occupation tactic, however. Rick, for example, was quite comfortable in his role as a non-participant on the basis that he saw himself as a useful conduit for spreading its message to a wider audience:

I think Appleton Tower was occupied for a while and I had classes in there, so I would walk past and they would have a banner and a little table saying 'Ask us about occupy' kind of thing. And I was just like, looking at this and thinking 'this is good' … and just continued on! (*laughs*) It was like, 'I support this' but I'm not going to sleep in Appleton Tower. … I think it's important for there to be people who aren't directly taking part saying 'I support this, I think it's a good idea' that gives them a bit more legitimacy. (Rick, Edinburgh)

Although supportive, Rick felt under no social obligation to join the occupation, admitting that most of his friends were like him in being opposed to the £9,000 fees cap, but unlikely to 'actually go out and join in a protest'. As has been argued in the previous chapters, research into non-participation tends

to prioritise *activists'* apparent mobilisation failures, rather than any properties unique to non-participants themselves. While Rick's non-participation
can again be explained by the weakness of his bridging ties (reinforced by
his relatively apolitical background), others' non-participation was more
informed by conflict. This recalls Oegema and Klandermans's (1994) distinction between 'nonconversion' and 'erosion', as well as the concept of
counter-networks. Arguably occupations' most immediate cause for conflict
was its commandeering of the space itself, as students would sometimes
find their lectures and seminars cancelled or relocated as a result. Occupiers would often try to negotiate ways of ensuring that classes could still go
ahead, though this would trigger internal disagreements over how disruptive
the occupation should aim to be. One prominent case was when the UCL
occupation's choice of venue forced the cancellation of rehearsal bookings
made by the Musical Theatre Society. The society favoured the space due to
its wooden floors, and requested that the occupation leave the room entirely
for its duration. Seeking to maintain their ownership of the space without
wishing to cause conflicts with other students, occupants engaged in a long
and intense discussion about the disruptive ethics of the occupation, and its
relationship to the wider student body:

> I remember facilitating – it was one of the more difficult GAs [general assem-
> blies] to facilitate. There was a whole heated debate about the various options –
> on the one extreme we get out and let them have it, and on the other extreme
> we don't let them in, or can we find a compromise where we move to one side
> of the room. Very long meeting, and whenever we eventually got to a proposal
> they were blocked. So we didn't achieve consensus on anything – there were a
> large amount of significant people blocking the idea of letting them in, because
> we were in occupation. (Graham, UCL)

With no consensus reached, the occupation had no choice but to stand its
ground. The cancellation caused a great deal of animosity between students, as various affected drama and dance societies united around this
counter-grievance and accused the occupation of lacking legitimacy as a
representation of the student voice. The occupiers, on the other hand, felt
that the society's lack of flexibility reflected the right-wing disposition of its
members. This may have had some validity, not least as a number of anti-
occupation Facebook groups and Twitter feeds sprung up shortly afterwards
(e.g. 'UCL Trespass', 'UCL Mockupation') claiming that it had caused
'financial and reputational damage to our university'.[7] Nevertheless, some
students involved in these societies *were* sympathetic to the anti-£9,000 fees
cause, but found themselves pitted against the occupation because of these
counter-grievances:

I did go in and try to speak to people because I was very interested in it all ... and it was very one-sided, and anybody who didn't completely agree with and 100 per cent support everything that was going on was just heckled and told that you were a Tory. It wasn't a very nice atmosphere at all. I'd imagine it would have been great for the people who were involved in it, but I thought it was quite unnecessary and immature in a way. (Sonya, UCL)

I think it's awful that tuition fees have changed, but I'm not sure than an occupation is the right way to do anything. ... It became a place for people partying, it was taking up space that was needed for exams and the like. ... I just saw people becoming 'martyrs to the cause'. Its supporters were in the minority across the university. ... Clubs and societies – zero support. (Louise, UCL)

Louise's position was especially interesting. She was against trebling the fees cap, and as an English student and sports societies member, belonged to two contrasting networks: the former had a critical mass of supportive and participating students and the latter, she claimed, had neither. As with Bekka from chapter 5, Louise's non-participation might be explained as a form of 'corrosion' as her initial anti-fees stance was compromised by her simultaneous membership of a counter-network. Another factor, too, was her lack of a political background growing up. This arguably left her veering towards the anti-occupation discourses shared among the sports societies network. Moreover, their solidarity with the Musical Theatre Society's grievances fuelled this counter-network's collective *dis-identification* with the occupiers, and the fees campaign more generally. As a concept, dis-identification has its roots in Bourdieu-influenced class analysis; particularly in the way individuals might ascribe specific cultural or behavioural signifiers to a group or class in order to draw distance from them (e.g. Savage et al., 1992; Skeggs, 1997; Savage et al., 2010). Although invoking these signifiers is usually designed to emphasise a group's perceived otherness or stigma, they also reveal something about the individual doing the ascribing, and what he or she wishes to dis-identify with. In the case of activism, this may relate to certain styles, behaviours, and practices that students feel uncomfortable with. This might be garnered from encounters with certain activists on campus, though it can also relate to more generalised media images and stereotypes. Both can be found in comments made by Mick, a Cambridge student:

When I came here I considered myself a left-winger, and then I actually met left-wingers at my college ... they were mental, so I jacked that in quite quickly! (*laughs*) It's full of the annoying side of the left – vegans and self-proclaimed Trotskyites, living in squats and stuff like it was a political statement or something. Also, people who tended to be from quite wealthy backgrounds, which is always hilarious. (Mick, Cambridge)

Perhaps surprisingly, according to the survey Mick qualified as a medium-cost/risk participant in the student protests: not only had he been to the NUS demonstration, he was even supportive of Millbank. Consequently, his non-participation in the Cambridge occupation was *socially* rather than politically motivated. The purpose of analysing dis-identification is not to capture the real practices, styles, and attitudes of activists – rather, it demonstrates how activist significations are used by *outsiders* as a means of drawing distance. Dis-identification, counter-grievances, and network position can be mutually reinforcing, because much like the selective attention strategies described by Norgaard (2006), collective dis-identification helps legitimise individuals' own non-participation – even when some might be sympathetic to a campaign's goals. This was arguably true for Louise, whose depiction of the occupation as a hedonistic, self-indulgent space was invoked as a means of questioning the sincerity of participants' actions. Similarly, Mick's reference to some activists' alleged 'wealthy backgrounds' draws on discourses of class-based 'lifestylism' in activist politics (Haenfler et al., 2012). Non-participants' dis-identification from activists will be explored in more detail in chapter 7.

THE TUITION FEES VOTE AND AFTER: IDENTITY, AFFINITY NETWORKS, AND CLIQUES

Although time spent in occupation had deepened many participants' political engagement, overturning the fees vote remained autumn's principal target. NCAFC and UCU arranged a further London demonstration on 30 November, and with an increasing number of Liberal Democrat MPs opposing the bill, NCAFC and University of London Union (ULU) called for a final London demonstration on 9 December to coincide with the Parliamentary vote.[8] Cambridge and Edinburgh's occupations had ended earlier that month, but both remained active mobilising networks: students from the latter joined NUS Scotland's march to Parliament on 8 December, and students from the former combined with CUSU to arrange coach travel for 300 students and sixth formers to attend the London demonstration. Still in occupation, UCL's Jeremy Bentham Room became a mass sleeping space for students from across the UK who had travelled down the night before.

With a reported 30,000 in attendance, the 9 December demonstration was perhaps the most violent protest of the whole campaign. Anticipating confrontations, the police and TSG officers soon cordoned marchers inside a large kettle in Parliament Square. Once news agencies revealed that the bill had been passed by Parliament – by a narrow majority of 21 votes – students began to fight their way out. Some interviewees recalled anticipating police clashes – and had 'masked up' accordingly – but many found themselves stuck in the middle of especially chaotic confrontations:

> I'd never seen that kind of violence up close. I could see people getting trampled, people getting their heads smashed in, and as the police charged I saw someone from Cambridge who was lying on the ground: I think she managed to break out and then got knocked over. So I and one of my friends picked her up and tried to carry her away, at which point the police charged again, and I ended up getting bashed on the head as I was trying to carry this really badly injured girl away. (Andrew, Cambridge)

> I think that was when Alfie Meadows was hospitalised, and that was something that really angered us. ... The police were forcing us into another police line, but neither police line realised this, and people at the back had police saying 'don't move forwards or we're gonna hit you'. I feel that what happened there was people ran because they felt powerful, they felt agents of change. ... Doing not what the police want you to do. ... That was the most empowered I've ever felt in my life. (Ronnie, Warwick)

The vote may have been lost, but the students' response reflected the radicalisation many had experienced in occupation spaces over the previous month. Having broken free from the police line, some smashed the windows of the HM Revenue and Customs Building, while others lit fires. In the West End, a breakaway group briefly attacked a Rolls Royce carrying Prince Charles and Camilla, Duchess of Cornwall – reportedly, to chants of 'off with their heads'. Many students suffered heavy sanctions, however: Alfie Meadows, a student from Middlesex University, underwent emergency brain surgery after being hit by a police baton – he, like many others, was later charged with violent disorder. Charlie Gilmour, a Cambridge student and Old Schools occupier, was arrested for swinging from a flag across the Cenotaph war memorial, and was later sentenced to 16 months imprisonment. Until midnight, several hundred protesters were forced to endure sub-zero temperatures while trapped inside a police kettle for several hours on Westminster Bridge, and along Whitehall. With academic term drawing to a close, most of the remaining occupations – including at UCL – ended the following day.

Although unsuccessful in their principal aims, and left exhausted by seven weeks of occupations and demonstrations, many students admitted to having undergone such a political – and arguably, emotional – transformation the previous autumn that they felt that there was now little point in turning back:

> I think because everyone felt their whole world-view changed quite drastically, nearly all of us carried on. I mean, the student fees were kind of over, but I think people had just been radicalised and wanted to do more political actions, so it didn't feel like people were defeated at all. (Donna, UCL)

I think one of the steps people make towards engagement is to realise that you're in this for the long haul. It's not like we're going to go on one demonstration and the Government are going to say 'oh, silly us – let's just revoke all this stuff'. (Andrew, Cambridge)

With the fees issue now in the past, core participants from each occupation network met up in early January to discuss where to go next. For many, the autumn campaign was felt to have instilled a sense of collective agency within the wider student population – one that could form the basis for a mass participatory student *movement* against higher education marketisation. Despite this, there was disagreement over how to proceed tactically. Some, for example, argued that mobilisation for the non-NUS demonstrations had been undermined by the reluctance of some student unions to promote and finance 'unofficial' protests. Moreover, the pressures and responsibilities of independent organising had left some activists fearing personal 'burnout'. To overcome this, they proposed forming informal free education 'slates' for upcoming student union elections, so that future campaigns would be better funded and resourced at a local level. Others took a different view. For them, the fees campaign's most powerful legacy had been the use of direct action, and if anything, the autumn protests had not been radical enough. From their perspective, this had been what had put students on the front pages, and the relationships of trust and solidarity that had formed between participants could be used to mobilise further actions, actions which could be used to build links with other groups in the wider anti-cuts and anti-capitalist movements.

Consequently, 2011 saw parts of the occupation networks slowly drift off into different directions. Although interviewees were usually keen to stress that these differences were tactical rather than political, some acknowledged that the split reflected the fragile nature of the political consensus that had been forged within activism networks the previous term:

That entire [previous] semester there wasn't much structured political discussion. We had a purpose – we were all there because of the fees thing, and the fact that some people were SJPs, and some were anarchists or whatever, it didn't matter – it was kind of like, 'We all agree on this'. That caused problems when the vote happened because it wasn't clear anymore what we were united on. (Peter, Edinburgh)

In many ways, such disagreements conform to Tarrow's (1989; 1998) theory of 'protest cycles', with one side advocating radicalisation and the other institutionalisation. This did not result in a complete fragmentation of the network, however, as activists retained strong affinity bonds through their experiences in occupation.[9] Indeed, both sides often helped out the other: union sabbatical officers would speak out in support of (and sometimes, albeit covertly, participate in) occupations, whereas direct action activists campaigned for union candidates. Yet these affinity bonds did not extend much beyond the original occupation cores, which created problems for mobilising students as quickly and widely as they had managed the previous autumn:

> The first thing we needed to deal with was a lot of people giving up because the bill had gone through, and our numbers shrank because of that. We decided to build for localised events, and for quite a long period that year we were just organising things like trying to get our MP to call to reinstate EMA (Education Maintenance Allowance), that kind of thing. (Andrew, Cambridge)

> We were still very high-profile, we had a lot of support – a lot of *latent* support – but when we didn't have an active issue to grapple around, that became a problem. ... Because we had attached our political actions to the actions of Parliament, we're then subservient to their timescale, and as soon as they stop doing things relevant to us, we cease to be relevant. (Gaz, UCL)

This pointed to two problematic legacies of the autumn protests. First, they had been mostly built around the grievance of the £9,000 tuition fees cap. In truth, fees were only one aspect of the Browne Review's recommendations, but activists nevertheless recognised that fees had represented a trump card for mobilising large numbers. Without this trump card, they lost an issue that appealed to the wider student body, and had provided campaigns with a clear political objective. Efforts to break out of the fees narrative and focus on other higher education grievances – such as EMA, or the higher education White Paper – did not carry the same universality, simplicity, or sense of betrayal that the fees issue had. To a large extent, this reflected how students' grievances had been characterised by mainstream media:

> The tuition fees were the tip of the iceberg, [but] the media would just drag the narrative back to (*reporter's voice*) 'Students protesting against higher tuition fees ...' – we're not protesting against higher tuition fees, we're protesting because there's eighty per cent cuts to university teaching! It's about far more than just tuition fees! (Gaz, UCL)

This played into a second legacy, that activists had become increasingly dependent on widespread media for mobilising the wider student population. As already noted, the fees grievance was an appealing narrative for the UK press, one which dovetailed with the already-prominent news story of the newly formed Coalition Government. With the controversy surrounding the Liberal Democrats' policy U-turn, followed by Millbank signalling the 'return of student activism', the media had good reasons to follow the campaign closely in the weeks leading up to the vote. Meanwhile, the absence of the NUS and its organisational resources had increased activists' dependency on social media and Facebook events for arranging mass mobilisations. This had produced remarkable results throughout autumn 2010, but as a strategy its successes were reliant on the campaign's amplification via mainstream media. This 'alternate reality' gave the campaign relevance and immediacy, ensuring that the fees grievance reached a wider pool of students hitherto-unattached to activism networks, and that its protest invites rose above Facebook's usual hubbub of requests and notifications. Once the bill passed, however, the press' fees-centric coverage of the student protests effectively ceased overnight. This exposed crucial shortcomings in activists' mobilising capacities once protests resumed in January:

> We started to call more days of action after Christmas, and like, three school kids would show up: the message wasn't really getting out there. There is a limit to how much you can use the press, the Guardian front page, as your main communications tool because they *can't* actually print it every other week. I guess the problem was the structures we were still using were defunct. (Damon, UCL)

Moreover, students' grievances were soon sidetracked by a series of major protest events throughout 2011, including the Arab Spring, the English riots, and the global Occupy movement. Given this shift in focus – and media interest – many activists put their energies into mobilising for other campaigns within the wider anti-cuts movement, including UK Uncut, anti-NHS privatisation campaigns, and trade union protests – notably, the TUC march in London on 26 March and the public sector strike on 30 November. Activists at UCL organised three further occupations in the spring term, the last of which was designed as an organising space in the build-up to the TUC rally. Their choice of space – UCL's Registry – reflected the extent that radical protest repertoires had gained traction among those involved in the previous autumn's occupation. It also represented a more 'ruptural' vision of an occupation's purpose: one which was not founded on a politics of demands – or, indeed, student outreach – but was more concerned with creating its own forms of counter-power (Aitchison, 2011; see also Pickerill and Chatterton, 2006).

Similar displays of radicalism took place on campuses during the second round of occupations in autumn 2011. Although their aim was to promote grievances related to the higher education White Paper, some core activists were intent on challenging some of the 'liberal' preconceptions of the previous year's fees campaign, and consequently sought to foreground direct action tactics. The most memorable example of this was when Cambridge students shut down a talk given by minister for universities, David Willetts. Reportedly organised by a subgroup within Cambridge's activism network, students chanted a specially written epistle from the audience, before occupying the stage. The protest sparked debates on campus about the meaning of freedom of speech, with many students angrily opposing the stunt. As well as damaging the mobilising power of the resultant campus occupation, it impeded activists' ability to promote and debate their original grievance:

> That was where one of the problems lay in our occupation because not only did people start screaming about freedom of speech, but also within the group there were divisions because this had been planned and hadn't been communicated to people. A lot of the time in the occupation was spent arguing why it wasn't breach of the freedom of speech, and hardly any time about the White Paper. (Andrew, Cambridge)

> I think in the 2010 occupation felt very busy, and [the 2011 occupation] definitely did not feel very busy – it felt quite empty most of the time. (Marianne, Cambridge)

The relative failure of the 15 occupations (and the NCAFC demonstration) to mobilise students in large numbers, or attract much in the way of mainstream media coverage, effectively sent plans for a mass student movement into hibernation. Consequently, activists would receive the Government's sudden and unexpected shelving of the White Paper two months later as something of a hollow victory. While the militancy of the Willetts protest could at least be taken as evidence of an overdue re-radicalisation of UK student activism,[10] it arguably also reflected the extent to which core members of the 2010 occupation had become socially and politically disconnected from the wider student body:

> People became slightly ghettoized, and there were fewer people joining in as the months progressed – it became much more of a group of friends. The idea that you have to be friends with the people you organise with, and you have to be ideologically correct and all this kind of stuff – that is quite pernicious. (Brett, UCL)

> This is something that I had an issue with, in the past year or so, which is that it's become this little clique of people who just kind of talk about things amongst themselves. (Angie, Cambridge)

To some extent, these 'cliques' were borne out of the increased costs and risks incurred by its participants over the past year. The experience of occupying spaces had resulted in many interviewees receiving threats of legal action or the termination of their degree registration. Some, too, had been arrested during the protests, and many spoke of personal connections to individuals who had received criminal charges, or had been seriously injured during the London demonstrations.[11] The victimisation students felt also left them increasingly wary of planning and promoting protests as openly as they had done in autumn 2010. In particular, the publicness through which occupation groups organised – both offline and online – had left them more vulnerable to forms of surveillance: some interviewees reported undercover police officers attending general assemblies, whereas others claimed that their phones had been tapped. Whether these students *were* actually under surveillance is a moot point; what remains significant is that they began to adapt their behaviour because they *felt* that they were being watched. As a result, groups became more selective in the sort of information and language they used to report meetings or planned actions. More problematic, however, was their increasing reliance on invitation-only 'secret Facebook groups':

> With Facebook groups, we have one which is a secret group, which has about 40 people on it, and then there is a broader one that has about 300, so I think that would be the core and periphery balance. We eventually became aware that we were being monitored from the Facebook group by security because they started turning up for our meetings, so we set up this secret group. (Raphael, Warwick)

> We have a [Facebook] page where we broadcast messages, and there's the secret group, which in a way isn't very healthy – it's a terrible way of organising. (Damon, UCL)

As Raphael suggests, students had originally been freely added to this group, but its settings were later changed to invitation-only. Meanwhile, a separate 'public' page was retained for forms of open discussion and micro-broadcasting. Partly the outcome of efforts to counter the threat of surveillance, by mid-2011 the invite-only group had effectively become a secret planning and discussion space. Although the two pages mimic the original occupations' core-periphery balance, the secret Facebook group crucially gave *structure* to these hitherto-implicit (and, initially at least, malleable) boundaries. This had consequences for students both inside and outside the 'secret' group. For those on the outside, the secret group represented a boundary between themselves and core activists. One student in the latter was Danny, who, as we saw in chapter 5, had attended the NUS demonstration but felt insufficiently connected socially to get involved in the Edinburgh occupation. Over time, he strengthened his social ties to activists, but still had to overcome certain barriers of affinity and trust:

> So there's a secret Facebook page and that's where a lot of organising used to happen. It used to be quite a little hub and I wasn't let on it for several months just to make sure I was alright – if I'm a cop I'm not going to tell you, right? (*laughs*) … If you've got connections then they assume you're good, whereas if they've seen you around campus, they sort of know who you are but they don't

really know your politics it takes a while to get their trust, which I felt a little bit alienating to be honest. (Danny, Edinburgh)

Among those on the inside, some admitted that the space had begun to function as an echo chamber for upholding certain beliefs: one interviewee voiced frustrations at how certain participants were given the freedom to dominate discussions in ways that would not have been tolerated in consensus meetings (see also Flesher Fominaya, 2015). Recalling Brett's earlier comments, this also contributed to core groups developing ideological consensus on a range of issues that extended beyond the politics of higher education and austerity. This reflected students' growing acceptance of a more holistic left-wing perspective, as well as the breadth of members' different campaign interests, but it also placed new, unexpected hurdles in front of non-members wishing to become involved. Interviewees from one university recalled an incident where a student requested to join a free education group which had evolved out of the occupation. The group responded by calling a private emergency meeting to discuss whether they should be allowed to do so. The reason for this was that some members – who were also active in the university's SJP branch – had accused the student of being a Zionist. Although evidence for this was disputed by some members, the group's SJP supporters considered these views tantamount to apologism for (Israeli) violence, and believed that allowing the student to join would violate the group's safer spaces policy. With no consensus reached, the student was ultimately refused membership.

Some members expressed their regret over the way the issue was handled, admitting that it had made the group look 'scary' and 'alienating' to outsiders. Its relevance to higher education campaigning was also considered a problem, especially given that the group apparently had no official position on Israel-Palestine politics. This example, along with Danny's belated entry into the Edinburgh occupation's 'secret Facebook group', both arguably illustrate some of the more problematic consequences of an outcome-based collective identity: for individuals who consider themselves part of the same movement but are outside certain schemes of experience, their integration into these networks is compromised. Although there was nothing 'official' to stop either individual from joining the free education group, the broad underlying political consensuses which had developed out of the sustained interaction of its core members posited certain invisible criteria to apparent 'outsiders'.

There is, of course, an irony to these 'clique' issues, given that one of the key successes of the 2010 occupations was their mobilising of students with little or no prior activism experience. Within the space of a year, however, students involved in these core occupation groups matured as activists with considerable speed. This radicalisation process put to the test efforts to build a multi-repertoire student movement – and cross-repertoire collective identity – that could transcend these different experience outcomes.

MEASURING SHARED EXPERIENCES AND SOLIDARITIES

Throughout this book, we have seen certain consistencies and inconsistencies when comparing the political views of students who participated in the 2010/11 protests. As found in chapter 4, the vast majority of low-, medium-, and high-cost/risk participants were united in their belief that access to an affordable university education is a right not a privilege, yet consensus fragmented when it came to assessing certain political policy solutions. Although these statistics do not demonstrate any causal effects, they do posit certain limitations in the extent to which protest participants might have shared a collective sense of 'we' – at least beyond a basic desire to pressurise Parliament into voting down the fees bill. Moreover, this chapter's discussion of high-cost/risk participation – and its reception by those on the periphery – points to fundamentally different experiences of protest. It is therefore useful to return to the survey in order to compare students' attitudes, experiences, and solidarities across *all* participatory categories.

Table 6.1 compares high-, medium-, and low-cost/risk participants' reasons for participating in the student protests. Given that barely any respondents outright disagreed with the statements put to them, the table compares the extent to which each category *strongly* agreed. This uncovers a consistent trend in which higher-cost/risk participants were more likely to strongly support statements. The biggest disparity (of 30 per cent) is found in the statement regarding the need to pressurise universities into publically opposing fees. This reflects the fact that occupations often appealed directly to university management to publically oppose higher fees in their list of demands. Moreover, as we saw earlier in this chapter, this purpose proved difficult for occupiers to explain to sceptical visitors. This suggests that low- and medium-cost/risk participants were less clear minded in their protest *targets* than high-cost/risk participants – it is noticeable, for instance, that both considered the more general notion of 'raising awareness' as considerably more important than directly pressurising politicians or universities.

Considering chapter 5's emphasis on social networks in protest mobilisation, it is perhaps surprising that the participation of 'friends and people I respected' should score comparatively poorly as a reason for participation. Although by no means an unpopular answer – more than 60 per cent of respondents agreed across all three categories – it clearly pales in comparison to the other available options. Admittedly, this may be a failing of the survey question, as it creates a false equivalency in situating a 'supply-side' reason in a list of reasons which are otherwise all directly political. In other words, regardless of political background respondents are unlikely to identify the participation of 'friends and people I respected' as *more* important than the political cause – as we saw in the cases of Danny, Jeremy, and Donna, their friends' involvement functioned more as the tipping-point to converting their latent interests into participation. This supports Klandermans's (1992) argument that strong identification makes participation more likely, but it does not necessarily capture *how* participation became more feasible for students, especially for those with little prior activism experience. Consequently, these sorts of paths and barriers are arguably better captured through the qualitative research found in chapter 5 – in terms of both high-cost/risk participation found through occupation recruitment and low-cost/risk participation typified by the forwarding of Facebook pages and e-petitions.

Statements related to collective identity – that is, acting in solidarity with fellow students, becoming part of a wider anti-cuts movement – elicit much stronger support from high-cost/risk participants in table 6.1, reflecting the networks of trust and commitment forged through involvement in occupations and the like. While the existence of UK-wide student and anti-cuts

Table 6.1 Comparing high-, medium-, and low-cost/risk participants' reasons for taking part in the student protests

	% High-cost/risk participants strongly agree	% Medium-cost/risk participants strongly agree	% Low-cost/risk participants strongly agree	% Total participants strongly agree
I want to express my views	75.4	72.2	57.8	65.7
We must pressurise politicians into making things change	80.0	67.9	55.2	63.3
We must raise public awareness	83.1	80.0	57.7	76.9
I wanted to express my solidarity with fellow students	70.3	54.2	43.5	51.1
Friends and people I respected were also getting involved	36.9	34.0	22.8	29.1
Students need to pressurise universities into publically opposing fees	83.1	60.4	53.0	59.8
It is important that students are part of a wider anti-cuts movement	83.1	69.4	56.7	65.1

N = 553 (excluding when respondents did not answer certain questions).
Question: If you HAVE taken part in the protests, how much do the following statements capture your reasons for protesting?

campaigns were hardly a secret, it raises the question of whether low-cost/ risk participants had fewer meaningful interactions with other participants than medium- and high-cost/risk participants. Certainly, the repertoires used to define the latter are more social in nature, and as we saw in chapter 5, low-cost/risk participants appeared notably less connected to other activists than medium- and high-cost/risk participants.

This adds weight to the earlier argument that the protests produced *layers* of collective identification based on the costs and risks that students' participation typically incurred. Further supporting evidence can be found in table 6.2, which compares the experience of participation across all participatory categories. The vast majority of high-cost/risk participants found their experience to have been enjoyable – and a source of pride – though only around half also felt that the experience had made them feel positive about the power of protest. This suggests that the experience of high-cost/risk participation has positive effects irrespective of its immediate political successes or failures – a point perhaps illustrated by the empowerment Warwick student Ronnie felt from participating in the 9 December demonstration. Moreover, the ostensible failure of the protests appears not to have deterred three-quarters of high-cost/risk participants from stating their preparedness to protest on similar issues in the future. A similar amount of pride could also be found among medium-cost/risk participants, which indicates that feelings of collective identity transcended occupation spaces. However, such feelings only extended to around half of low-cost/risk participants: 82.2 per cent may have claimed to have 'felt good' about their personal contribution, but less than half claimed to have actually 'enjoyed' participating.

These findings point to a clear divide in the social and personal consequences of protest participation between high- and low-cost/risk participants. Less than half of the latter claimed to have become more politically knowledgeable, gained a strong sense of solidarity with fellow protesters, or felt more positive about the power of protest as a consequence of their participation. Similarly, only 12.1 per cent claimed that their experience led to them making more friends when the corresponding figure for high-cost/risk participants is 69.2 per cent. This correlation implies that friendship forming and feelings of collective identity are mutually reinforcing. The scale of new friendships made also suggests that the more trust-heavy protest activities were not the sole preserve of already-experienced and socially connected activists. This recalls students' earlier accounts of occupations bringing together different overlapping networks and allowing for unlikely friendships and affinities to develop (e.g. Justine and Noel at the UCL occupation).

In view of the fact that experiences of protest might be positive or negative, respondents were asked if they had any regrets about their participation.

Table 6.2 Comparing high-, medium-, and low-cost/risk participants' experiences of and attitudes towards taking part in the student protests

	% High-cost/risk participants agree	% Medium-cost/risk participant agree	% Low-cost/risk participants agree	% Total participants
It felt good to do something about an issue important to me	95.3	97.4	82.2	89.8
My involvement has made me more politically knowledgeable	87.7	69.1	52.6	63.8
My involvement has led to me making new friends	69.2	35.6	12.1	28.9
Overall, I enjoyed getting involved in the student protests	96.9	82.2	46.3	67.3
I am proud to be part of a UK-wide student movement	86.2	81.6	54.8	69.5
My involvement has made me feel positive about the power of protest	50.0	43.2	29.8	37.7
I wish I had expressed my views on the student fees issue in a different way	9.2	16.7	22.2	18.2
I now regret getting involved in the student protests	6.2	5.2	3.9	4.7
The student protests will be remembered more for violence than politics	35.4	52.5	63.3	55.7
The student protests have made me more prepared to protest on issues of importance to me in the future	75.4	72.9	46.3	59.1

N = 553 (excluding when respondents did not answer certain questions).
Questions: If you HAVE taken part in the protests, to what extent do you agree with the following statements? This question is for all respondents. To what extent do you agree with the following statements?

Overall, the vast majority reported no regrets in getting involved. Given this broad consensus, it is interesting that 22.2 per cent of low-cost/risk participants admitted wishing that they had expressed their views on the fees issue 'in a different way' – more than both other categories and twice that of high-cost/risk participants. One can hypothesise that these participants might have liked to have undertaken more costly or risky activities than they ended up doing, which, given the findings of chapter 5, may reflect a lack of network connectedness.

As found in chapter 5, networks played a key part in how different students responded to the events of Millbank at the 2010 NUS demonstration. Although 'violence' is not defined in the question, it is perhaps telling that whereas 52.5 per cent of medium- and 63.3 per cent of low-cost/risk participants agreed that 'the student protests will be remembered more for violence than politics', only 35.4 per cent of high-cost/risk participants agreed with this view. Continuing with this theme, table 6.3 compares participants' general trust in state bodies. Trust in the UK Government is unsurprisingly low for all three participation categories. The slightly higher percentage of trust among low-cost/risk participants supports findings in chapter 4 which indicated that they were less likely to treat the fees issue in ideological terms than medium- or high-cost/risk participants. Complementing this apparent ideological separation are the different forms of knowledge flowing between high- and medium-cost/risk participants. In particular, high-cost/risk participants display remarkably low levels of police trust – 46.2 per cent claimed to '*strongly* distrust' the police, with 70.8 per cent distrusting overall.[12]

This disparity arguably reflects the nature of the protest activities undertaken by high-cost/risk participants and the sorts of insider information pooled and distributed between participants. As noted in the previous section, many high-cost/risk participants recalled first-hand experiences of police violence in interviews, along with friends who had faced criminal prosecutions following their involvement in the London demonstrations. With information related to certain cases being shared across activism networks, it is perhaps unsurprising that high-cost/risk participants developed a strong distrust of the police. One such case is recalled by Brett:

> I had this sort of 'idea' that the police lied all the time, and now I've seen them *repeatedly* lie systematically, to try and send people I know to prison. Like one friend, six police officers went on record in court saying he assaulted a police officer. The defence kept a piece of evidence on YouTube till the day of the trial. And the video showed it was the copper assaulting him! And it was like, 'In light of new evidence that has cast *significant* doubt in the testimony of the officers we are going to be withdrawing the prosecution'. We were, like, pissing ourselves, but probably no repercussions for those police officers. (Brett, UCL)

Table 6.3   Comparing high-, medium-, and low-cost/risk participants' trust in the UK Government and police

	% High-cost/risk participants trust	% Medium-cost/risk participants trust	% Low-cost/risk participants trust
UK Government	6.2	13.5	19.6
The police	18.5	42.5	54.1

N = 553.
Question: Please indicate, in general, how much you trust each of the following.

Table 6.4 **Comparing students' knowledge of local university cuts with participatory cost/risk**

		Low-cost/risk participants (%)	Medium-cost/risk participants (%)	High-cost/risk participants (%)
Are you aware of any recent/	Yes	53.0	63.5	89.2
ongoing cases of cuts being	No	2.5	2.0	0.0
made at your own university?	Don't know	44.5	34.5	10.8

N = 553. *Note*: Percentages by column.

For an impression of how much participants diverged in their experiences of the police, it is worth comparing Brett's quote to those of Laura and Hayley in chapter 5. The divergence of information and experiences being shared among different social networks is also reflected in table 6.4, which finds that a higher proportion of high- and medium-cost/risk participants claimed to be aware of cuts taking place at their own university than low-cost/risk participants. Although it is not possible to test if cuts actually *were* taking place at each university – such information may not have been widely reported in the national or local press – the perception is nevertheless significant: whereas only 10.8 per cent of high-cost/risk participants admit to being unsure of the situation, the figure is 44.5 per cent for low-cost/risk participants. In other words, high-cost/risk participants were more likely to belong to networks where more specific grievances and forms of campaign information were shared and discussed.

CONCLUSION

This chapter has emphasised the different participatory experiences that exist within a single, multi-repertoire campaign, and how they can produce multiple layers of collective identity. In the case of the 2010/11 protests, one can draw a basic distinction between the campaign's collective identity product and the outcome identities that emerged from different forms of participation. In the case of the former, survey data found a strong shared consensus with regard to the campaign's basic aims, and a sense of pride and solidarity that extended to more than two-thirds of participants. In the case of the latter, interview accounts revealed distinct group affinities emerging from demonstration and occupation participants, affinities which not only strengthened their commitment to each other but also increasingly separated them politically and socially from the rest of the student population. This created complex relations of affinity and trust within the fees campaign, relations which arguably became more problematic once activists sought to build a multi-repertoire student movement.

During the autumn campaign at least, differences in students' participatory experience did not particularly matter. The range of tactics deployed – from petitions to blockades – was illustrative of the strength of feeling among a diversity of students in opposition to higher fees. Nevertheless, relations of solidarity and trust were strongest among high-cost/risk participants. This owed to the intensity of the experiences they shared – be they sleeping in lecture rooms, negotiating threats from university management, being kettled at national demonstrations, or confronting police – which created an outcome identity quite removed from other participants. Indeed, low-cost/risk participants – who made up the majority of participants overall – had comparatively little in the way of a 'transformative' political experience. This reflected the fact that their chosen forms of participation – for example, signing petitions, liking Facebook pages – were less likely to involve strong, sustained, face-to-face social interactions. As a result, they gained relatively little in the way of affinity ties, political knowledge, or enjoyment from their participation.

Differences were also found in how students framed their own participation. Survey data found that high- and medium-cost/risk participants had a clear sense of their intended audience – the Coalition Government, local MPs, university management – whereas for low-cost/risk participants their action was borne out of a more generic need to 'raise awareness'. This echoes findings from chapter 4 on students' confusion as to the purpose of protest, with low-cost/risk participants arguably feeling a desire to at least do *something* to register their views. This again hints at deeper issues of knowledge and confidence in students' engagement with politics – issues that will be explored in greater detail in the next chapter.

Given these different participatory experiences, occupation groups were particularly keen to engage and politicise the rest of the student population so that their 'outcome' identity could be shared more widely. This was successful insofar as occupiers harnessed their surrounding social networks on campus to visit the occupation and mobilise for local marches. This process recalled Crossley's (2008) 'self-perpetuating dynamic of politicisation' in student activism recruitment, but it also revealed key limitations. First, individual mobilisation required social ties that were strong enough to support and encourage high-cost/risk participation – especially among those lacking prior experience in such activities. Second, the disruptive nature of occupations generated its own grievances, causing some students to dis-identify with occupiers and the wider campaign. Significantly, the sharing of dis-identification discourses was not limited to those who already opposed the protests – they also extended to students who opposed fees but resided within counter-networks. In this context, it is important to consider not only the collective self-identities as generated by the activists themselves but also the identities externally *ascribed* to them, as these can deter participation.

Whereas these tensions and conflicts could be managed during autumn 2010, they arguably became more problematic once the fees bill was passed by Parliament. As per Diani and Bison's definition (2004: 283), activists' efforts to build a multi-repertoire student *movement* required a strong, enduring collective identity that could transcend individual events, campaigns, or coalitions. Students' collective identity in the run-up to the fees vote had rested on the shared goal of forcing Parliament to vote down the fees bill, but these conditions evaporated as soon as the bill passed. This included their mainstream media attention, which had proven so valuable for amplifying students' grievances – and publicising its protests – to a wider audience. Second, the absence of a uniting campaign issue exposed conflicting views in activists' tactical preferences, as well as the increasing radicalisation of the occupying core. In this respect, the dense solidarity bonds forged through the occupations became activists' strength and curse: although continuing to drive protest organisation and mobilisation on campus and across the UK, politically and tactically they were becoming more and more removed from the ideas and values of the wider student population (see Hirsch, 1990).

While activists failed to sustain a multi-repertoire collective identity beyond the autumn fees campaign, it at least succeeded in expanding the support base of the smaller, pre-existing free education movement. Many core occupiers took part in follow-up occupations in autumn 2011 and became involved in union politics or NCAFC with the intention of promoting the principle of free education on their respective campuses and across the UK.[13] This return to grassroots activism also reflected the fact that for all the protests had achieved in revitalising student politics, they still mobilised less than a quarter of the total student population. This brings us to questions fundamental to this book, namely why the majority of students chose not to convert their political interests and sympathies into *any* form of collective action. This will be a focus for the next chapter.

NOTES

1. A 'safer spaces policy' typically sets ground rules against forms of discrimination and promotes inclusivity and a respect for individuals' physical and emotional boundaries. It often, though not always, involves the banning of alcohol and drug consumption in the space. An example of this in a student activism context can be found here: http://anticuts.com/ncafc-policy/safer-spaces-policy/

2. UCL's occupation (2010), for example, demanded that the university publically condemned 'all cuts to higher education and the rise in tuition fees', implemented an open books policy on budget constraints, made assurances of no redundancies, reversed its outsourcing policy, implemented the London Living Wage to all staff, and made guarantees for the protection of occupation participants.

3. UCL's contribution can be found here: https://www.youtube.com/watch?v=jEkk2eUCY1Y

4. Aided by its central London location, the UCL occupation was especially successful in attracting a range of speakers including journalists Polly Toynbee and Suzanne Moore, Labour MPs Jeremy Corbyn and John McDonnell, and comedians Mark Thomas and Richard Herring.

5. Yvonne is speaking about Warwick's 2011 occupation.

6. Lawrence is speaking about Warwick's 2011 occupation.

7. Facebook page entitled 'no ifs, no buts, this occupation sucks' https://www.facebook.com/pages/No-ifs-no-buts-this-occupation-sucks/172862326072135?id=172862326072135&sk=info. This also reflected an accompanying grievance brought about by the occupation, namely the practice of 'chalking', that is, writing political slogans in chalk on university buildings. Arrests were made after slogans had been found drawn on UCL's portico war memorial.

8. NUS hosted a rally and candlelit vigil in Central London on 9 December, as its National Executive voted against organising its own 'official' demonstration. The NUS remained keen not to directly associate itself with the NCAFC/ULU demonstration taking place elsewhere in the city.

9. Nor was the tactical split as extreme as it had been in the 1960s. According to interviewees, some activists later left university to pursue more alternative, anarchistic lifestyles, and others briefly toyed with the idea of more radical direct action tactics. Generally speaking, however, students eschewed violence as a collective action repertoire.

10. The Willetts protest resulted in a 30-month suspension of studies for one of its participants, though following large-scale protests from students the sentence was reduced to one term (*The Cambridge Student*, 2012).

11. This collective bearing of costs and risks saw many former occupiers become involved in groups such as Defend the Right to Protest, as well as campaigns to support students charged with violent disorder as a result of the protests.

12. $p = 0.00$.

13. The endurance of a free education group in UK student politics owes, in part, to the wider NUS system and electoral process. Following on from CFE and ENS, NCAFC positions itself as the campaign group responsible for maintaining a free education voice within NUS. In practical terms, this involves putting candidates forward for NUS elections and holding information stalls at the annual conference. This effectively operates as an 'abeyance structure', giving campaign groups a purpose and continuity in spite of the constant cohort turnover and occasional fallow periods for fees-based collective action frames.

Chapter 7

Being a Non-Participant

Uncertainty, Dis-Identification, and the 'Caring But Not Committed'

Non-participation is a key theme for this book, but so far has been invoked mainly as a means of comparison with participants. The purpose of this chapter is to consider non-participation as a social and political phenomenon in its own right. Although this subject is becoming more prominent in political science – especially regarding young people – recent studies have tended to focus more on emerging gaps between patterns of engagement and public policy (e.g. Marsh et al., 2007; O'Toole et al., 2003; Pattie et al., 2004; Loncle et al., 2012). Though this has helped reframe the debate to include 'supply-side' factors (Hay, 2007: 56), it still undervalues the possibility that non-participation might also be *socially produced* at an agency level. Rational choice theories of participation (e.g. Olson, 1965; McCarthy and Zald, 1977) have addressed this insofar as they depict non-participation as the outcome of the incompatibility between a group's goals and an individual's personal interests. Yet, as we saw in chapter 2, this perspective does not fully flesh out the social context of non-participants' decision-making, nor whether rational 'decisions' have even been made.

The shortcomings in rational choice theories have helped inspire more sociological approaches (e.g. Norgaard, 2006; Oegema and Klandermans, 1994; Eliasoph, 1998), and developing these further will help us to understand not only how non-participants differ from participants but also how non-participation is produced and sustained in everyday life. As noted in chapters 5 and 6, counter-networks (and accompanying counter-grievances) held back some budding activists from getting involved in certain activities, whereas other, less-engaged students were more likely to convert their political sympathies into action *because of* their network position. Moreover, students' dis-identification with activism groups suggests 'supply-side' factors come into play at a campus as well as governmental level, as everyday encounters with political actors may generate feelings of wariness or hostility. In this sense, if collective identity helps to produce and sustain participation, collective dis-identification may help to produce and sustain non-participation.

This chapter consists of two substantive sections. The first considers students who did not participate in the 2010/11 protests and features a comparative analysis of students who identified in the survey as 'supportive', 'unsupportive', and 'undecided'. The second section considers non-participation in broader terms. Drawing on the book's recurrent themes of knowledge, connectedness, and identity, it examines the sociological factors that appear to leave many students 'caring but not committed' about politics today.

EXPLORING NON-PARTICIPATION TRENDS

With non-participants amounting to 77.7 per cent of the total sample, the survey provides considerable analytical potential. According to table 7.1, two-thirds of non-participants 'broadly supported' the student protests, with only 15.3 per cent – 11.9 per cent of students overall – outright opposed to them. This provides evidence not only of majority opposition to higher fees, but also of widespread support for the protests themselves. Although this does not capture the different layers of collective identification examined in chapter 6, one can combine percentages of participants and supportive non-participants to claim that three-quarters of all students were at least positively disposed towards the protests.

Before breaking down analysis into these three categories, it is useful to compare supportive, unsupportive, and undecided non-participants demographically. Chapter 4 discussed differences between participants and non-participants, with the former featuring a higher proportion of students studying the social sciences, undergraduates in their second year or above, UK domiciles, and students identifying as working class. Comparing the three non-participatory categories, table 7.2 shows a much higher proportion of male non-participants opposed the student protests than female

Table 7.1   Non-participants' attitudes towards the student protests

	No. of students	% Non-participants	% Students overall
Supportive of the student protests	1,268	65.6	51.0
Unsupportive of the student protests	296	15.3	11.9
Undecided	343	17.8	13.8

$N = 1,932$ (excluding respondents who 'did not answer').
Question: If you have NOT participated in the student protests, do you broadly support students' campaigns and protests on the issue?

non-participants (accounting for the survey's gender bias). There appears to be no single explanation for this, although it is perhaps significant that a higher proportion of non-participating male students studied science subjects (46 per cent) than female students (37.6 per cent).[1] It is also noticeable that supportive non-participants have a stronger lower-middle/working-class profile than the other categories, again suggesting that concern over higher fees was felt more strongly among those from lower-income backgrounds.

Survey data from chapter 4 found that non-EU international students were significantly underrepresented among protest participants, with only 6 per cent taking part. Despite this, table 7.2 shows that just over half of non-EU non-participants were supportive of the protests. This might be attributable to the fact that international students normally pay fees at least twice as high compared to UK and EU students, though their low conversion rate arguably reflects their relative network disconnectedness on campus. Findings from table 7.3 appear to support this hypothesis: although international categories draw on smaller sample sizes, non-EU students appear to have been less connected through social media to receive Facebook invites from active students, or to have known UK- or EU-based course colleagues well enough to have been aware of their participation.

This disconnectedness reflects two underlying factors: first, the propensity for international students to be housed in separate halls of residence to UK students and, second, the existence of certain cultural boundaries that

Table 7.2 Comparing social demographics of supportive, unsupportive, and undecided non-participants

		Supported protests (N = 1268) (%)	Unsupportive (N = 296) (%)	Undecided (N = 343) (%)
Sex	Male (N = 573)	59.9	24.1	16.1
	Female (N = 1,322)	69.5	11.9	18.6
Domicile	UK students (N = 1,581)	68.1	15.7	16.3
	EU students (N = 152)	66.4	11.8	21.7
	Non-EU students (N = 170)	51.2	17.6	31.2
Class identification	Upper-middle class (N = 577)	60.5**	19.1**	20.5**
	Lower-middle class (N = 782)	69.1**	13.8**	17.1**
	Working class (N = 348)	73.0**	12.1**	14.9**
	No class identification (N = 183)	61.2**	18.6**	20.2**
Degree subject	Art and design (N = 101)	70.3	12.9	16.8
	Humanities (N = 587)	64.6	15.7	19.8
	Social sciences (N = 456)	56.8	21.6	21.6
	Natural sciences (N = 527)	68.7	13.5	17.8
	Logic and technology (N = 236)	70.6	15.1	14.3

N = 1,932 (excluding respondents who 'did not answer'). *Note*: Percentages by row. **$p < 0.05$.

Table 7.3   Comparing network disconnectedness to the student protests according to domicile

	Not invited to participate (%)	Knew nobody who participated (%)
UK students (N = 2,104)	28.1**	40.7**
Other EU students (N = 193)	30.6**	41.5**
Non-EU students (N = 184)	38.6**	50.0**

N = 2,485. **p < 0.05.

Question: Have you been invited to participate in the student protests against fees by any of the following? Yes/no binary aggregated from the following available options: student union; course colleagues; friends from your university; friends from other universities; Facebook group/event invitation. How many people (other than yourself) do you know personally who have participated in the student protests against fees at your university?

make integration into UK university life sometimes difficult, especially for students from non-English-speaking countries. Schweisfurth and Gu (2009: 468) observed from interviews that UK-based international students often felt alienated by the social practices of the home student body, particularly the focus on alcohol and clubbing. As a result, students would often 'self-select into peer groups consisting mainly of people from their own, or similar cultures', while avoiding 'intercultural' situations. This tendency was observed by Rhiannon, a non-EU protest participant and international representative for her student union:

> A lot of universities basically segregate international students. So when I was in halls – but flats – in my first year all my flatmates were international students. ... It became this insular thing where they just hung out with each other. I would meet international students 6–8 months into my course and they had not met a Scottish person! (Rhiannon, Edinburgh)

Rhiannon's political background, combined with her network access to politically active UK students on campus, led to her joining the autumn 2010 occupation, which in turn helped her become strongly involved in fees and cuts campaigns at Edinburgh. But her participation was constrained by her visa status, which placed high levels of risk on her involvement in any protest activity that carried the threat of arrest. Moreover, in her role as union representative, she recognised how these constraints limited opportunities for mobilising international students – even when they related to grievances specific to this group:

> Mobilising [non-EU students] is almost impossible, so it's all petitions and anonymous things. I want to go out and picket the UKBA but no-one will do it, and in fairness I probably wouldn't either. ... I'm on a student visa, which is why my interest in things like Millbank is very academic – I'm *never* going to

do anything like that because the second I'm near a policeman I'm like, 'fuck, I'm going to get deported'. (Rhiannon, Edinburgh)

Of course, such risks did not apply to UK-domiciled non-participants, but table 7.3 indicates that they shared similar levels of network disconnectedness. Taking this further, table 7.4 finds that two-thirds of supportive non-participants had at least been invited to participate, but 47.8 per cent did not personally know anybody who participated. With chapter 5 finding that personal connections were a much stronger pathway to participation than anonymous mass invitations, this suggests that nearly half of supportive non-participants (a quarter of the total survey population) felt little *social* encouragement or pressure to participate in the protests. The importance of network positioning is clearly evidenced in the accounts of Christine and Cynthia:

> In terms of Edinburgh, I suppose I don't have many friends, but I didn't really hear anybody saying 'We're going to the student protests' or 'We went to the student protests', so I wasn't just going to go along. ... I was just doing my thing in college that day. (Christine, Edinburgh)

> I read a bit about it, I don't think I discussed it with many people. There were a few marches I think. ... I don't remember much of the details. I didn't go on any of them. I think my problem at that time was that I didn't know people around. (Cynthia, Cambridge)

As a supportive non-participant, Christine's lack of a network context to broker participatory opportunities corresponds very clearly to Oegema and Klandermans's (1994) concept of 'nonconversion'. Cynthia's experience as an undecided non-participant, however, highlights the absence of *deliberation* networks that might have helped her form a clear opinion of the fees issue. As we saw in chapter 5, Cynthia saw politics as something of a taboo subject for everyday conversation – an attitude that reflected her upbringing where politics was never discussed at home. To some extent, this is true for undecided non-participants more generally – table 7.5 finds that only 38.8 per cent grew up in a household where politics was discussed regularly/fairly often. Although marginally higher than the corresponding figure for supportive non-participants, only 37 per cent currently discuss politics regularly/fairly often – comfortably the lowest among the three categories. Unsupportive non-participants, on the other hand, possess the strongest political background, and claim to discuss politics the most frequently. These findings indicate different levels of political knowledge and confidence among supportive, unsupportive, and undecided students, necessitating a closer inspection of each category in their own right. This is the focus for the following three sections.

Table 7.4   Non-participants' invitations and connectedness to the student protests

		Supported student protests (N = 1,268) (%)	Did not support student protests (N = 296) (%)	Undecided over student protests (N = 343) (%)
Have you been invited to participate in the student protests against fees by any of the following?	Invited	68.0	61.1	54.5
	Not invited	32.0	38.9	45.5
How many people (other than yourself) do you know personally who have participated in the student protests against fees at your university?	Nobody	47.8	45.9	56.3
	One person	8.3	11.5	9.9
	Two to four people	25.2	27.7	19.5
	Five people or more	18.7	14.9	14.3

N = 1,932. *Note*: Percentages by column.
Question: Have you been invited to participate in the student protests against fees by any of the following? Yes/no binary aggregated from the following available options: student union; course colleagues; friends from your university; friends from other universities; Facebook group/event invitation.

Table 7.5   Comparing participants and non-participants' political background and discussion of politics

		Non-participants		Participants	
		Supportive (%)	Unsupportive (%)	Undecided (%)	Participated (%)
At the time when you were growing up, how often was politics discussed at home?	Regularly/ fairly often	36.2**	43.6**	38.8**	49.7**
	Rarely/never	33.8**	28.0**	31.5**	23.3**
How often do you discuss politics?	Regularly/ fairly often	43.0**	52.7**	37.0**	63.8**
	Rarely/never	26.7**	21.3**	31.2**	13.2**

N = 2,485. **p < 0.05.

SUPPORTIVE NON-PARTICIPANTS

Supportive non-participants are at the heart of this book, and at 51 per cent of the total survey population, represent its biggest analytical category. Table 7.6 looks at their reasons for not taking part, and perhaps unsurprisingly, the most popular claim is having been 'too busy with academic work'.

There are opportunities for a rational choice interpretation here, with a third also admitting that the issue did not personally affect them, and 37.7 per cent agreeing that their involvement would not have made any difference. This feeling was reflected in some ways by Julian (Leeds) and Rick (Edinburgh), both of whom had friends on the NUS demonstration, but felt that they were too busy with their studies to take part:

> At the time I was just like, I'm going to just go do some work – there's no point in me going down, it's a waste of time, I've got better things to do essentially. [Protest] is effective, but only if enough people take part ... and obviously it's a bit contradictory for me to say 'It works only if enough people take part so I'm not gonna go', but at the same time for some reason I've got the attitude that all those other people are going on the demonstration so I don't need to be there. (Julian, Leeds)

Table 7.6 Reasons for supporters' non-participation in the student protests

	Agree (%)	Neither agree or disagree (%)	Disagree (%)
The student fees issue is not important enough for me to protest	14.6	14.5	71.0
I feel that I do not know enough about the student fees issue to make an informed decision	27.3	13.1	59.6
I was undecided about how good or bad the Government's proposals were	21.8	16.8	61.4
I support the Government's changes to Higher Education funding	3.9	13.1	83.0
I was too busy with academic work to participate	64.1	15.5	20.4
I didn't participate because the fees and funding issue does not personally affect me	33.4	12.6	54.0
Personal commitments (job, family, etc.) prevent me from participating in the protests	44.6	20.3	35.1
I am concerned about clashing with police and/or getting arrested during student protest marches	48.0	15.5	36.5
I do not approve of the protest tactics used by students	34.7	30.0	35.4
I do not personally identify with or feel comfortable around the people involved in the protests	33.8	25.6	40.6
My involvement wouldn't have made any difference	37.7	25.7	36.6
It is right to protest against public sector cuts, but wrong to prioritise the student cause	17.4	31.9	50.7
The student protests were not radical enough	8.5	25.5	66.0

$N = 1,268$ (excluding respondents who did not answer). *Note:* Percentages by row.
Question: If you have NOT participated in the student protests, to what extent do you agree with the following statements?

I knew lots of people who went down to London but I was kind of thinking that I wanted to keep on with my studies, and also thinking that I had a bad feeling about what was going to happen with these protests, when you see the amount of policeman riding into students and stuff – I was thinking that I didn't want to go down and get involved in that at the moment, it's a bit too dangerous. That's just self-preservation, but I definitely felt that the protests were good. (Rick, Edinburgh)

Focusing on academic work is by no means an illegitimate reason for non-participation, but one should avoid taking such explanations at face value. The 'barrier' of study time should – at least in theory – apply to all students, just as none can legitimately claim that they were any less affected materially by the fees increase than those who participated. Instead, these explanations may reflect differences in students' *priorities*. It was found in chapter 5 that both Julian and Rick admitted to having little in the way of an active political background growing up and, as political science students, preferred to view politics from a more detached, 'academic' perspective. Rick's earlier mention of concerns about violence at the NUS demonstration also reflects his more general tendency to consider protest in 'rational' rather than 'emotional' terms:

I really tend to think through the pros and cons of doing something, and I try to put my personal feelings on the back-burner a bit more, I think – it's like, 'Do I want to be spending a lot of time in St Andrews Square protesting, or should I really be working on my dissertation' or 'Do I want to stay in the warm more than I want to do that?' (Rick, Edinburgh)

Although Rick's comment fits with a classic rational choice deliberation, it is worth pointing out that neither he nor Julian had ever been on a demonstration. This arguably skews the rationality of their decisions insofar as the 'process' and 'outcome' incentives to participation – from the satiation of moral emotions, to making new friends – remained either abstract or unconsidered. Furthermore, these were outweighed by more easily perceivable *disincentives* – notably the fear of arrest and missing out on study time. As we saw in chapter 5, Rick's recollection of his parents' experience of being accidentally kettled appeared to heighten his impression of protest as a high-risk and volatile activity. This returns us to issues surrounding students' political backgrounds, with table 7.5 pointing out that only 36.2 per cent grew up in a household where politics was discussed regularly or fairly often. This means that the majority of supportive non-participants may have lacked a political background which allowed activism participation to be considered a normal, legitimate, and broadly 'safe' activity. In this context, *not* participating therefore felt like the 'rational' option for Julian and Rick to take.

Chapter 5 also found that some students became more active by virtue of their social network position on campus. Table 7.7 indicates that connectedness varies by degree subject, with a higher proportion of natural science and technology students claiming to have known nobody who participated. The table also reveals correlations between supportive non-participants' network connectedness and their claims to 'busyness'. Natural science students – more than a quarter of supportive non-participants overall – were the least-connected degree subject group and also the most likely to consider themselves as 'too busy' with work to participate. This partly reflects the fact that natural science degrees are usually more heavily timetabled, raising the possibility of marches and demonstrations clashing with lectures.[2] Yet this was unlikely to have prevented students from participating in low-cost/risk activities, especially online. In other words, considering oneself 'too busy' may also reflect the *absence* of social pressure to participate: fewer natural science students claimed to know protest participants or have been invited by course colleagues, meaning that converting their support into action carried little social incentive or reward.

It was noted earlier in this chapter that supportive non-participants featured an above-average proportion of female students. Considering that the survey is already biased in favour of female students, this creates a considerable gender imbalance: table 7.2 finds that 72.5 per cent in this category are female and 27.1 per cent male. With the former amounting to 37 per cent of the total survey population, it would seem that supportive non-participation might carry gender-specific properties. To test this, table 7.8 compares male and female supportive non-participants' political engagement. The first three statements, all of which relate to the moral properties of the fees issue, elicit extremely similar responses from male and female students. The fourth statement, however, concerns a basic policy proposal for funding higher

Table 7.7 **Supportive non-participants' availability and network connectedness by degree subject**

	Art and Design (N = 71) (%)	Humanities (N = 379) (%)	Logic and technology (N = 134) (%)	Natural science (N = 362) (%)	Social science (N = 322) (%)
% were 'too busy with academic work to participate'	61.4	64.7	65.6	70.4	56.2
% were invited to protest by course colleagues	18.3	25.1	13.4	14.6	26.1
% knew 5 or more participants	23.9	22.4	13.4	12.4	52.2
% knew no participants	40.8	46.4	53.7	52.8	42.9

N = 1,268.

education and reveals a notable gap between male and female students, with only 29.2 per cent of women agreeing. This suggests that while female non-participants were engaged on the campaign's central grievances, they were either more circumspect towards certain policy solutions than men or generally less sure of their views.

This raises the question of whether female supportive non-participants may have lacked opportunities to express their views on the fees grievance and, in the process, develop their own opinions on policy alternatives. Table 7.9 finds little difference between male and female supportive non-participants in terms of network connectedness, or disapproval of protesters' tactics. Where they *do* differ is in their everyday discussion of politics: only 39.6 per cent of female students claim to do this often – 13.5 per cent less than male students. Moreover, two-thirds of female students agree to often feeling that they 'don't know enough about politics to fully engage in it' – 24.5 per cent higher than for male students. In other words, women are no less politically engaged or connected to protest participants than men, yet they discuss politics far less regularly. This raises key questions about women's engagement in politics

Table 7.8 Comparing male and female supportive non-participants' political engagement

	Male (N = 343)	Female (N = 919)
% agree that 'access to an affordable higher education is a right is a right, not a privilege'	86.6**	90.5**
% agree that 'I feel let down by the Liberal Democrats over their reversal of tuition fees policy'	81.0*	80.5*
% agree that 'I am concerned that higher fees will put off some strong candidates off applying for university altogether'	87.2	92.3
% agree that 'higher education funding should be maintained through higher taxes'	43.7	29.2

$N = 1,268$. *$p > 0.05$; **$p < 0.05$.

Table 7.9 Comparing male and female supportive non-participants' political discussion

	Male (N = 343)	Female (N = 919)
% knew 5 or more participants	44.9*	43.7*
% knew no participants	46.4*	48.1*
% agreed that 'I do not approve of the protest tactics used by students'	32.4*	34.3*
% discuss politics regularly/fairly often	53.1	39.6
% agreed that 'I often feel that I don't know enough about politics to fully engage in it'	43.1	67.6

$N = 1,268$. *$p > 0.05$.

in general – particularly why they feel less confident in discussing politics than men (or conversely, why men claim to be more confident in discussing politics than women).

Of course, activists recognised the powerful simplicity of the fees grievance, and its potential as a hook for stimulating deeper engagement among the wider student body. This is partly borne out in the survey: table 7.10 indicates that the tuition fees issue increased engagement for 42.6 per cent of supportive non-participants, which at 21.7 per cent of the total sample is almost as many as those who actually participated in the protests. Similarly, 29.1 per cent claimed to have become more politically engaged as a result of the *protests* – 14.8 per cent of students overall. Notwithstanding students who may have been unavailable to participate because of health or childcare concerns, it bears thinking that persuading these individuals to take part in anything from signing petitions to attending marches would have almost doubled the overall participation rate for the whole UK student population. Whether this would have made the protests any more successful is a moot point: what is clear, however, is that the protests – well attended though they were – did not mobilise anywhere near as many students as they could have done.

Certainly, supportive non-participants were not impervious to the costs and risks of protest participation. By the time of the autumn 2011 NCAFC demonstration, a number of activists and academics were arguing that police

Table 7.10 Supportive non-participants' attitudes towards the legacy of the student protests

	Agree (%)	Don't know/ neither agree or disagree (%)	Disagree (%)
The tuition fees issue has made me more politically engaged	42.6	28.2	29.3
The student protests have made me more politically engaged	29.1	34.5	36.4
The student fees and anti-cuts protests will make the Government pay more attention to the views of its citizens in the future	27.4	28.2	44.3
The student protests will be remembered more for violence than politics	56.9	23.0	20.0
The student protests have made me more prepared to protest on issues important to me in the future	27.4	35.7	36.9
The Government and police force have made protest appear an illegitimate and deviant act	60.3	26.7	13.1

N = 1,268. *Note*: Percentages by row.
Question: If you have NOT participated in the student protests, to what extent do you agree with the following statements?

tactics and custodial sentences had been deployed as a deliberate deterrent to students' participation in demonstrations (Power, 2012). Table 7.10 indicates that this deterrent may have been successful: 60.3 per cent of supportive non-participants agreed that 'the Government and police force have made protest appear an illegitimate and deviant act'. Moreover, those who agreed with this statement *and* admitted to police clashes and fear of arrest factoring in their decision not to participate totals at 31.5 per cent of supportive non-participants – 16 per cent of all students.[3]

Considering supportive non-participants' general lack of political sociali-sation and network connectedness, one can therefore argue that many were sympathetic to protesters' treatment by police, but lacked much encour-agement or motivation to get involved themselves. While this suggests 'nonconversion' on a mass scale, one should also be aware that many non-participants' stated 'support' for the protests may have been purely notional, with little or no expression in practice. Despite this, table 7.10 at least shows 27.4 per cent claiming that the protests have made them more prepared to protest on issues important to them in the future. Of course, there is no indica-tion what 'participation' might involve, but it at least implies that the protests were partially successful in promoting activism as a valid form of political expression. Nevertheless, converting this willingness into *action* will likely depend on many of the perceived barriers to participation highlighted in this section being overcome.

UNSUPPORTIVE NON-PARTICIPANTS

Given their self-identification, it would be easy to overlook this category when analysing the social production of non-participation. Yet students might have had many different reasons for not supporting the protests: as we saw in chapter 6, interviewees' hostility to the occupations was sometimes a response to specific counter-grievances rather than support for £9,000 fees per se. To effectively understand participation and mobilisation processes, it is therefore important to understand the criticisms that anti-fees campaigns had to counter, and how they may have corroded some students' initial sup-port for the protests.

Recalling data from table 7.5, the unsupportive represent the most politi-cally engaged of the three non-participating categories. A higher proportion grew up in households where politics was discussed regularly/fairly often, and a higher number still claimed to now discuss politics regularly/fairly often. This would suggest that the unsupportive were more likely to have debated the protests and higher education funding than other non-participants. Perhaps surprisingly, table 7.11 paints a fractured picture: around half supported the

Table 7.11 Reasons for unsupportive students' non-participation in the student protests

	Agree (%)	Neither agree or disagree (%)	Disagree (%)
The student fees issue is not important enough for me to protest	47.5	17.4	35.1
I feel that I do not know enough about the student fees issue to make an informed decision	19.9	15.2	64.9
I was undecided about how good or bad the Government's proposals were	16.3	25.5	58.2
I support the Government's changes to Higher Education funding	50.7	22.7	26.6
I was too busy with academic work to participate	37.1	21.1	41.8
I didn't participate because the fees and funding issue does not personally affect me	42.5	16.4	41.1
Personal commitments (job, family, etc.) prevent me from participating in the protests	13.8	22.0	64.2
I am concerned about clashing with police and/or getting arrested during student protest marches	32.0	22.8	45.2
I do not approve of the protest tactics used by students	72.6	15.3	12.1
I do not personally identify with or feel comfortable around the people involved in the protests	61.0	19.1	19.9
My involvement wouldn't have made any difference	40.4	30.9	28.7
It is right to protest against public sector cuts, but wrong to prioritise the student cause	27.4	34.9	37.7
The student protests were not radical enough	5.0	19.1	75.9

$N = 296$ (excluding respondents who 'did not answer'). *Note*: Percentages by row.
Question: If you have NOT participated in the student protests, to what extent do you agree with the following statements?

Government changes to higher education funding (only 6 per cent of students overall), whereas 26.6 per cent opposed them and 22.7 per cent were unsure. This reveals a significant split between unsupportive non-participants who opposed the protests *because* they supported higher fees, and those who opposed the protests *in spite* of their opposition to higher fees.

To explore these fractures further, table 7.12 compares attitudes towards the fees, the protests, and activism according to unsupportive non-participants' views on higher education reforms. Unsurprisingly, the majority of students who supported Government reforms displayed right-wing views, with two-thirds currently identifying with the Conservative Party. Moreover, 44.1 per cent agreed with the libertarian position that non-university-educated taxpayers should not have to pay towards funding the higher education system. In other words, two-thirds of students in this category were opposed to the protests' *political* rationale.

Table 7.12   Comparing attitudes towards the fees, the protests, and activism of unsupportive non-participants according to their views on the Government's higher education reforms

	Supported higher education reforms (N = 143)	Unsure about higher education reforms (N = 64)	Did not support higher education reforms (N = 75)
% agreed that 'I do not approve of the protest tactics used by students'	81.8	62.5	56.0
% agreed that 'I feel that I do not know enough about the student fees issue to make an informed decision'	11.9	28.1	28.0
% agreed that 'Protest suffers because the actions of a minority usually spoil it for the majority'	81.8	70.3	68.0
% agreed that 'Maintaining higher education funding is not a priority when public service cuts have to be made'	56.6	43.8	36.0
% agreed that 'I am concerned that higher fees will put some strong candidates off applying for university altogether'	34.3	59.4	77.3
% agreed that 'Taxpayers who did not go through higher education should not be expected to pay for the higher education of others'	44.1	9.4	21.3
% currently identifies with the Conservative Party	64.3	37.5	40.0

N = 296 (14 respondents did not answer).
Question: If you have NOT participated in the student protests, to what extent do you agree with the following statements? 'I support the Government's changes to Higher Education funding'.

Pro-fees attitudes were expressed in the majority of interviews with unsupportive non-participants, many of whom gave their own counter-arguments to those put forward by activists. Most prominent among these was the perceived decline in the standard of university education in the UK. Specifically, it was claimed that Tony Blair's famous policy target of getting 50 per cent of young people going to university by 2010 had diluted the overall quality of undergraduates and was devaluing their own degrees. Given the fact that students frequently invoked personal experiences when discussing this issue, this effectively functioned as a counter-grievance to student protest campaigns:

> The reason I backed the tuition fee rise is that fewer people will go to uni, and what a degree is worth would increase because you will have fewer people doing the – I hate to pick on it – performing arts and theatre studies degrees.

So you would have fewer people going to uni just for the sake of having a degree – you would have more dedicated students, and possibly a higher quality of graduates. (Dennis, Warwick)

I think Tony Blair's whole 'Everyone should go to university' campaign was a really bad idea. There's a massive difference between the expected level at different unis, and if you have everyone going to university it does kind of devalue some degrees. Because a degree's not for everyone, not everyone benefits from spending three years at university studying, like, travel and tourism. I think there are too many courses, too many universities. (Louise, UCL)

There are people at my school who I don't think should have gone to university. Some of my friends dropped out because they were just not that interested. I think there's this stigma attached to not going to university – if you don't go then you must be really stupid or lazy. I think the 50 per cent target is a big problem, actually. (Anita, Cambridge)

It is worth noting that concerns related to Labour's '50 per cent' ideal were also shared by a minority of interviewees who had participated in the protests (though never high-cost/risk participants). In other words, unsupportive non-participants felt that the protests were effectively defending a system that many students believed to be deeply flawed. Of course, activists would likely contest the counter-argument that higher fees might drive up standards as it rests on the spurious assumption that they will only deter the 'bad' or 'uninterested' students from going to university. But unsupportive students such as Pattie also felt that the anti-fees campaigns had intentionally depicted the tuition fees increase in catastrophic terms, while obfuscating the terms of its loan repayment scheme:

Most of the people I know who went on the protests were saying 'It's completely unjust that students should have to pay more for their education'. And that spurred me to go online and find the documents that set out what the proposed changes were, and I actually decided that in an economy where cuts had to be made in order to reduce the deficit, tertiary education *is* a privilege. ... The rate in which you pay it back is quite low – if after graduation your degree is only getting you into a job where you're at the minimum of paying it back, the cost of paying it back is one less pint a week – it's not that much money! (Pattie, Cambridge)

To explain the non-participants who did not support the protests *or* the fees cap increase (7.2 per cent of all non-participants), we can return to table 7.12. In some ways, this group is more closely aligned politically to supportive non-participants: 77.3 per cent were 'concerned that higher fees will put some strong candidates off applying for university altogether', and only 21.3 per cent agreed that 'taxpayers who did not go through higher education should not be expected to pay for the higher education of others'. What remains strong, however, is their dis-identification with the activists themselves, and their scepticism towards the efficacy of protest. One interviewee who fell into this category was Louise. As we saw in chapter 5, the combination of her relatively apolitical background and counter-network membership meant that she opposed the protests. This contributed to a fatalistic view of electoral politics, leaving her feeling powerless to change anything about higher fees, yet cynical about the actions and motives of those trying to prove otherwise:

> It is a constant problem in education that there isn't very much money – particularly in humanities subjects. And I think it's unfair because it means some people are pushed out of education because they haven't got the funds to do without. But I just feel that I can't really see a way around it – there's nothing I can do. (Louise, UCL)

Students' feelings of powerlessness and uncertainty over political action will be discussed in more detail in this chapter's third section. But such feelings also play a significant part in explaining the non-participation of the final subcategory, namely those who were 'undecided' whether they supported the student protests or not.

UNDECIDED NON-PARTICIPANTS

Perhaps predictably, analysis of undecided non-participants tends to position them somewhere between supportive and unsupportive non-participants, though more emphasis is placed on students' uncertainty and lack of engagement with politics in general. Looking at tables 7.13 and 7.14, it is noticeable how few strong feelings undecided non-participants appear to hold: no single statement achieves 60 per cent agreement or disagreement, including the widely-contested claim that 'the student protests weren't radical enough'. Around half of students in this category were relatively disengaged from the fees grievance as well as the protests, with only 21.3 per cent disagreeing that they were undecided about how good or bad the Government's proposals were. A similar proportion also claimed that the fees issue did not personally affect them, as well as expressing a dis-identification with the activists and the tactics they used.

Table 7.14 considers the protests' legacy, and finds that they had relatively little impact on the thought and behaviour of undecided non-participants. Only 11.7 per cent felt that they had become more politically engaged as a result, with 7.6 per cent claiming that they were more prepared to protest on other issues in the future. Significantly, nearly half held no view on whether

Table 7.13   Reasons for 'undecided' students' non-participation in the student protests

	Agree (%)	Neither agree or disagree (%)	Disagree (%)
The student fees issue is not important enough for me to protest	29.8	32.7	37.5
I feel that I do not know enough about the student fees issue to make an informed decision	46.4	20.7	32.9
I was undecided about how good or bad the Government's proposals were	48.3	30.3	21.3
I support the Government's changes to Higher Education funding	13.5	44.6	41.9
I was too busy with academic work to participate	50.1	26.9	23.0
I didn't participate because the fees and funding issue does not personally affect me	49.9	16.7	33.4
Personal commitments (job, family, etc.) prevent me from participating in the protests	23.3	33.4	43.3
I am concerned about clashing with police and/or getting arrested during student protest marches	41.6	28.4	30.0
I do not approve of the protest tactics used by students	54.0	33.4	12.5
I do not personally identify with or feel comfortable around the people involved in the protests	51.7	31.8	16.5
My involvement wouldn't have made any difference	42.0	39.0	18.9
It is right to protest against public sector cuts, but wrong to prioritise the student cause	26.9	46.7	26.3
The student protests were not radical enough	3.6	35.8	41.9

N = 343 (excluding respondents who 'did not answer'). *Note:* Percentages by row.
Question: If you have NOT participated in the student protests, to what extent do you agree with the following statements?

the student protests had failed in their aims, suggesting a limited awareness of what its aims and outcomes even were. This points to their broader disengagement from UK politics in general: 58.3 per cent said that they were certain to vote in the next election,[4] and only 45.5 per cent believed that their participation could have an impact on UK Government policy. Faith in *protest* was lower still, at 33.2 per cent. In other words, not only were undecided non-participants unsure about the fees grievance, two-thirds disagreed that protest could help change Government policy anyway.

To some extent, undecided non-participants' lack of strong feelings might be explained by results presented earlier in this chapter. Table 7.5 found that 38.8 per cent grew up in a home where politics was discussed regularly or fairly often, with 37 per cent claiming to now discuss politics regularly or fairly often. This lack of political engagement may have also been sustained by their network position on campus, with table 7.4 showing that a higher

Table 7.14 'Undecided' non-participants' attitudes towards the legacy of the student protests and the efficacy of political participation

	Agree (%)	Don't know/ neither agree or disagree (%)	Disagree (%)
The tuition fees issue has made me more politically engaged	20.7	38.2	41.1
The student protests have made me more politically engaged	11.7	40.8	47.5
The student protests have failed in their aims	45.2	45.5	9.3
The student protests will be remembered more for violence than politics	58.3	32.4	9.3
The student protests have made me more prepared to protest on issues important to me in the future	7.6	40.2	52.2
I am definitely going to vote in the next election	58.3	32.1	9.6
My participation can have an impact on government policy in this country	45.5	26.5	28.0
If a person is dissatisfied with the policies of government, he/she has a duty to do something about it	53.9	32.1	14.0
Protest can help change UK Government policy	33.2	41.1	25.7

N = 343. *Note:* Percentages by row.
Question: To what extent do you agree with the following statements?

proportion of undecided non-participants were not invited to participate in the protests (45.5 per cent) and knew nobody who participated (56.3 per cent) than supportive and unsupportive non-participants. These factors are well illustrated in the case of Cynthia, whose lack of confidence discussing politics combined with her political network disconnection meant that she felt ill-equipped to weigh up the pros and cons of the fees increase. Despite this disconnectedness, however, she often put forward her desire to be rational and methodical as a contrast to students who *did* participate:

> Lots of people that were protesting I thought – rightly or wrongly – probably only know one side of the story, and are not willing to discuss the issue properly. ... I think lots of people had already made up their minds, and I felt like I didn't have enough information to take part. But on the other hand, I don't think you're ever going to know *everything* about an issue, so you have to make some kind of preliminary decision and work with that. (Cynthia, Cambridge)

Although slightly more confident in their views, this perception of 'political students' was shared by Sharon and Sonya, both of whom also self-identified as undecided non-participants. This reflects a slightly different type of dis-identification, namely a dis-identification with a more general 'student activist' identity:

> I just felt that the same buzzwords were being brought up over and over again, and I didn't get much in the way of information or reasonable discussion. ... It was that kind of very scandalised take on it all, which again I think is a part of the reputation students have – you know, they get to university and they go crazy and they think that they know everything. (Sonya, UCL)

> I was sceptical about those protests because a lot of it was people just being self-centred and not wanting to pay personally for what they enjoy. (Sharon, Warwick)

This pejorative characterisation of protesters as self-interested egoists masquerading as selfless arbiters for the common good is typical of long-standing struggles in student activism history. Whereas Sonya's comments reflect her first-hand encounters with the UCL occupation (as discussed in chapter 6), Sharon's observations draw little on personal connections with protest participants. In both cases, however, their argument is that student activists were overly dogmatic, and that this had overridden their ability to objectively analyse the conditions and origins of the fees increase. As we saw earlier, these criticisms were expressed by students who opposed the protests – such as Pattie – but they were also shared by some students who participated in the protests:

> I was actually down in London, and there were people shouting for Labour, and I turned round to these guys and said 'Do you realise that it was Labour who brought in fees in the first place you bloody idiot – we're only here because they started it!' (Mick, Cambridge)

Irrespective of how informed or uninformed student activists were, this sort of dis-identification points to many students' more fundamental problems with politics in general. This relates not only to the shortcomings of democratic systems, but also to the perceived failure of political actors – from cabinet ministers to student activists – to practise politics in the way it *should* be done. This dissatisfaction arguably transcends both the case study and distinctions between participants and non-participants, and it this that we shall focus on in the next section of this chapter.

THEORISING NON-PARTICIPATION: THE 'CARING BUT NOT COMMITTED'

Findings throughout this book have pointed to ambiguities in students' experience of non-participation: while many frequently voiced disappointment and frustration with politics as performed in government and on campus, a large proportion were often also conscious of their own limitations as political actors. This was especially true among the 51 per cent of survey respondents who supported the 2010/11 protests but did not participate in them. Although less sympathetic to the fees grievance, some unsupportive and undecided non-participants also admitted to lacking confidence in their political knowledge. Moreover, as we saw in chapter 6, similar uncertainties and dis-identifications were experienced by some students who had participated in the protests. This suggests, somewhat paradoxically, that studying political non-participation as a sociological phenomenon necessitates moving beyond a simple participation/non-participation binary. With findings from chapter 4 indicating that only 7 per cent of students qualified as 'pure' non-participants, it is perhaps significant that the majority of one-off, low-cost/risk participants admitted to often feeling that they 'don't know enough about politics to fully engage in it'.

This final section is divided into four themes that help explain those students who were found to be *caring* about politics, but not *committed* to any sustained forms of participation. As a theoretical concept, the 'caring but not committed' recalls similar intersectional categories such as Eden and Roker's (2000) 'engaged cynic' and Jordan and Maloney's (2007) 'concerned, unmobilised' insofar as they emphasise dissatisfaction with 'supply-side' factors in the contemporary delivery of politics. However, one should also pay attention to the negative emotions and collective narratives of self-preservation that produce and legitimise non-participation *sociologically* in everyday life. In exploring these themes, this final section gets to the heart of why students – and potentially, young people more generally – are less active in politics than one might expect.

Dis-identification with political parties

A principal theme in the caring but not committed phenomenon is students' widespread dis-identification with political parties. Although the swing towards 'no party identification' identified in chapter 4 is unsurprising midway through an election cycle, interviews pointed to deeper misgivings in their relationship with formal politics. Party dis-identification is a well-studied area in political science, with numerous studies pointing to the decline in electoral turnout and party memberships since the 1980s (Henn and Foard, 2012: 47–48). These trends are connected to wider societal transformations, in which the increased mobility demands of the labour market has resulted in individuals becoming more and more 'disembedded' from their local environment (Giddens, 1991; Beck, 1992). This, in turn, has contributed to the decline of 'mass politics' which political parties traditionally depended on for their support (Putnam, 2000). In its place are forms of political participation more congruent to the contemporary labour ethic of mobility and flexibility, such as single-issue social movements and campaigns reflective of an identity-based or 'post-material' politics (Inglehart, 1997).

Reflecting these transformations, recent research in the UK has found that young people prefer to practise politics on their own terms, evidenced through their increasing engagement in non-traditional 'one-off' forms of 'consumer citizenship' (Pattie et al., 2004; Marsh et al., 2007; Bang, 2004). Interviews suggest that this has impacted on how formal political participation processes are now perceived by young people. The clearest expression of this was students' rejection of party identification and a fixed political spectrum on the basis that it would compromise their desire to be flexible in their political opinions on a range of issues:

> I don't really buy the whole political spectrum anymore. ... I don't see the point of wedding myself to one sort of programme come up by some dead guy yonks ago. (Mick, Cambridge)

> I've voted in elections for different parties each time, because policies change, and political parties change. Yes, you've got a traditional model of what a Tory is and what a Labour supporter is, but I think you're getting yourself into trouble if you take that model as gospel. (Sonya, UCL)

> I'm open-minded, and if something makes sense, whoever's saying it, I'll go along with it. So it's never really been a case of me wanting to wage an ideological war against Conservatives or whoever's in power – I always criticise things based on policy. (Julian, Leeds)

> If you vote Lib Dem you are supposed to agree with X, X and X – but I might not, it might be the first two things and the third thing I disagree with completely. So it's difficult to give a fully-rounded view of one's political views if you mainly politically identify with a party. (Anita, Cambridge)

In other words, choosing to identify with a political party risks allowing the party to eventually identify *you*.[5] Given these concerns, it is perhaps significant that each of the four students quoted above voted Liberal Democrat in the 2010 general election. As noted in chapter 4, many considered the party a left-of-centre alternative to Labour prior to the election, and so felt wrong-footed by the formation of the Coalition Government. These students' prioritisation of 'pragmatism' and 'open-mindedness' above party loyalty arguably reflects their original motives for voting Liberal Democrat and their subsequent desire to reassert their political autonomy. This is because of a desire to do politics on their own terms. Party identification, in contrast, is seen as sticky, restrictive, and defining, with supporters expected to automatically subscribe to the party line on a range of issues they might not agree with or feel sufficiently knowledgeable about. Although the students disagreed on whether party identification wedded them to an impregnable historical ideology (as suggested by Mick), or a party programme that was constantly changing (argued by Sonya), the effect is much the same. Instead, they favoured a political engagement process in which they could personally acquire and consider knowledge carefully and impartially before making a decision:

> I don't like pinning myself to any kind of allegiance without doing proper research on the party, and I haven't had the time or impetus to do that yet. (Rick, Edinburgh)

> Someone [who] declares themselves a left-winger and then goes and finds out what that entails for them to believe, rather than making up their mind what should be the case and sticking to that – it seems like the wrong way round. (Mick, Cambridge)

> If you're a Lib Dem or whatever, you'll vote for this because you're with them ... which I don't think is a particularly good thing if they're changing things about their party. [But] I'm not personally convinced that I have every-thing clear in my head in order to be able to judge what the most important issues are. (Cynthia, Cambridge)

Despite their desire for a methodical process, it is questionable how success-fully this can be practised in reality. As Rick admits, he requires 'the time and impetus' to engage fully, neither of which he claims to have had during his four years at university. Moreover, practising this process is harder still when political issues are numerous and complex. Cynthia's comment alludes to political parties' responsibility to help voters judge what the most impor-tant issues are, yet widespread cynicism towards the actions and motivations of political parties and politicians has seemingly broken this relationship of trust (see Stoker, 2006; Hay, 2007). This leaves the caring but not committed with the arduous task of undergoing this time-consuming engagement process largely alone.

Of course, part of the reason why so many students were prepared to mobilise for the fees protests was that the issue could be interpreted on a basic moral level, that is, the *right* to an affordable education. Further-more, an anti-£9,000 fees position could also be taken from a strictly non-partisan perspective: Labour had originally introduced fees and later commissioned the Browne Review; the Liberal Democrats had campaigned to abolish fees only to then U-turn on the policy, and the Conservatives were ultimately responsible for pushing the fees bill through Parliament. Yet as we saw earlier in this chapter, majority support did not translate into anything approaching majority participation. To a significant extent, this reflects many students' specific uncertainties over *protest* as a means of participation.

Protest and Efficacy

For most activists, protest represented the only available form of participation that could have influenced the Parliamentary vote in December 2010. But with the resultant campaign mobilising only a fraction of its support base, it is significant that the caring but not committed often spoke of discomfort specifically at the idea of protesting. Somewhat inevitably, the use of direct action tactics was a particular source of unease as it went against their pre-conceptions of protest being most efficacious when its primary goal was to 'raise awareness':

> It's always a bit tricky with protest and activism to tell whether they've made a really palpable difference, but I think that more often than not they do the job of raising awareness among the public rather than the government. (Rick, Edinburgh)

> I can't think of many instances in the recent past where protest has made a notable difference, at least not a protest where you take to the streets. (Sonya, UCL)

This combination of a strong respect for the *principle* of protest and a general lack of faith in its power to provoke change – especially at a governmental level – arguably reflects the often gradual and diffusive nature of its historical outcomes (at least in the UK). For the caring but not committed, this also generates uncertainties in *how* one should protest, and for what purpose. Whereas students involved in direct action repertoires often cited the 2003 Iraq War demonstrations as showing the limitations of what 'polite protest' could achieve, the caring but not committed often cited it as showing the limitations of what protest of *any* kind could achieve:

> What have protests done for us lately? All the major ones we've had in the past few years – the budget cuts, the student one, Iraq ... you know, the Iraq one was *huge*, and it was completely ignored. I support the right to protest, you know – that's fundamental – but because they don't get listened to, it's not really worth it. (Sharon, Warwick)

Debates over protest tactics became especially prominent on campuses in the aftermath of Millbank. Exploring this further, interviewees were invited to consider activists' defence of the event: that it represented a controversial-but-necessary 'moment of excess' to give the fees grievance wider coverage. Most responded by claiming arguments for the use of 'violence' were incompatible with any legitimate claims to the moral high ground in a political debate:

> It's not productive to get aggressive and angry in that way – it just looks like you're a mob. If you *reason* with someone it's more productive than if you threaten them. I just think it's counterproductive, and now they're gonna pay a fuck-load of money to fix the building – it doesn't really benefit anyone. (Heather, Leeds)

> To an extent I can see that you have to inconvenience people to make them listen, but I don't think you have to make people feel afraid – and I don't just mean David Cameron. If I were to go on a big demonstration, to be perfectly frank I would be slightly afraid that I'd end up dead, or injured in some way. It's a big crowd, it can be volatile. (Anita, Cambridge)

> A large chunk of them are just along for the ride, I think, and the violence comes from people who are just looking for an excuse to go out and be violent – I'm sorry, but not wanting to pay higher fees isn't a valid reason for smashing a window. It definitely does undermine the goal, because it portrays these protests as being just people wanting to yell for the sake of yelling. (Sharon, Warwick)

As with students' preferred method for party identification, emphasis is again placed on rationality rather than emotion. It is also revealing that, when asked to clarify what the ideal model for protest might look like in practice, many students cited the 'peaceful' and 'dignified' historical examples of Mahatma Gandhi, Nelson Mandela, and the US civil rights movement. With instances of radical or violent tactics effectively written out of anti-apartheid and civil rights movements, this suggests that protest is perhaps easier to consider as 'effective' or 'legitimate' once history has framed it as such. However, whereas Heather and Sharon dismiss direct action and property violence on almost Habermasian grounds, others were more willing to rationalise such tactics as the necessary outcome of the *failure* of communicative reason:

> I think it's going to get people's attention more than a march would, because it's prolonged, and it can cause more disruption than a march might, so I do think it's a valuable political tool. (Julian, Leeds)

> Realistically, if a government knows that all you're going to get out of a movement is peaceful protest, you know, you can just write them off – like, 'Oh, the peaceful protesters are outside again' – like, what does that mean? Absolutely nothing to anyone! The public will forget about it within a week. They need to be disruptive. (Mick, Cambridge)

> If I were in a situation where I felt extremely strongly about something, I think I would probably be happy to commit a criminal offence. (Lawrence , Warwick)[6]

Of course, these comments are hypothetical responses to hypothetical situations, and of these three students only Mick had recently attended a demonstration – the NUS march in November 2010. Although supportive of Millbank, he also admitted being too worried about his own career prospects to personally participate in such acts. This not only reveals the limitations of debating direct action participation in the abstract; it also belies a desire for personal autonomy when participating. Mick was certainly not alone in this regard; as we saw in chapter 5, fellow NUS demonstration attendees Hayley and Laura resented being made to feel 'responsible' for Millbank. Anita expressed similar reservations about attending demonstrations on the grounds that 'it only takes one person [to act violently] for everyone to get tarred with the same brush' extended to grievances as well as tactics: Mick expressed anger that fellow marchers on the NUS demonstration were displaying pro-Palestine and Labour Party banners, neither of which he wanted to be seen to be endorsing by association. This represents a very individualistic reading of collective action repertoires, where actors' desire to maintain a favourable (and flexible) impression of the self (Goffman, 1971) is always potentially compromised by the unpredictable actions of other, unfamiliar protesters. Such readings also reflect and reinforce a basic dis-identification with political actors.

Dis-identification with Political Actors

Dis-identification has been a prominent theme in the past two chapters – for participants as well as non-participants. To explore this further, interviewees were invited to describe and compare themselves to the most political person they knew personally. This had the dual purpose of clarifying the extent of their ties to activism networks on campus and revealing how they saw themselves as political actors. Broadly speaking, the caring but not committed regularly characterised themselves as rational, reasoned, and open-minded in their political decision-making, whereas their more-active peers were depicted as lacking in these qualities:

> I like to think I think about the other side. And I think he is generally more extreme in his views, so every little thing that springs up about politics he's very quick to get on his soapbox. (Sonya, UCL)

> I don't chat with her [about politics] because it goes into a big mess and it isn't what I would consider a proper debate because it just gets emotional and not logical. It's self-preservation! (Sharon, Warwick)

> I don't want to debate with somebody when I'm being forced into the position of defending a party that I don't agree with, just because I can't bear to be in a debate where only one party is represented. Because I will misrepresent the

argument, and it will sound like I am agreeing with them, when in fact I am just trying to understand them. (Cynthia, Cambridge)

Evident in each of these accounts is the perception that politically active actors frequently fail to live up to interviewees' ideal standard of political decision-making. Sonya's chosen activist is perceived as dogmatic rather than rational, whereas Sonya and Sharon claim to feel uncomfortable with their activists' tendency to politicise everyday conversations and get on their 'soapbox'. As recipients of this behaviour, it is again noticeable how Sharon and Cynthia draw attention to their lack of *control* in how discussions proceed. For Sharon, her inability to impose 'rational' rules of debate in the face of 'emotional' arguments leads her to withdraw from the debate completely ('it's self-preservation!'). Also implicit within these criticisms is the belief that political actors are not always as well informed and knowledgeable as they think they are. Some interviewees were able to identify specific cases where student activists shared information which they knew to be inaccurate or misrepresentative. These were often invoked as evidencing arrogance and confirmation bias, or their blind loyalty to the politics of a particular group or party. This left the caring but not committed feeling sceptical towards the information and motivation behind student activism campaigns more generally.

In activists' defence, accusations of 'groupthink' might be misrepresenting a consistent, shared philosophy that is too abstruse to outsiders – particularly those who reject the political spectrum in favour of a case-by-case approach. For the caring but not committed, though, activists' shared politics is viewed with greater suspicion when it is perceived to be inseparable from their shared *lifestyles*. Here, the political becomes distorted by the social. Anita and Cynthia recalled experiences as freshers of wanting to join political groups – the feminist society for the former, and the college student council for the latter – but finding that their political similarities were ultimately outweighed by their cultural incompatibility with existing participants:

I felt like we weren't alternative enough – we didn't only go and shop at the fair trade market and every time someone made a joke about women we didn't pounce on them and go 'Actually that's derogatory'. I don't see how [radical feminism] translates to other lifestyle choices. … It made me feel that if I came back wearing dungarees and Doc Martens and been a bit more 'yeah, screw the patriarchy' I would have fitted in a bit more. (Anita, Cambridge)

I went to some of the open meetings in college but I was a bit disillusioned with that because they were incredibly cliquey. … They were all from pretty similar backgrounds – or if they weren't, they pretended that they were – and cultivated similar interests, and bought the same clothes, and you got the sense that politics came with that. (Cynthia, Cambridge)

Both identified what they felt to be the group's key 'tie-signs' – clothes, language, food preferences – as a stronger basis for dis-identification than the group's politics or organisation. Indeed, similar feelings were also expressed by Mick about the 2010 Cambridge occupation ('it was run by a lot of the hipstery, vegany bits of the left'). Although these tie-signs are usually invoked to emphasise otherness or stigma, they also reveal something about the individual doing the ascribing, and what she or he wishes to dis-identify with. On the one hand, it reflects the desire not to be defined by one's politics: for Anita, the Cambridge feminist society's behaviour and dress were considered too dominant and restricting for her preferred mode of feminism. On the other hand, the specific nature of students' dis-identification with activists may reveal certain confirmation biases of their own. Some questioned the authenticity of activists' political identity, believing them to mask more nefarious personal motivations, such as narcissism (Louise bemoaning Facebook being filled of 'arty' Instagram photos of students 'suffering for the cause'), self-interest (Sharon claiming that students attending protest marches 'are just trying to get a day off'), or 'lifestylism':

> It's the dishonesty and hypocrisy. … Seeing one of these guys after graduation being driven by his dad in his enormous Jaguar – like, one of these really prominent left-wingers, I think you are a ridiculous person, telling everyone that you're bloody poor. (Mick, Cambridge)

Accusations of 'radical chic' have been a regular issue for activists since the 1960s and do not necessarily warrant deep analysis here. For the caring but not committed at least, these *ad hominem* remarks reflect a perceived contradiction between activists' political and social identities that fatally undermines their credibility as political actors. According to Runciman (2008), however, demand for a politics free from all perceived hypocrisies is both unrealistic and naïve. Accusations of narcissism and self-interest seem to reflect a suspicion towards individuals who have ultimately taken the 'leap of faith' into the complex world of political activism and self-identification – a leap which the caring but not committed feel unable or unwilling to take themselves. This forms the basis of the final discussion.

Civic Anxiety or Civic Ambivalence? Knowing Enough to Care, but not Enough to Participate

At a basic level, nearly all students have converted political engagement into some form of action at one time or another: as we saw in chapter 4, only 7 per cent of survey respondents participated in *none* of the listed activities over the past three years. Inviting students to reflect on their personal decision-making process, however, reveals a degree of ambivalence. While the caring but not committed feel equipped to broadly follow politics, appreciate its importance, and sporadically engage in forms of participation, they do not feel engaged or confident enough to commit to any forms of action that feel particularly meaningful or efficacious.

Knowledge accumulation and confidence have been prominent themes throughout this book, as well as in political surveys more generally: Henn and Foard (2012) found that 47 per cent of 18-year-olds felt they did not know enough about politics, and only 24 per cent felt that they did. There are also gender properties within these trends: Hansard's (2011: 91) survey finds that 62 per cent of men feel knowledgeable about politics, compared with only 42 per cent of women. Not only do these findings chime with earlier analysis of supportive non-participants, table 7.15 suggests that this gender imbalance extends beyond non-participants as well. Among those who participated in the student protests, the proportion of women claiming that they 'often feel that they don't know enough about politics to fully engage in it' is almost double that of men.

The literature on gender and political participation has variously cited as potential explanations the lack of female role models in formal politics (Taft, 2006), women's hesitancy and uncertainty over feminist identifications (Aronson, 2003; Crossley, 2010), and depictions of political activism as being somehow incompatible with women's gender identity (Freeman, 2005; Hercus, 2005). Historical accounts of student activism have also highlighted the macho, male-centric culture of certain groups and campaigns as triggering female dis-identification and demobilisation (Hoefferle, 2013). The extent to which these factors impact on women's ordinary, everyday discussion of politics is perhaps less clear and warrants investigation in future research. In this study at least, female *and* male interviewees often claimed insufficient

Table 7.15 Comparing male and female students' political confidence and discussion

		Participated in the student protests		Did not participate in the student protests	
		Male %	Female %	Male %	Female %
'I often feel that they	Agree	27.3	49.2	39.1	66.4
don't know enough	Neither agree	9.3	12.4	16.0	12.9
about politics to fully	nor disagree	63.4	38.3	44.9	20.8
engage in it'	Disagree				
How often do you	Regularly	53.4	32.4	29.4	16.2
discuss politics?	Fairly often	22.4	26.4	25.5	22.1
	Sometimes	13.0	26.9	25.6	31.8
	Rarely	9.3	13.2	16.2	25.1
	Never	1.9	1.0	3.3	4.8

N = 2,485. *Note:* Percentages by column.

knowledge about politics as a key reason for their non-participation in activities and campaigns about topics that interested them:

> I don't think I understand politics very well. I appreciate that lots of people who vote probably don't understand politics very well, but it's often difficult for me to try to weigh up which particular points are the most important. It seems to be very easy to form initial impressions of political parties or political figures which are very superficial and based on things that don't really matter. (Cynthia, Cambridge)

> I'm always aware that stuff's more complicated than what I know generally, so I was a bit dubious to get involved unless I'm aware of what I'm doing. (Mick, Cambridge)

> I would [like to be more politically active] but I'd like to know more about it. I tend to like to know a *lot* about something before I'll argue about it normally. I don't know how much I'd have to know before I'd want to argue about it! (Heather, Leeds)

Given students' earlier criticisms of political actors for possessing an inflated confidence in their own views, the caring but not committed were usually keen not to fall into these traps themselves. Like many students, Heather found it fairly easy to take a basic moral position on tuition fees, but was less sure if this alone was a strong enough reason for participating. Compounding this uncertainty was a desire for self-preservation and the avoidance of hypocrisy, as publically stating one's opinion on an issue ran the risk of being exposed as insufficiently informed, and subject to the sort of ridicule the caring but not committed might normally direct at activists:

> I'd say one of the things that has happened to me at university is in general I've become less sure of my views. Like, a lot of the time I'm thinking okay, I know I think this, but not with enough confidence to try and persuade other people of it. So I might support a cause, but I'll be aware that there are people who are far more intelligent than me who don't and say that it isn't a good way of doing this. And I don't feel confident enough to go preaching my views to other people. I mean, I'm happy to have them myself – I'm not insecure in having them – but at the same time I don't want to go shouting it from the roof if I'm not sure of it. (Lawrence, Warwick)

> I don't want to be the person shouting about politics when I only know enough to be spouting the opinion I've heard from someone else, and I don't know enough to base it on an actual thought-process. (Heather, Leeds)

> In an ideal world you would find a party or a movement where you think that their views are roughly the right opinion, and follow them and what they say. I don't think that will ever really happen, but even if you did, you would still

need to read the opinions of your opponents otherwise how are you going to understand the logic of anyone who believes differently? The problem is basically there's always other things I could be doing than sitting and reading about politics, and you know, most of the time I'm going to pick them, because I have things that I need to do. (Cynthia, Cambridge)

This perhaps gets to the core of why many students are 'caring but not committed' about politics. Cynthia's advocacy of a rational and well-informed decision-making process leaves her with the prospect of an arduous, time-consuming task each time a participatory opportunity presents itself. Yet in the absence of a social environment where participation is encouraged or rewarded, she faces little pressure or motivation to ever carry this out. Furthermore, the social environment she and other members of the caring but not committed belongs to helps preserve this position of stasis. Just as activists' mobilisation is partly driven by the expectation of their surrounding networks, the networks that surround the caring but not committed expect them *not* to participate. This outlook is typically maintained by the absence of any conversational trigger to stimulate political thought and action. In the event of specific grievances, however, participatory opportunities might be corroded by the hostility or scepticism of one's peers (Oegema and Klandermans, 1994; see also van Stekelenberg, 2013). In either case, this surrounding counter-network implicitly precludes and discourages participation via the casual, periodic reiteration of 'perspectival selectivity' narratives (Norgaard, 2006) – namely, dis-identification with political parties, scepticism over protest, and dis-identification with political actors.

While this shows how the caring but not committed withdraw from political commitment, ascertaining this process's emotional significance provides further insights. In her study of non-participation in climate change activism, Norgaard (2006) found that individuals' uncertainty over how best to convert their engagement into participation caused feelings of helplessness and guilt. Students, however, generally gave little impression that being caring but not committed over tuition fees or other contemporaneous grievances was a source of personal anxiety. Indeed, Cynthia's non-participation reflected a position of relative comfort, as her instincts ultimately steered her away from undertaking a largely thankless and never-ending task of political self-education. As Warde (1994) argues, individuals are only likely to feel a 'choice anxiety' if subjected to expectations that their deliberations will produce an outcome. For most caring but not committed students, their non-participation was seldom subjected to any emotional pressure.

This brings us to fundamental issues about the sociology of networks. To conceptualise the social production of non-participation, we can return to Putnam's (2000) distinction between bonding and bridging forms of social capital from chapter 2. Given their non-participatory norms and perspectival selectivity narratives, one can argue that counter-networks fall into the former category. This may seem unusual in a campus context, since the overlapping networks which comprise the student body have been depicted as potentially creating a 'self-perpetuating dynamic of politicisation' (Crossley, 2008: 18). Research presented in this book, however, has identified more complex social relations in the experience of non-participation, as counter-networks bond non-participants together using comparable social mechanisms to activism networks. Yet through their dis-identification with political actors, non-participants are also protecting themselves from confronting their *own* political indecisions and uncertainties.

For activists wishing to transcend this malaise and mobilise the student body, these findings place large emphasis on the importance of 'advocates' who can broker access to activism networks which are open and welcoming enough to challenge students' grounds for dis-identification. Without such advocates, their cycle of non-participation is likely to remain unbroken.

CONCLUSION

Through its focus on the 2010/11 fees protests and contemporary trends more generally, this chapter has advanced a more sociological approach for studying political non-participation. Although non-participation is often characterised as a direct response to specific grievances and mobilisations, the evidence presented indicates that it may also be socially produced and maintained independently of such contexts. Only a small minority opposed the protests for outright political reasons, and the high proportion of supportive non-participants – 51 per cent of all students – hinted at deeper issues regarding students' political engagement and confidence. In addressing these issues, the chapter closed by conceptualising the social production of non-participation, a process that left many students feeling 'caring but not committed' about politics today.

At one level, the high proportion of supportive non-participants in the 2010/11 protests can be seen to confirm activists' claims that their anti-fees stance reflected the vast majority of student views. But the majority's explanation of having been 'too busy with academic work' to take part belies a social network context in which political participation is seldom afforded any value. For some students, this simply meant not receiving personal invitations to participate, or even learning that protests were happening nearby. For others, mobilisation opportunities were distorted by social cross-pressures, as any ties to participants were ultimately superseded by the participatory disincentives propagated through their surrounding counter-networks. Most prominent among these was the protests' sometimes violent nature, though counter-grievances related to the current standard of higher education also chipped away at students' participatory potential. For individuals belonging to these counter-networks – especially those lacking much of a political family background – the 'rational' decision was therefore *not* to participate.

The emphasis on 'rationality' might be easily taken as an endorsement of Olson's (1965) theory of collective action, but one should highlight the significance these counter-networks have in shaping non-participants' knowledge and attitudes. In this regard, it is perhaps better to follow Glaesser and Cooper's (2014: 466–467) lead by considering the resultant decision-making as a process of *subjective* rationality (see also Passy and Monsch, 2014; Hensby, 2015). Certainly, many students advocated a highly individualistic, knowledge-intensive process of political decision-making – one that necessitated a great deal of time spent learning and deliberating on all sides of an issue. While this process was partly shaped by their frustrations with the perceived dogmatism of student activists on campus, it also demanded standards of engagement that they themselves were unable or unwilling to live up to. This left them ultimately feeling 'caring but not committed' about politics, wary as they were of being pushed into participating on someone else's terms (such as a party or movement), or expressing an opinion on something that others might be better informed about. In this context, it often felt easier to avoid politics as a topic of conversation altogether (see Eliasoph, 1998).

There is also evidence to suggest that the caring but not committed phenomenon is especially relevant to female students. Not only were women over-represented among supportive non-participants, the survey found significant gender disparities in students' discussion of, and confidence in, politics. Given the emphasis throughout this book on everyday conversation as a driver of engagement and politics as a legitimate activity, this hints at fundamental barriers to the political participation of women. Yet this does not necessarily reflect the absence of surrounding social networks in which to discuss politics: rather, it points to fundamental problems in the *quality* of everyday political discussion on campus. This raises questions about the performance of men in this context, with women either lacking the confidence to join in with these debates or feeling wary and cynical of their purpose and efficacy.

Despite these uncertainties over political discussion and engagement, being 'caring but not committed' seemed to represent a state of relative autonomy and self-control. This stasis was socially maintained and legitimated by certain 'self-preservation narratives' – particularly those identifying the foibles and shortcomings of political actors. Despite the sharing of these narratives, however, the caring but not committed generally took an individualised approach to politics – one that rendered the whole process of collective action as potentially problematic. This recalls Bauman's (2000) consumer-centric 'task' of identity in a society that increasingly prioritises mobility and flexibility. While this admirably eschews some of the more nefarious aspects to participation – dogmatism, hypocrisy, cliques – this desire for self-preservation leaves individuals more comfortable as 'caring but not committed' than getting their hands dirty in the messy (but potentially more efficacious) reality of political participation.

NOTES

1. $p = 0.00$.

2. For example, the autumn 2010 and 2011 NUS/NCAFC demonstrations both took place on Wednesdays.

3. $p = 0.00$.

4. Admittedly, this reflects the category's above-average proportion of international students: the percentage of those 'certain to vote' jumps to 69.3 per cent when limited to UK students only ($N = 257$), whereas 66.3 per cent of undecided international students ($N = 86$) offered no opinion of whether the protests had failed or not.

5. One may reasonably claim that these risks are at odds with the recent election of Jeremy Corbyn as Labour Party leader. Corbyn's initial campaign saw the party's membership rise to 350,000 – more than the Conservatives, Liberal Democrats, and the SNP combined (Gamble, 2015). However, this does not necessarily contradict analysis of students' dis-identification with political parties insofar as Corbyn promised a left-wing programme that was at odds with the centrist, technocratic politics of the previous two decades, while seeking to use the party's expanded membership to turn it into a 'social movement' (BBC, 2015).

6. Though these anti-violence quotations are drawn exclusively from female interviewees, and quotations from 'open-minded' are all male, this might reflect selection bias rather than a 'gendered' trend per se: the survey, for example, shows that a slightly higher proportion of female students considered 'direct action protest (e.g. occupations, sit-ins, blockades)' very/somewhat effective (48.1 per cent) than male students (46.0 per cent).

Chapter 8

Conclusion

This book has sought to unpack the experience of contemporary student activism, and explain why some students are more likely to be mobilised than others. As a case study of participation and non-participation, the UK Government's proposal to treble the cap on tuition fees in autumn 2010 represented an issue of widespread grievance for students, yet few converted this grievance into collective action. Investigating this further, chapters 4–7 have drawn on survey and interview data to identify patterns that separate participants from non-participants; uncover what sort of paths and barriers enable or preclude mobilisation; foreground the role of collective identity in building and sustaining campus activism networks; and explain how non-participation is collectively produced and sustained in everyday life.

At a basic level, the vast majority of students *are* political participants in some form: recalling survey findings from chapter 4, only 7 per cent had not taken part in any of the listed activities in the past three years. This reveals certain limitations in employing a participation/non-participation binary, prompting this book to explore some of its key intersections. On the one hand, the case study identified key differences in the participatory experiences of students who typically engaged in low-cost/risk activities, and those involved in high-cost/risk activities. On the other hand, a number of participants and non-participants were found to be 'caring but not committed' about politics more generally, revealing deeper concerns over students' knowledge of, and confidence in, political thought and action.

Bringing the book to a conclusion, this final chapter has three purposes. First, it summarises its key empirical themes, namely the role of social networks, the formation of collective identities, and the social production of non-participation. Second, it evaluates the legacy of the 2010/11 student protests for higher education and anti-austerity campaigns in the UK, as well as for the participants themselves. Third, and finally, it considers the future of student activism – in terms of its capacity to continue engaging and mobilising students for collective action, and its ability to influence the wider political process.

HABITUS, NETWORKS, AND MOBILISATION

It's *so* to do with the people that surround you the whole time. If I had got in with the sports crowd or something at UCL, god knows, I could have been running the *Mockupation* Twitter account! (*laughs*) (Justine, UCL)

A fundamental question for this book has been how students access political knowledge, discussion, and participatory opportunities. The availability and quality of each of these is critical to shaping the subjective rationality of individuals' political thought and decision-making, that is, what *feels* rational in the context of the norms, values, expectations, and conversations surrounding them. For students, this context is usually provided by family, school, and social ties made at university. Family background is arguably the strongest of these, as it offers the earliest forms of political education which can be built on in later years (see Bourdieu, 1984: 440). This was evidenced by the fact that most high-cost/risk participants grew up in a household where politics was discussed often, and had been politically active prior to arriving at university. Recalling Braungart and Braungart's (1990) study, this did not involve the verbatim inheritance of a political ideology or party identification: rather, it provided students with the tools of politicisation – including access to knowledge, the normalisation of political debate, and the legitimation of protest as an activity. Once at university, these formative experiences equipped students to easily assimilate into the campus's activism network and further develop their 'radical habitus'.

In contrast, students who grew up in a household where politics was discussed rarely or never arrived at university in possession of a comparatively *apolitical* habitus. For them, politics often felt like a 'taboo' subject, with many admitting to not even knowing who their parents voted for. The campus provided resources and opportunities for freshers to subvert this background, though much depended on the sorts of friendships and social networks they formed in their first year. As implied by Justine's comment above, residing in networks where protest was considered 'normal' behaviour provided opportunities for these students to become more politically engaged and active. Conversely, some already-engaged students found themselves belonging to the 'wrong' networks where politics and activism were either afforded no social value, or actively discouraged. For students lacking the confidence to ignore these pressures and seek out new social ties, their participation was held back by these 'counter-networks'.

Consistent with Crossley and Ibrahim's (2012) study, most opportunities for activism participation on campus were attributable to the efforts of an interconnected network of political groups and societies, and the student union. These 'political worlds' were found to be especially powerful and well resourced at Cambridge, Edinburgh, UCL, and Warwick, even if their density of mutual affinities and loyalties lent themselves to the formation of cliques and factions. These networks are not wholly impenetrable, however, as specific collective action frames generate opportunities to mobilise a wider population of students. Although higher education funding had long been a campaigning issue for students, the Government's proposal in autumn 2010 to treble the fees cap, combined with the sense of betrayal felt by many Liberal Democrat voters over the party's fees policy U-turn, represented an issue of grievance for the vast majority of students.

Subsequent mobilisations drew strongly on social media for communicating with students quickly and directly, but also benefitted from the grievance's amplification via mainstream media. Through this coverage, the protests were afforded a national significance that transcended the usual hubbub of campus politics. This generated a 'pull-up' effect where groups of students unattached to campus activism networks were spurred into mobilising for local and national protests. The most prominent of these was the NUS demonstration in November 2010, though the attack on Conservative HQ at Millbank represented the significant 'event within the event'. Controversial and certainly divisive among students, networks were key to its subsequent framing and defence. Many high-cost/risk participants admitted to initial reservations, but through discussions with fellow activists were eventually won over to its value as a paradigm-shifting 'moment of excess'. In contrast, students who were critical of Millbank and resided outside of activism networks were less likely to be confronted with counter-arguments, thus giving them little cause to reconsider their views.

Networks also played a key role in protest mobilisations after Millbank. With the NUS reluctant to preside over a campaign featuring direct action tactics, student groups and networks took it upon themselves to organise their own local and national protest events. The most prominent and coordinated of these was NCAFC's 'National Walkout and Day of Action', which served as the springboard for the majority of campus occupations across November and December. Occupations brought together students from a range of backgrounds and quickly coalesced into a single, multilayered activism network. These spaces functioned as the campaign's political hub on campus, with students encouraged to visit the space, participate in meetings and debates, and mobilise for impromptu marches and flash mobs.

In general, though, students were less inclined to spend time in occupations if they did not possess strong ties to people involved, even though the space was ostensibly open to all. This again points to the significance of networks in shaping individuals' subjective rationality. In the absence of activist 'advocates' who spanned multiple networks and could broker participatory opportunities, students were more likely to anticipate the potential costs and risks of participation (notably sanctions from university management) than the potential benefits (empowerment, education, developing strong social affinities). Students' non-participation was also to some extent *sustained* by their network position. For those residing in counter-networks, the dissemination of 'counter-grievances' and narratives of 'dis-identification' generated a non-participatory consensus in much the same way as a campus's activism networks generated a participatory consensus.

BUILDING COLLECTIVE IDENTITY: A CAMPAIGN OR A MOVEMENT?

Looking back it was kind of the golden days of the anti-cuts group. We actually did something; students were a bit radical – it was good. Lots of friendships. Almost all of my friends are from that group. And my girlfriend as well. (John, Edinburgh)

Given the range and diversity of tactics, it should come as no surprise that participants differed in their experiences of the student protests. For John, participation in the Edinburgh occupation helped him strengthen his political views and develop close relationships with many of those involved. While similar experiences were relayed by many high-cost/risk participants at Cambridge, Edinburgh, and UCL, they were by no means typical of participants as a whole. Survey findings found that low-cost/risk activities such as petition signing and joining/'liking' Facebook groups were by far the most popular forms of participation, yet few could claim to have undergone a transformative radicalising experience in the process. With only 4 per cent claiming to have participated in campus occupations, this raises questions over the extent to which a single, coherent 'collective identity' can emerge out of such a divergent, multi-repertoire campaign.

Certainly, in the autumn 2010 protests, strong feelings of solidarity and affinity emerged out of the more high-cost/risk activities. Campus occupations operated as 'liminal' spaces for intensive debate and knowledge sharing, as well as the practising of politics through working groups and consensus meetings. Much like Gitlin's (2013) depiction of Occupy Wall Street participants, however, occupiers at Cambridge, Edinburgh, and UCL spoke in terms of cores and peripheries. For core members, their participation had radicalising effects, with many reconsidering the fees increase as symptomatic of broader marketisation trends. Moreover, the costs and risks involved in maintaining the space helped develop strong mutual relations of trust, strengthening their commitment to more radical protest repertoires. In contrast, students on the occupation's periphery were less likely to access the space's liminal powers, with its more infrequent visitors struggling to fully understand the occupation's purpose and value to the wider campaign.

If these tactical differences reflected some of the limitations in building a cross-repertoire campaign, one should stress that participants remained united by the goal of pressurising Parliament into voting down the fees bill. According to the survey, this generated a basic sense of collective identity for the majority of participants, with two-thirds claiming to have felt 'proud to be part of a UK-wide student movement'. Whether the fees campaign *can* be seen as the work of a wider 'movement', however, is less clear. Tilly's (1984: 306) emphasis on a *sustained* series of interactions in his classic definition implies that social movements are not reducible to an individual campaign goal. This would require the fees campaign functioning as a catalyst to a more general movement encompassing multiple higher education grievances. Certainly, occupation groups were keen to *talk* such a movement into existence, with their media outputs frequently citing polling data, demonstration turnout, and the network of campus occupations as evidence of students' shared consensus. Yet this consensus was firmly rooted in the fees grievance, and once the bill was passed in Parliament, conditions for a student-wide collective identity quickly evaporated. Follow-up grievances concerning the Government's White Paper achieved only limited engagement, thereby restricting activists' capacity to mobilise students on the same scale as they had managed in autumn 2010.

This book has also drawn attention to the ambiguous role of social media networks in building and sustaining collective identities. Although undoubtedly valuable for mobilising online and offline activism, their powers rest on certain temporalities. During the autumn fees campaign, social media was extremely valuable for mobilising students on a large scale at short notice, and at little cost. Through their blog sites, Facebook pages, and Twitter feeds, occupations were able to 'expand the room' and attract a much bigger audience online. Yet within a year, social media was being used as a space for core activists' covert planning and organisation – effectively giving structure to occupations' initially fluid core-periphery boundaries. With the secrecy of the latter contradicting the openness of the former, one can highlight social media's capacity to support and sustain some of the more pernicious aspects of an 'outcome' collective identity – namely, cliques and implicit hierarchies (Hensby, 2016b; see also Kavada, 2009; Flesher Fominaya, 2015).

In sum, student activism can be seen to generate multiple layers of collective identity. These layers can broadly coalesce and complement each other for popular, goal-based campaigns (as the fees campaign demonstrated), but they might be too divergent and contradictory for building wider student movements in the long term – especially given the limiting effects of constant cohort turnover. While the fees campaign rested on a common uniting grievance, the fundamental differences in students' experiences of protest revealed underlying conflicts in their ideological perspectives and tactical preferences. These came to the fore once the fees bill was passed, revealing little common ground for the creation of a mass movement.

THE SOCIAL PRODUCTION OF NON-PARTICIPATION

I don't see that my participation would have changed the way that things were going. I didn't think it was going to do anything, so why take part, why bother! (Julian, Leeds)

Any sociological study of non-participation is confronted with the seemingly paradoxical challenge of identifying trends and commonalities among individuals who are grouped only by something they do *not* do. This book's case study, however, has provided a rare opportunity to compare non-participants quantitatively and qualitatively. Central to this analysis is the sizeable category of students who were supportive of the 2010/11 protests but did not participate in them. Most appeared to engage with the grievance on a moral basis, but lacked the participatory ethos or social network context to convert this into any meaningful action. Findings not only highlight the importance of accessing micro-mobilisation networks to provide social pathways for formal mobilisation drives (McAdam, 1986; Oegema and Klandermans, 1994), but also suggest that non-participation should be studied as a social phenomenon in its own right.

Despite the ubiquity of the protests in autumn 2010, the campaign's mobilising power varied across the campuses studied. With just over a third of supportive non-participants growing up in a household where politics was discussed regularly/often, many had since ensconced themselves in friendship groups at university where politics played only a limited role in everyday conversation. This was especially the case among students studying science and technology subjects. Consequently, their non-participation was often simply the unconscious outcome of not knowing many people who protested, and not having been invited by anyone to take part – what Oegema and Klandermans (1994) term 'nonconversion'. For non-participants in the humanities and social sciences, however, their closer proximity to participants generated stronger network cross-pressures. The majority opposed the £9,000 fees cap, but their potential mobilisation was negated by a personal stronger affiliation to counter-networks. In other words, conversations about the inarticulacy and inefficacy of protest as a means of political expression (as voiced by Julian, above), and the personal costs and risks incurred through participating, ultimately cancelled out any weak-tie claims about the benefits and virtues of taking part.

In some instances, students' participatory potential was more actively corroded by counter-arguments and counter-grievances from the small minority who supported the fees increase. With public debates sometimes guilty of oversimplifying or obfuscating the precise terms of the Government's proposals, these counter-arguments were able to chip away at students' confidence in their anti-fees position. The sharing of activist dis-identifications was also significant to counter-networks' legitimation of non-participation. This emphasises the significance of social conflict, as the desire not to be personally associated with the people leading or embodying activism campaigns is clearly a fundamental impediment for repertoires predicated on collective action and shared solidarity. Negative perceptions of their styles, attitudes, and practices were informed either by specific counter-grievances with activists on campus (such as the UCL occupation's dispute with the Musical Theatre Society) or more general images and stereotypes of student activism over the course of its history. Although it is true to say that occupation cores often exhibited subcultural tendencies, they comprised only a tiny fraction of participants overall, implying that invoking dis-identifications may have also functioned as a self-preservation narrative for some non-participants (Norgaard, 2006).

Self-preservation narratives moreover hinted at a social production of non-participation in everyday life – one which did not necessarily preclude sporadic, one-off forms of participation, but nevertheless pointed to deeper uncertainties in students' self-confidence as political actors. Recalling the work of Bang (2004), many expressed a dissatisfaction and cynicism over the contemporary supply of politics – both at a campus and UK level. In rejecting displays of partisanship or narcissism in favour of a decision-making process predicated on knowledge, objectivity, and independence, students accused political actors of all-too-often failing to live up to these expectations. However, a lack of time, motivation, or self-confidence meant that these students struggled to live up to these expectations as well – leaving them 'caring but not committed' about politics. Networks also played a part here, as the absence of peer expectation to show political engagement meant that non-participants had few social motivations to challenge this stasis. As a result, non-participation represented a position of comfort and self-preservation rather than anxiety or guilt.

Survey evidence also implied that this tendency might be especially pertinent to female students. A lower proportion of women – including participants as well as non-participants – discussed politics regularly/fairly often, whereas two-thirds of female non-participants agreed that they 'often feel that they don't know enough about politics to fully engage in it'. This implies persistent barriers to female political engagement via the way politics is discussed and debated in everyday life. It also suggests that women might be generally more self-critical than men in their role as political actors – potentially giving a gender slant to some of the activist dis-identifications covered in this book. This characteristic might be self-fulfilling insofar as it deters a willingness to partake in political conversations if they are routinely dominated (and undermined) by men.

As an emerging theme in this book, the caring but not committed phenomenon arguably warrants further study in a range of other fields. In this context, the concept might admittedly reflect temporary 'life cycle' effects symptomatic of young people's limited agency in formal political processes (Henn et al., 2002). Its particular emphasis on knowledge and rationality might also betray a specific relevance to university students, rather than young people more generally. That said, there is a wealth of literature pointing to the growth of political individualism and citizens' preference for more sporadic, impulsive, and autonomous participatory practices, even if there remains disagreement over whether this is producing empowered 'everyday makers' or bumptious 'slacktivists' (Bennett, 1998; Pattie et al., 2004; Bang, 2004; Morozov, 2011). For the caring but not committed at least, their feelings of cynicism and uncertainty towards the efficacy of formal *and* contentious politics hints at a 'civic ambivalence' comparable to more wide-ranging participation studies (e.g. Jordan and Maloney, 2007; Putnam, 2000). One might also see this phenomenon as symptomatic of 'depoliticisation' trends in governmental politics, especially given their eschewing of ideology and partisanship in favour of individualistic, knowledge-intensive deliberation processes (see Burnham, 2001; Flinders and Wood, 2014). In any case, the continued research and study of similar 'negative identities' is crucial to understanding the political *and* social factors that preclude citizens' knowledge, confidence, and participation in contemporary society.

THE LEGACY OF THE UK STUDENT PROTESTS

I don't think any of us expected to win [the fees vote] – we'd always seen that this was something greater, and that all we could really do was be detonators to wider society. I mean, the student movement blew apart any consensus that the cuts were inevitable or necessary, and they played a very strong part of the resistance. The Lib Dems' electoral haemorrhaging, I think, stems directly and irrevocably from the student movement. We were eleven [sic] votes away from winning. So we had an absolutely massive impact, even if we didn't win what we wanted. (Gaz, UCL)

Ostensibly, the protests failed in their principal aim of preventing the Government from raising the cap on tuition fees for students in England, and since 2012/13 undergraduates have faced a future of £27,000 in debt repayments from fees alone.[1] As a headline issue in autumn 2010, it is perhaps surprising that only around half of survey respondents agreed that the protests had 'failed in their aims' (see chapter 4). This chimes with Gaz's claim that the legacy of the student protests should not be judged purely on the outcome of the fees vote. Certainly, there is a literature in social movement studies that seeks to broaden the analysis of outcomes to include forms of cultural, ethical, and institutional change (Giugni, 1998). Moreover, as we saw in chapter 3, the significance of student activism has often been found more in long-term societal changes, such as the shifting of dominant norms and values. While wider societal effects might be difficult to gauge still relatively soon after the protests took place, one can at least consider their recent impact on higher education campaigns, social movements, and UK party politics.

To begin with the issue of higher education, one can reiterate Gaz's argument that pressurising Parliament into voting down the fees bill was always going to be a steep task for students. The fees grievance drew widespread sympathy from students and the general public, but protest campaigns were faced with the Coalition Government's all-encompassing austerity mantra of *there is no alternative*, and even opponents to this programme were liable to claim that student grievances were 'low in the pain pecking order' (Toynbee, 2010). Protest, too, was only an indirect means of effecting change. In this context, the narrowness of the bill's passing is something of a testament to the pressure students exerted on MPs, especially Liberal Democrats. It has also been argued by McGettigan (2013: 24) among others that a desire to avoid repeating the scale and radicalism of the 2010 protests likely factored in the Government's decision in 2012 to shelve its White Paper. This represented only a temporary respite, however: following the Conservative Party's outright election victory in 2015, it is expected that the fees cap will soon be extended – or possibly even removed altogether.

Although it is presently unclear how much future campaigns will benefit from the organisational legacy of the 2010/11 protests, the memory of Millbank and the occupations should at least inspire new cohorts to make their voices heard loud and clear. Nevertheless, the years since have witnessed more sober evaluations of the protests' legacy from activists and commentators. McGettigan (2013), for example, questioned how activists framed their campaign grievances, arguing that prioritising tuition fees came at the expense of any detailed discourse about the conditions of the repayment mechanism, or the Browne Review's broader recommendations for the marketisation of higher education. Gilbert (Gilbert and Aitchison, 2012) claimed that the emphasis on fees reflected the fact that the protests were 'overwhelmingly ... by and for the children of the professional classes' rather than those students already faced with a reality of long-term debt repayment. Both Gilbert and McGettigan were also critical of the way campaigns sometimes misleadingly gave the impression that students would be expected to pay £27,000 fees upfront. As we saw in chapter 7, similar accusations fuelled unsupportive non-participants' counter-arguments, lending credibility to those who questioned campaigners' personal motivations for participating.

At the same time, however, activists' depiction of the fees issue primarily as a *moral* grievance (Ibrahim, 2011) was arguably vital to the campaign gaining as much support and participation as it did. Not only did its simplicity make the issue easy for most students to understand, it also functioned as an important hook for mobilising cohorts who were themselves unaffected by the increase. Moreover, the Government's decision to hold a 'snap' vote necessitated a 'snap' response, with students given only seven weeks to digest the recommendations of the Browne Review and build a UK-wide campaign. In this sense, the fees grievance gave the autumn protests a clear sense of narrative: a common goal, a preset timeframe, a sense of who 'us' and 'them' were, and the possibility of agency through pressurising of MPs to vote down the bill. This narrative was then amplified through the media, which served to promote and legitimise the campaign's goals to a wider audience. At the same time, however, the focus on fees arguably placed limitations on its capacity to sustain the level of momentum it had created: once the bill passed, the media (and many students) considered the campaign to have served its purpose, and subsequent protests struggled to mobilise on the same scale as before.

With much emphasis placed on creating media spectacles, one can also argue that the student protests generated a significant tactical legacy. Key to this was the use of direct action, evidenced by Millbank and the UK-wide network of campus occupations. For many activists, memories of the 'million march' against the Iraq War were a stark reminder of the limits to 'peaceful' mass participation. Although direct action tactics were by no means new, their deployment against *government* gave them far greater public prominence than in Climate Camp and Free Palestine campaigns. This helped inspire a number of anti-austerity protests throughout 2011 and 2012, including the work of UK Uncut, trade unions, and even the English riots. They also influenced the global Occupy movement, as well as student protests in Quebec (Palacios, 2013). At the same time, however, these tactics reflected a more problematic legacy, namely the trend towards 'command and control' forms of protest policing. Activists have warned that such tactics are more successful in provoking public order situations than preventing them, though police will likely see the value of intensifying the individual costs and risks to protest participation (see also Dauvergne and LeBaron, 2014).

Beyond the field of social movements, one of the most remarkable – and perhaps unexpected – legacies of the 2010/11 protests has been its impact on UK party politics, particularly for Labour and the Liberal Democrats. The protests drew significant attention to the role of the latter in the Coalition Government, causing substantial damage to the party's image – especially among young people. This was made apparent in September 2012 when Nick Clegg took the unusual step of personally apologising for the breaking his pledge on fees (even if he did not apologise for backing the policy itself). The fees grievance was cited as a factor when the Liberal Democrats lost 695 seats in 2011's local council elections (*Daily Mail*, 7 May 2011), but the ultimate humiliation came when it lost 57 of its 65 seats in the 2015 general election – prompting Clegg's resignation as party leader.

The Conservatives' victory in 2015 also forced Ed Miliband's exit as leader of the Labour Party, with veteran socialist backbencher Jeremy Corbyn elected as his surprise successor. With Miliband's Labour having advocated a graduate tax as a policy alternative to £9,000 fees, Corbyn's championing of *free* higher education bore the influence of the 2010/11 student protests very clearly. He and Shadow Chancellor John McDonnell had been invited speakers at the UCL occupation in autumn 2010, and some of the campaign's core activists would turn their mobilising energies to Corbyn's leadership campaign five years later. Moreover, his campaign drew heavily on activism tactics central to the 2010/11 student protests – from clicktivism to flash mobs organised via social media – in order to make voting feel akin to participating in an empowering national *event*. While Labour's leftward shift and rediscovery of social movement repertoires may indeed reflect the transformation of the student 'class of 2010' into the 'Corbyn generation' (Chessum, 2015), it remains to be seen – at the time of writing – whether the party will be able to harness its highly active membership to win over the wider electorate.

Finally, it is important to consider the legacy of the protests on the participants themselves. Given the fraction of participants identified in this book's survey, it is not unreasonable to estimate that approximately half a million students took part in the protests – a third of whom may not been active prior to university. For students such as Justine, Donna, Jeremy, and Danny, their participation had transformative effects, both personally and for the people around them.[2] Of course, it is not yet clear whether this transformation will steer these students towards certain career and lifestyle choices akin to Sherkat and Blocker's (1997) 1960s activists. What can be claimed, however, is that the fees protests provided many students with a strong belief in the importance and meaningfulness of political participation. Much of this owed to the multiple participatory opportunities the fees campaign provided, but also the initial openness of campus occupation networks. Through these networks, students not only became more politically engaged and knowledgeable, they also built affinities, loyalties, and relations of trust which encouraged further participation. Maintaining trust and solidarity within these networks, while ensuring they remain open and available to new students, is arguably crucial to the future of student activism in the UK. This is because, to quote Damon, 'ideally, the networks never stop'. The further the networks extend, the greater are the opportunities for mass mobilisation, politicisation, and participation.

THE FUTURE OF STUDENT ACTIVISM

I said this to my tutor the other day, 'I love everything I've done in this degree, and I've had such a good time, but the three weeks I spent in the first occupation I learned more than I have in my entire three years at UCL'. (Justine, UCL)

With the forces of marketisation continuing to professionalise and rationalise the higher education sector, questions are raised as to universities' perceived value and purpose in contemporary society. Whereas the Humboldtian ideal has traditionally emphasised the importance of institutional and academic autonomy (Baert and Shipman, 2005), the neo-liberal rationale of market competition and 'value for money' dictates that universities consider students in more consumerist terms. While any state education system is to some degree subservient to the national (and global) economy it serves, this rationale risks compromising students' freedoms to explore new interests, ideas, and identities, as well as narrowing time and space allocated for personal growth and the building of meaningful social and intellectual relationships. Moreover, the combination of expensive fees and a precarious graduate labour market puts students under increased pressure to rationalise their own university experience, and ensure they have maximised their employability prospects. Student unions, too, are falling under this rationality, with their mandate for political representation increasingly twisted into arbitrating the university's 'student satisfaction' metric (Brooks et al., 2014).

Against this backdrop, the notion of student activism might appear incongruous and almost anachronistic. No student has been awarded any qualification for attending a demonstration, and no careers adviser would recommend 'occupying campus facilities' be included on a graduate's CV. While activism work can, of course, lead to the acquisition of skills and experiences that may help advance a graduate's professional career, his or her driving motivation should transcend such rationalisations, instead reflecting the pursuit of what she or he finds interesting, important, and worthwhile. One can also highlight its benefits to the broader democratic process: protest participation can strengthen students' confidence in consuming political knowledge, develop their ability to critically reason, and increase their access to forms of cultural and social capital – all of which will continue to inform and enhance their engagement as citizens after graduation. Though the 2010/11 protests failed in their immediate aims, the campaign featured a number of markers – from Millbank to the narrowing of the fees bill's parliamentary majority – which equipped participants with a sense of *agency*, that their collective participation had the power to be noticed, listened to, and shape public discourse.

This brings us to students' much-maligned role as society's 'incipient intelligentsia'. In some ways, the constant renewal of student activism through cross-cohort turnover represents student activism's blessing and its curse. On the one hand, struggles to sustain institutional memory across generations not only restrict the building of a durable movement, but also consign student activism to a state of permanent arrested development: frequently prone to displays of ahistorical neophilia and susceptible to repeating the same tactical or organisational mistakes as previous cohorts. On the other hand, students' verve and righteous anger (and occasionally, youthful naivety) operates as a vital *rupturing* force to the often-impervious technocracy of governmental and parliamentary politics. In this respect, the pejorative characterisation of student activists as living in their 'bubble' also reflects one of their key strengths: within the creative, knowledge-intensive campus space, students are encouraged to be idealistic and to develop new ideas, critiques, and practices. Indeed, recent campaigns and debates related to mental health, transgender rights, and black lives matter have demonstrated the key role students play in civil society as engineers of progressive moral and ethical thought.

For this role and purpose to endure, however, the 'value' of a university education must continue to transcend neo-liberal rationalisations of institutional performance. As Justine's above comment attests, a student's learning experience at university is not wholly reducible to time spent in lecture theatres and examination halls, nor should it be. Although it is true that the professionalisation of student unions in the UK has compromised their structural independence as campaigning organisations, it is the overarching *network* of groups and societies that continues to drive activism and protest on university campuses. This partly reflects recent shifts in social movements from institutional to network-based organising structures (Diani and McAdam, 2002; Castells, 2004; Hensby et al., 2012), though the 2010 NUS demonstration showed that the availability of union resources remains vital to converting emerging grievances into mass actions. Given this shift, social media has a clear role to play in augmenting these institutions, as it can exploit mainstream media traction and accelerate communication and mobilisation processes quickly and directly.

It is also crucial that activism remains a valued and legitimate part of a student's university experience. This ensures that campus groups and societies are founded and passed onto new cohorts, so that a campus's overarching 'activism world' and campaign history will continue to serve as a draw for prospective students (Van Dyke, 1998). Yet in this book's research, as well as Crossley and Ibrahim's (2012) similar study, the maintenance of these worlds arguably rests on a number of assumptions, including the endurance of universities that encourage and facilitate student representation and community, and students with the time and impetus to explore these opportunities. Certainly, in the emerging context of alternative higher education providers and 'massive open online courses' (MOOCs), it is harder to see where student networks and collective identifications would find the time and space to build. Yet for as long as universities retain a diversity of subjects and curricula, combined with a dense and overlapping network of well-connected undergraduates, they will continue to function as spaces for stimulating political ideas and mobilising provocative actions.

FINAL WORDS

> We're going to be better people for this having happened. We're not going to do shit things with our lives, and maybe we'll become teachers and social workers and human rights lawyers. ... We're not the Baader-Meinhoff gang. (Donna, UCL)

The aim of this book was to advance our knowledge and understanding of contemporary student politics and activism. In particular, I hope that it has revealed insights in how we might best understand non-participation – not only through the barriers to mobilisation generated by activism groups and networks but also through its social production in everyday life. Though short-lived, the 2010/11 protests marked a significant moment in the fight-back against austerity politics, and the politicisation and radicalisation of many of their participants. Among those interviewed for this book, the protests created significant and unique personal experiences: feelings of pride and solidarity, moments of anger and empowerment, and friendships made. And as shown in Donna's reflections, these experiences have generated for many participants a desire to change the way they live their lives for the better. I hope that this study, in the stories it tells and the analysis it makes, has done those experiences justice.

NOTES

1. From 2017/18, the fees cap will be indexed to inflation – resulting in a further increase to £9,250 per year.

2. Some students spoke of the residual politicising effects on friends and family members, particularly younger siblings. This was recalled by Jeremy, for example: "I have friends outside politics, but they end up being political, just through osmosis. Like, with my little sister, suddenly it was like, 'what do you want for Christmas?' 'I want some books on feminism'".

Appendix A

Survey Sample of UK Universities and Academic Departments

Appendix A Survey sample of UK universities and academic departments

	University	Region	Est.	Campus Structure	No of students	No of depts	Departments sampled
1	University of Edinburgh	Scotland	1583	Multi-site city	457	4	Social and Political Science, Arts, Biological Sciences, Chemistry
2	University of Nottingham	East Mids	1948	Multi-site city	248	10	Sociology, Physics & Astronomy, Music, Theology & Religious Studies, Computer Science, Philosophy, Mathematics, Biology, Education, History
3	Plymouth University	South West	1992	Multi location	157	4	Social Science, Psychology & Criminology, Marine Science & Engineering, Arts
4	University of York	North	1963	Single campus	155	4	Sociology, Health Science, Mathematics, History
5	Aberystwyth University	Wales	1872	Dual campus	149	4	Management & Business, Geography and Earth Sciences, International Politics, Art
6	University of Liverpool	North West	1903	Single campus	141	5	Dentistry, Veterinary Science, Biological Sciences, Politics, History
7	University of Warwick	West Mids	1965	Multi-campus	138	6	Economics, Sociology, Classics & Ancient History, Law, Medicine, Engineering
8	Nottingham Trent University	East Mids	1992	Multi-campus	123	4	Arts & Humanities, Education, Physics, Mathematics
9	University of Cambridge	East	1209	Multi-site city	118	7	Social & Political Science, Divinity, Economics, Archaeology, English, Geography, King's College
10	Newcastle University	North East	1963	Single campus	116	4	Geography, History & Classics, Psychology, Modern Languages

11	University of Sussex	South East	1961	Single campus	105	7	Sociology, Physics & Astronomy, Law, Informatics, English & Drama, Politics, Philosophy
12	University of Leeds	North	1904	Multi-site city	93	3	Politics & IS, Food Science, Biological Sciences
13	University of Roehampton	London	1992	Dual campus	91	4	Social Sciences, English & Drama, Education, Business
14	Cardiff University	Wales	1883	Multi-site city	69	4	Social Sciences, Welsh, Law, Computer Science & Informatics
15	University of Abertay Dundee	Scotland	1994	Single campus	69	1	Social Sciences
16	University College London	London	1826	Multi-site city	61	5	Engineering & Computing, English, Anthropology, Philosophy, History
17	Brunel University	London	1966	Multi-campus	57	4	Health Science, Sports Science & Education, Law, Sociology
18	University of Derby	East Mids	1992	Multi-site city	48	4	Sociology & Cultural Studies, Geology, Film & Television Studies, Biological Sciences
19	Birmingham City University	West Mids	1992	Multi-campus	42	2	Social Science & Education, Health Science
20	Queen Margaret University	Scotland	2007	Single campus	29	2	Sociology & Psychology, Nursing & Occupational Therapy
21	University of The West Of England	South West	1992	Multi-campus	14	1	Journalism & Creative Writing
22	Swansea University	Wales	1920	Single campus	5	1	Computer Science

Appendix B

Student Survey Questionnaire

1. How important were the following in your decision to study at your current university?

(1) Very important; (2) Slightly important; (3) Neither important or unimportant; (4) Not very important; (5) Not at all important

1.a. Improving career chances
1.b. An opportunity to meet new people
1.c. A chance to learn more about the world
1.d. I have a passion for the subject I am studying
1.e. An opportunity to become more socially and politically aware
1.f. A chance to discover a new town/region
1.g. An opportunity to have fun

2. What, in your opinion, is the purpose of university?

(1) Strongly agree; (2) Slightly agree; (3) Neither agree or disagree; (4) Slightly disagree; (5) Strongly disagree

2.a. To prepare students for a career
2.b. To help students gain a clearer sense of what he or she is good at
2.c. To help students learn more about their personal interests and perspectives
2.d. To make students better citizens
2.e. To make students more free-thinking and independent

3. What sort of extra-curricular activities did you expect to participate in when you started at your current university?

(1) Yes; (2) No; (3) Don't know

3.a. Join societies
3.b. Take a part-time job
3.c. Become involved in student politics/councils
3.d. Make friends with people different to you
3.e. Become more politically aware/active
3.f. Take up an internship/voluntary work

4. Tick if you HAVE done any of the following since starting at your current university

(1) Yes; (2) No

4.a. Joined societies
4.b. Taken a part-time job
4.c. Become involved in student politics/councils
4.d. Made friends with people different to you
4.e. Become more politically aware/active
4.f. Taken up an internship/voluntary work

5. How active are you in the student societies you belong to? (If you belong to more than one society, select the one you are most involved with)

(1) I am involved with the society's organization and decision-making; (2) Regularly attend meetings and events; (3) Occasionally attend meetings and events; (4) Passive, little involvement; (5) I do not belong to any student societies

6. Have you done any of the following activities relating to your student union/guild/association?

(1) Yes; (2) No but might do in future; (3) No and not interested

6.a. Taken part in a student union-led campaign
6.b. Participated in a student union-led volunteer scheme
6.c. Voted in a student union meeting/assembly
6.d. Voted in student union elections
6.e. Stood as a candidate in student union elections

6.f. Campaigned on behalf of someone else standing in student union elections

7. How much of a say do you think students should have in influencing the following issues related to their university? (tick all that apply)

(1) A right to vote on the outcome; (2) A right to be consulted; (3) A right to campaign on the issue; (4) Students don't need to get involved with this; (5) Don't know

7.a. The selection of university chancellor
7.b. Financial investments undertaken by the university
7.c. University stance on Government Higher Education policy
7.d. Provision of student facilities i.e. Halls of Residence, Common rooms etc.

8. To what extent do you feel that your university student union represents your interests?

(1) A lot; (2) A little; (3) Not very much; (4) Not at all; (5) Don't know

9. To what extent do you feel that the National Union of Students (NUS) represents student interests in wider society?

(1) A lot; (2) A little; (3) Not very much; (4) Not at all; (5) Don't know

10. To what extent do you agree with this statement? 'Everyone would benefit from a university education'

(1) Strongly agree; (2) Slightly agree; (3) Neither agree or disagree; (4) Slightly disagree; (5) Strongly disagree

11. How much did the cost of fees/subsistence come into your thinking when deciding whether to go to university or not?

(1) A lot; (2) A little; (3) Not very much; (4) Not at all

12. To what extent do you agree with the following statements about recent changes to the funding of Higher Education in the UK?

(1) Strongly agree; (2) Slightly agree; (3) Neither agree or disagree; (4) Slightly disagree; (5) Strongly disagree

12.a. Access to an affordable university education is a right, not a privilege

12.b. I feel let down by the Liberal Democrats over their reversal of tuition fees policy

12.c. Politicians don't care about the interests of young people

12.d. Parties should always be held accountable for their election pledges once they become part of government

12.e. I am concerned that higher fees will put some strong candidates off applying for university altogether

12.f. Maintaining higher education funding is not a priority when public service cuts have to be made

12.g. Higher Education funding should be maintained through higher taxes

12.h. Taxpayers who did not go through higher education should not be expected to pay for the higher education of others

13. Are you aware of any recent/ongoing cases of cuts being made at your own university? (e.g. course or departmental closures, staff redundancies etc)

(1) Yes; (2) No; (3) Don't know

14. At the time when you were growing up, how often was politics discussed at home?

(1) Regularly; (2) Fairly often; (3) Sometimes; (4) Rarely; (5) Never; (6) Don't know

15. How politically active were your parents/guardians when you were growing up?

(1) Very active; (2) Fairly active; (3) Not very active; (4) Not at all active; (5) Don't know

16. How often do you discuss politics?

(1) Regularly; (2) Fairly often; (3) Sometimes; (4) Rarely; (5) Never

17. Do you use any of the following to access news and information about political issues?

(1) Regularly; (2) Fairly often; (3) Sometimes; (4) Rarely; (5) Never

17.a. Television

17.b. Newspapers (print and online)

17.c. Alternative news websites

17.d. Independent blogs
17.e. Social networking sites (Facebook, Twitter etc.)
17.f. Emails/newsletters etc from a group that you belong to

18. With which political party, if any, do you most closely identify right now?

19. Did you vote in the 2010 UK general election?

(1) Yes; (2) No; (3) Prefer not to say; (4) Was ineligible to vote

19.a. If you answered 'yes', who did you vote for? (Optional)

20. Please indicate, in general, how much you trust each of the following:

(1) Strongly trust; (2) Quite trust; (3) Neither trust or distrust; (4) Slightly distrust; (5) Strongly distrust; (6) Not applicable

20.a. UK Government
20.b. Scottish Government (if applicable)
20.c. Welsh Assembly (if applicable)
20.d. London Assembly (if applicable)
20.e. Political parties
20.f. Trade unions
20.g. Judicial system
20.h. The Police

21. To what extent do you agree or disagree with the following statements?

(1) Strongly agree; (2) Slightly agree; (3) Neither agree or disagree; (4) Slightly disagree; (5) Strongly disagree

21.a. Most politicians make a lot of promises but do not actually do anything
21.b. I don't see the use of voting, parties do whatever they want anyway
21.c. My participation can have an impact on government policy in this country
21.d. Organized groups of citizens can have a lot of impact on public policies in this country
21.e. If a person is dissatisfied with the policies of the Government, he/she has a duty to do something about it

21.f. I often feel that I don't know enough about politics to fully engage in it

21.g. I'm usually too busy with other commitments to engage in politics

22. It has sometimes been argued that democracy in the UK needs to be reformed to allow for greater voice from its citizens. What is your view of the following?

(1) Strongly agree; (2) Slightly agree; (3) Neither agree or disagree; (4) Slightly disagree; (5) Strongly disagree

22.a. Democracy in the UK would be improved by having more referenda on major issues of public interest

22.b. Democracy in the UK would be improved if a system of Proportional Representation was introduced for general elections

22.c. True democracy in the UK is only possible through the abolition of parliament and the creation of a new system of direct democracy

22.d. I see no problem with the current democratic system in the UK

22.e. Democracy in the UK already gives people too much of a say on political issues

23. Please tick if you have done any of the following political activities in the last three years (select all that apply)

(1) Yes, I have done this more than once; (2) Yes, I did this once; (3) I have not done this

23.a. Signed a petition

23.b. Boycotted certain products and services for political, ethical or environmental reasons

23.c. Bought certain products and services for political, ethical or environmental reasons

23.d. Worn or displayed a campaign badge or sticker

23.e. Presented my views to a local councillor or MP

23.f. Been a member of a social movement organization (e.g. Amnesty International, Greenpeace)

23.g. Worked or campaigned on behalf of a political party

23.h. Stood as a candidate for school/student/local elections

23.i. Distributed flyers for a political campaign

23.j. Taken part in a protest march

23.k. Taken part in strike action

23.l. Taken part in an occupation/sit-in

23.m. Taken part in the blockade of a building or meeting

24. How effective a form of political participation do you think are each of these activities?

(1) Very effective; (2) Somewhat effective; (3) Not very effective; (4) Not at all effective; (5) Not sure

24.a. Voting in elections
24.b. Petitions
24.c. Consumer boycotts of products and services
24.d. Contacting an MP
24.e. Joining/financially supporting a social movement organization (e.g. Amnesty International, Greenpeace)
24.f. Joining or forming a civic association (e.g. Fathers 4 Justice)
24.g. Protest marches
24.h. Strike action
24.i. 'Direct action' protest (e.g. occupations, sit-ins, blockades)

25. People might choose to protest for a variety of different reasons. What sort of impact do you think protest can have?

(1) Strongly agree; (2) Slightly agree; (3) Neither agree or disagree; (4) Slightly disagree; (5) Strongly disagree

25.a. Protest can positively influence the views and interests of the wider population
25.b. Protest can increase the wider population's knowledge and awareness of an issue
25.c. Protest can help change UK Government policy
25.d. Protest can help change the policy of corporations
25.e. Protest can gain the support of the mainstream media
25.f. Protest can strengthen the ideals and values of the people involved
25.g. Protest does not make a difference

26. To what extent do you agree with the following statements about protest?

(1) Strongly agree; (2) Slightly agree; (3) Neither agree or disagree; (4) Slightly disagree; (5) Strongly disagree

26.a. Protest is an essential form of political engagement
26.b. Protest is the last meaningful form of political engagement available in the UK
26.c. Protest can only be effective if it involves taking power by force

26.d. Protest is a legitimate form of political expression, but only when campaigning on more important issues like civil rights

26.e. There are always better ways of making your views heard than by protesting

26.f. Protest is not a legitimate form of political participation

26.g. Protest suffers because the actions of a minority usually spoil it for the majority

26.h. Protest has never had the power to change things

27. Please tick if you have been involved in any campaigns and protests relating to the following issues (select all that apply)

(1) Yes, before I became a student; (2) Yes, since I have become a student; (3) No, Never

27.a. Human rights/global justice

27.b. The environment

27.c. Anti-racism/ethnic discrimination

27.d. Gender rights and sexual politics

27.e. Anti-war campaigns

27.f. Anti-capitalism/neoliberalism

27.g. Campaigns against cuts to the public sector in the UK

27.h. Other

28. Please tick if you have been involved in any of the following campaign groups/networks

(1) Yes; (2) No

28.a. Climate Camp

28.b. People & Planet

28.c. UK Uncut

28.d. Free Gaza campaign

29. Have you been invited to participate in the student protests against fees by any of the following?

(1) Yes; (2) No; (3) Don't remember

29.a. Student union

29.b. Course colleagues

29.c. Friends from your university

29.d. Friends from other universities

29.e. Facebook group/event invitation

30. How many people (other than yourself) do you know personally who have participated in the student protests against fees at YOUR university?

(1) 5 or more people; (2) 2-4 people, (3) One person; (4) Nobody

30.a. What about at OTHER universities excluding your own?

(1) 5 or more people; (2) 2-4 people, (3) One person; (4) Nobody

31. Have you participated in any way in the student protests against fees?

(1) Yes; (2) No

32. If you clicked 'YES' to the last question, please tick if your participation in the student protests involved any of the following activities. (If you clicked 'NO', skip this and go straight to Q36).

(1) I have done this more than once; (2) I did this once; (3) I did not do this; (4) Did not participate

32.a. Signing a petition

32.b. Wearing or displaying a campaign badge or sticker

32.c. Distributing flyers

32.d. Attending a national/regional level student march

32.e. Attending a student march in your own/nearest town or city

32.f. Taking part in the blockade of a building or meeting

32.g. Taking part in an occupation/sit-in

32.h. Taking part in the organizing of a protest event

32.i. Attending a student-led teach-in or activism workshop

32.j. Attending a university or union-arranged debate or meeting about student fees

32.k. Like/join a protest page/group on Facebook

32.l. Follow a protest group on Twitter

32.m. Other

33. If you ticked 'other' in the last question, please explain what sort of activity you are referring to

34. If you HAVE taken part in the protests, how much do the following statements capture your reasons for protesting?

(1) Strongly agree; (2) Slightly agree; (3) Neither agree or disagree; (4) Slightly disagree; (5) Strongly disagree; (6) Did not answer; (7) Did not participate

34.a. I want to express my views
34.b. We must pressure politicians into making things change
34.c. We must raise public awareness
34.d. I protest to express my solidarity with fellow students
34.e. Friends and people I respected were also getting involved
34.f. Students need to pressurize universities into publically opposing higher fees
34.g. It is important that students are an active part of the wider anti-cuts movement

35. If you HAVE taken part in the protests, to what extent do you agree with the following statements?

(1) Strongly agree; (2) Slightly agree; (3) Neither agree or disagree; (4) Slightly disagree; (5) Strongly disagree; (6) Did not answer; (7) Did not participate

35.a. It felt good to do something about an issue important to me
35.b. My involvement has made me more politically knowledgeable
35.c. My involvement has led to me making new friends
35.d. Overall, I enjoyed getting involved in the student protests
35.e. I am proud to be part of a UK-wide student movement
35.f. My involvement has made me feel very positive about the power of protest
35.g. I wish I had expressed my views on the student fees issue in a different way
35.h. I now regret getting involved in the student protests

36. If you have NOT participated in the student protests, do you broadly support students' campaigns and protests on this issue? (If you HAVE participated, skip this and go straight to Q38)

(1) Yes; (2) No; (3) Undecided

37. If you have NOT participated in the student protests, to what extent do you agree with the following statements?

(1) Strongly agree; (2) Slightly agree; (3) Neither agree or disagree; (4) Slightly disagree; (5) Strongly disagree

37.a. The student fees issue is not important enough to me to protest

37.b. I feel that I do not know enough about the student fees issue to make an informed decision

37.c. I was undecided about how good or bad the Government's proposals were

37.d. I support the Government's changes to Higher Education funding

37.e. I was too busy with academic work to participate

37.f. I didn't participate because the fees and funding issue does not personally affect me

37.g. Personal commitments (job, family etc) prevent me from participating in the protests

37.h. I am concerned about clashing with police and/or getting arrested during student protest marches

37.i. I do not approve of the protest tactics used by students

37.j. I do not personally identify with or feel comfortable around the people involved in the protests

37.k. My involvement wouldn't have made any difference

37.l. It is right to protest against public sector cuts, but wrong to prioritise the student cause

37.m. The student protests were not radical enough

38. This question is for all respondents. To what extent do you agree with the following statements?

(1) Strongly agree; (2) Slightly agree; (3) Neither agree or disagree; (4) Slightly disagree; (5) Strongly disagree (6) Don't know

38.a. The tuition fees issue has made me more politically engaged

38.b. The student protests have made me more politically engaged

38.c. The student fees and anti-cuts protests will make the Government pay more attention to the views of its citizens in the future

38.d. The student protests have failed in their aims

38.e. The student protests will be remembered more for violence than politics

38.f. The student protests have made me more prepared to protest on issues important to me in the future

38.g. I am definitely going to vote in the next general election

38.h. The Government and police force have made protest appear an illegitimate and deviant act

39. Which year were you born?

40. Your sex

(1) Male; (2) Female; (3) Prefer not to say

41. When you are not studying at university, in which country do you normally reside?

42. Which university do you currently attend?

(1) Aberystwyth University; (2) Birmingham City University; (3) Brunel University; (4) Cardiff University; (5) Newcastle University; (6) Nottingham Trent University; (7) Plymouth University (8) Queen Margaret University; (9) Swansea University; (10) University College London; (11) University of Abertay; (12) University of Cambridge; (13) University of Derby; (14) University of Edinburgh (15) University of Leeds; (16) University of Liverpool; (17) University of Nottingham; (18) University of Roehampton; (19) University of Sussex; (20) University of the West of England (21) University of Warwick; (22) University of York

43. Are you currently studying as an...

(1) Undergraduate; (2) Postgraduate

44. What is your current year of study?

(1) First year; (2) Second year; (3) Third year; (4) Fourth year; (5) Fifth year or more

45. What degree and subject are you currently studying for?

46. If you had to choose which social class group you belonged to, which would it be?

(1) Upper class; (2) Upper middle class; (3) Lower middle class; (4) Working class; (5) None

Bibliography

Adams, N., Macintosh, A., & Johnston, J. (2005). E-Petitioning: Enabling Ground-Up Participation. *5th IFIP Conference e-Commerce, e-Business, and e-Government (I3E'2005), October 28–30, 2005, Poznan, Poland* (pp. 265–279). US: Springer.

Agger, B. (2009). The Pulpless Generation: Why Young People Don't Protest the Iraq War (or Anything Else), and Why It's Not Entirely Their Fault. *Cultural Studies – Critical Methodologies, 9*, 41–51.

Aitchison, G. (2011). Reform, Rupture or Re-imagination: Understanding the Purpose of an Occupation. *Social Movement Studies, 10*(4), 431–439.

Alinsky, S. D. (1971). *Rules for Radicals*. New York: Random House.

Altbach, P. G. (1989). From Revolution to Apathy: American Student Activism in the 1970s. In P. G. Altbach (Ed.), *Student Politics: Perspectives for the Eighties*. Metuchen: The Scarecrow Press.

Anderson, T. H. (1999–2000). 1968: The End and the Beginning in the United States and Western Europe. *South Central Review, 16*(4), 1–15.

Anduiza, E., Cantijoch, M., & Gallego, A. (2009). Political Participation and the Internet. *Information, Communication & Society, 12*(6), 860–878.

Aronson, P. (2003). Feminists or 'postfeminists'? Young Women's Attitudes toward Feminism and Gender Relations. *Gender and Society, 17*(5), 903–922.

Baert, P., & Shipman, A. (2005). Universities Under Siege? *European Societies, 7*(1), 157–185.

Bailey, M., & Freedman, D. (Eds.) (2011). *The Assault on Universities: A Manifesto for Resistance*. London: Pluto Press.

Banaji, S., & Buckingham, D. (2012). Young People and Online Civic Participation: Key Findings from a Pan-European Research Project. In P. Loncle, M. Cuconato, V. Muniglia, & A. Walther (Eds.), *Youth Participation in Europe*. Bristol: Policy Press.

Bang, H. (2004). *Everyday Makers and Expert Citizens: Building Political not Social Capital*. Retrieved October 15, 2013, from ANU School of Social Sciences: https://digitalcollections.anu.edu.au/handle/1885/42117

Barker, C. (2008). Some Reflections on Student Movements of the 1960s and Early 1970s. *Revista Crítica de Ciências Sociais, 81*, 43–91.

Barr, N., & Crawford, I. (1998). Funding Higher Education in an Age of Expansion. *Education Economics, 6*, 45–70.

Bartlett, J., Bennett, S., Birnie, R., & Wibberley, S. (2013). *Virtually Members: The Facebook and Twitter Followers of UK Political Parties.* London: Demos.

Bauman, Z. (2000). *Liquid Modernity.* Cambridge: Polity.

BBC News (July 26, 2015). *Labour Leadership: Jeremy Corbyn Rejects 'entryism' Claims.* Retrieved September 4, 2016, from http://www.bbc.com/news/uk-politics-33667761

Beck, U. (1992). *Risk Society: Towards a New Modernity.* London: Sage.

Becker, H. (1991). *Outsiders: Studies in the Sociology of Deviance.* New York: The Free Press.

Bennett, W. L. (1998). The Uncivic Culture: Communication, Identity, and the Rise of Lifestyle Politics. *PS: Political Science and Politics, 31*(4), 740–761.

——— (2008). Changing Citizenship in the Digital Age. In W. L. Bennett (Ed.), *Civic Life Online: Learning How Digital Media Can Engage Youth.* Cambridge, MA: The MIT Press.

———, & Segerberg, A. (2012). The Logic of Connective Action: Digital Media and the Personalization of Contentious Politics. *Information, Communication & Society, 15*(5), 739–768.

Biddix, J. P., & Park, H. W. (2008). Networks of Student Protest: The Case of the Living Wage Campaign. *New Media & Society, 10*(6), 871–891.

Biekart, K., & Fowler, A. (2013). Transforming Activisms 2010+: Exploring Ways and Waves. *Development and Change, 44*(3), 527–546.

Binder, A. J., & Wood, K. (2012). *Becoming Right: How Campuses Shape Young Conservatives.* Princeton: Princeton University Press.

Blackstone, T., & Hadley, R. (1971). Student Protest in a British University: Some Comparisons with American Research. *Comparative Education, 15*(1), 1–19.

Bobel, C. (2007). 'I'm not an activist, though I've done a lot of it': Doing Activism, Being Activist and the 'Perfect Standard' in a Contemporary Movement. *Social Movement Studies, 6*(2), 147–159.

Boren, M. E. (2001). *Student Resistance: A History of the Unruly Subject.* New York: Routledge.

Bourdieu, P. (1977). *Outline of a Theory of Practice.* Cambridge: Cambridge University Press.

——— (1984). *Distinction.* London: Routledge.

Braungart, M. M., & Braungart, R. G. (1990). The Life-Course Development of Left and Right-Wing Youth Activist Leaders from the 1960s. *Political Psychology, 11*(2), 243–282.

Brooks, L. (April 26, 2003). *Kid Power.* Retrieved October 14, 2013, from The Guardian: http://www.theguardian.com/politics/2003/apr/26/schools.antiwar

Brooks, R., Byford, K., & Sela, K. (2014). The Changing Role of Students' Unions Within Contemporary Higher Education. *Journal of Education Policy, 30*(2), 165–181.

Burnham, P. (2001). New Labour and the Politics of Depoliticisation. *The British Journal of Politics and International Relations, 3*(2), 127–149.

Calhoun, C. (1993). 'New Social Movements' of the Early Nineteenth Century. *Social Science History, 17*(3), 385–427.

The Cambridge Student (June 27, 2012). *Owen Holland's Rustication Sentence Reduced to One Term*. Retrieved September 4, 2016, from http://www.tcs.cam. ac.uk/news/0017401-breaking-news-owen-hollands-rustication-sentence-reduced-to-one-term.html

Casquette, J. (2006). The Power of Demonstrations. *Social Movement Studies, 5*(1), 45–60.

Castells, M. (2004). *The Power of Identity* (2nd ed.). Oxford: Blackwell.

——— (2007). Communication, Power and Counter-Power in the Network Society. *International Journal of Communication, 1*, 238–266.

——— (2009). *Communication Power*. Oxford: Oxford University Press.

——— (2012). *Networks of Outrage and Hope: Social Movements in the Internet Age*. Cambridge: Polity.

Chadwick, A. (2012). Web 2.0: New Challenges for the Study of E-Democracy in an Era of Informational Exuberance. In S. Coleman, & P. Shane (Eds.), *Connecting Democracy: Online Consultation and the Flow of Political Communication* (pp. 45–75). Cambridge, MA: MIT Press.

Channel 4 (November 10, 2010). *Student Protest: An Ugly Turn to a Peaceful Demo*. Retrieved October 15, 2013, from Channel 4 News: http://www.channel4.com/news/student-protest-an-ugly-turn-to-peaceful-demo

Chessum, M. (October 2, 2015). *How the Student Protesters of 2010 Became the Corbyn Generation*. Retrieved September 4, 2016, from The Guardian: https://www.theguardian.com/commentisfree/2015/oct/02/student-protesters-2010-jeremy-corbyn-election-labour-party?CMP=twt_gu

Clarke, J. W., & Egan, J. (1972). Social and Political Dimensions of Campus Protest Activity. *The Journal of Politics, 34*(2), 500–523.

Coleman, S., & Blumler, J. G. (2009). *The Internet and Democratic Citizenship*. Cambridge: Cambridge University Press.

Coles, R. (1986). *The Political Life of Children*. Boston: Atlantic Monthly Press.

Collini, S. (2012). *What are Universities For?* London: Penguin.

Crossley, A. D. (2010). 'When it Suits Me, I'm a Feminist': International Students Negotiating Feminist Representations. *Women's Studies International Forum, 33*, 125–133.

Crossley, N. (2002). *Making Sense of Social Movements*. Milton Keynes: Open University Press.

——— (2003). From Reproduction to Transformation: Social Movement Fields and the Radical Habitus. *Theory, Culture & Society, 20*(6), 43–68.

——— (2007). Social Networks and Extraparliamentary Politics. *Sociology Compass, 1*(1), 222–236.

——— (2008). Social Networks and Student Activism: On the Politicising Effect of Campus Connections. *The Sociological Review, 56*(1), 19–38.

———, & Ibrahim, J. (2012). Critical Mass, Social Networks and Collective Action: Exploring Student Political Worlds. *Sociology, 46*(4), 596–612.

Crouch, C. (1970). *The Student Revolt*. London: Bodley Head.

Cunningham, S., & Lavalette, M. (2004). 'Active Citizens' or 'Irresponsible Truants'? School Student Strikes against the War. *Critical Social Policy, 24*(2), 255–269.

Daily Mail (May 7, 2011). *Humbling of Nick Clegg: After Polls Humiliation He is Warned to Stop Tory Love-in or You're History*. Retrieved December 19, 2013, from http://www.dailymail.co.uk/news/article-1384135/Local-elections-2011-Lib-Dem-leader-Nick-Clegg-faces-1st-resign.html

Daily Mail (November 8, 2011). *Police Will Have the Right to Fire Rubber Bullets on Student Protesters as They Prepare for Huge London Demonstration.* Retrieved December 19, 2013, from http://www.dailymail.co.uk/news/article-2058726/Police-right-rubber-bullets-Wednesdays-student-protests-London.html

Dauvergne, P., & LeBaron, G. (2014). *Protest Inc: The Corporatization of Activism.* Cambridge: Polity.

De Luca, K. M., & Peeples, J. (2002). From Public Sphere to Public Screen: Democracy, Activism, and the 'Violence' of Seattle. *Critical Studies in Media Communication, 19*(2), 125–151.

Dean, J. (2016). 'Angelic Spirits of "68": Memories of 60s' Radicalism in Responses to the 2010–11 UK Student Protests. *Contemporary British History, 30*(3), 305–325.

Della Porta, D. (1988). Recruitment Processes in Clandestine Political Organizations: Italian Left-Wing Terrorism. In B. Klandermans, H. Kriesi, & S. Tarrow (Eds.), *International Social Movement Research Vol 1: From Structure to Action.* Greenwich: JAI Press.

———, & Diani, M. (2006). *Social Movements: An Introduction* (2nd ed.). Malden: Blackwell.

Department for Business, Innovation & Skills (2011). *Higher Education: Students at the Heart of the System [White Paper].* Retrieved October 16, 2013, from https://www.gov.uk/government/uploads/system/uploads/attachment_data/file/31384/11–944-higher-education-students-at-heart-of-system.pdf

Deuze, M. (2003). The Web and Its Journalisms: Considering the Consequences of Different Types of News Media Online. *New Media & Society, 5*(2), 203–230.

Diani, M. (1992). The Concept of Social Movement. *The Sociological Review, 401*, 1–25.

——— (2000). Social Movement Networks Virtual and Real. *Information, Communication and Society, 3*(3), 386–401.

——— (2004). Networks and Participation. In D. Snow, S. Soule, & H. Kriesi (Eds.), *The Blackwell Companion to Social Movements.* Oxford: Blackwell.

———, & Lodi, G. (1988). Three in One: Currents in the Milan Ecology Movement. In B. Klandermans, H. Kriesi, & S. Tarrow (Eds.), *From Structure to Action.* Greenwich: JAI Press.

———, & McAdam, D. (2003). *Social Movements and Networks.* Oxford: Oxford University Press.

Docherty, T. (2011). *For the University: Democracy and the Future of the Institution.* London: Bloomsbury Academic.

Dunt, I. (February 6, 2015). *Safe Space or Free Speech? The Crisis Around Debate at UK Universities.* Retrieved September 4, 2016, from The Guardian: https://www.theguardian.com/education/2015/feb/06/safe-space-or-free-speech-crisis-debate-uk-universities

Dutton, W. H., & Blank, G. (2011). *Next Generation Users: The Internet in Britain.* Retrieved October 15, 2013, from Social Science Research Network: http://microsites.oii.ox.ac.uk/oxis/

Eden, K., & Roker, D. (2000). 'You've Gotta Do Something...': A Longitudinal Study of Young People's Involvement in Social Action. *ESRC Conference: Youth Research*. Keele: University of Keele.

Einwohner, R. L., Hollander, J. A., & Olson, T. (2000). Engendering Social Movements: Cultural Images and Movement Dynamics. *Gender and Society, 14*(5), 679–699.

Eliasoph, N. (1998). *Avoiding Politics: How Americans Produce Apathy in Everyday Life*. Cambridge: Cambridge University Press.

Ellis, S. (1998). 'A Demonstration of British Good Sense?' British Student Protest During the Vietnam War. In G. J. De Groot (Ed.), *Student Protest: The Sixties and After*. London: Longman.

EUSA (November 12, 2010). *Edinburgh Students March against Cuts*. Retrieved December 19, 2013, from http://www.eusa.ed.ac.uk/news/article/6001/79/

Fendrich, J. M., & Lovoy, K. L. (1988). Back to the Future: Adult Political Behavior of Former Student Activists. *American Sociological Review, 53*, 780–784.

Fine, S. (1965). The General Motors Sit-Down Strike: A Re-examination. *The American Historical Review, 70*(3), 691–713.

Flesher Fominaya, C. (2010). Collective Identity in Social Movements: Central Concepts and Debates. *Sociology Compass, 4*(6), 393–404.

———— (2015). Unintended Consequences: The Negative Impact of E-mail Use on Participation and Collective Identity in Two 'Horizontal' Social Movement Groups. *European Political Science Review, 8*(1), 95–122.

Flinders, M., & Wood, M. (2014). Depoliticisation, Governance and the State. *Policy & Politics, 42*(2), 135–149.

Free Association (2011). *Moments of Excess: Movements, Protest and Everyday Life*. Oakland: PM Press.

Freeman, J. (1970). *The Tyranny of the Structureless*. Retrieved October 15, 2013, from http://struggle.ws/pdfs/tyranny.pdf

———— (2005). *No More Miss America (1968–1969)*. Retrieved December 21, 2013, from http://www.jofreeman.com/photos/MissAm1969.html

Friedersdorf, C. (November 2015). *The New Intolerance of Student Activism*. Retrieved September 4, 2016, from The Atlantic: http://www.theatlantic.com/politics/archive/2015/11/the-new-intolerance-of-student-activism-at-yale/414810/

Furlong, A., & Cartmel, F. (2012). Social Change and Political Engagement among Young People: Generation and the 2009/2010 British Election Survey. *Parliamentary Affairs, 65*, 13–28.

Gamble, A. (2009). *The Spectre at the Feast: Capitalist Crisis and the Politics of Recession*. Basingstoke: Palgrave MacMillan.

———— (September 24, 2015). *After New Labour: The Corbyn Surge and the Future of Social Democracy in Britain*. Retrieved September 4, 2016, from Policy Network: http://www.policy-network.net/pno_detail.aspx?ID=4978&title=After-New-Labour-The-Corbyn-surge-and-the-future-of-social-democracy-in-Britain

Gamson, W. A. (1992). *Talking Politics*. Cambridge: Cambridge University Press.

Gerbaudo, P. (2013). Protest Diffusion and Cultural Resonance in the 2011 Protest Wave. *The International Spectator: Italian Journal of International Affairs, 48*(4), 86–101.

Giddens, A. (1991). *Modernity and Self-Identity.* Cambridge: Polity.

Gilbert, J. (2008). *Anticapitalism and Culture.* Oxford: Berg.

———, & Aitchison, G. (2012). *Reflections on Britain's Student Movement.* Retrieved October 14, 2013, from Open Democracy: http://www.opendemocracy.net/ourkingdom/jeremy-gilbert-guy-aitchison/reflections-on-britains-student-movement

Giroux, H. A. (2013). The Quebec Student Protest Movement in the Age of Neoliberal Terror. *Social Identities, 19*(5), 515–535.

Gitlin, T. (1981). *The Whole World is Watching: The Mass Media in the Making and Unmaking of the New Left.* Berkeley: University of California Press.

——— (2013). Occupy's Predicament: The Moment and the Prospects for the Movement. *British Journal of Sociology, 64*(1), 3–25.

Giugni, M. G. (1998). Was It Worth the Effort? The Outcomes and Consequences of Social Movements. *Annual Review of Sociology, 24,* 371–393.

Gladwell, M. (October 4, 2010). *Small Change: Why the Revolution Will Not Be Tweeted.* Retrieved October 15, 2013, from The New Yorker: http://www.newyorker.com/reporting/2010/10/04/101004fa_fact_gladwell?currentPage=all

Goffman, E. (1971). *Relations in Public.* Harmondsworth: Penguin.

Goodwin, J., & Jasper, J. M. (2006). Emotions and Social Movements. In J. E. Stets, & J. H. Turner (Eds.), *Handbook of the Sociology of Emotions* (pp. 611–635). New York: Springer.

Goodwin, J., Jasper, J. M., & Polletta, F. (2001). *Passionate Politics: Emotions in Social Movements.* Chicago: University of Chicago Press.

Gordon, B. (1998). The Eyes of the Marcher: Paris, May 1968 – Theory and its Consequences. In G. J. De Groot (Ed.), *Student Protest: The Sixties and After.* London: Longman.

Graeber, D. (2009). *Direct Action: An Ethnography.* Oakland: AK Press.

——— (2013). *The Democracy Project.* London: Allen Lane.

Granovetter, M. S. (1973). The Strength of Weak Ties. *American Journal of Sociology, 78*(6), 1360–1380.

Gripsrud, K. (2002). *Understanding Media Culture.* London: Arnold.

Guardian (February 25, 2004). *Strike Leaders Claim to Have 'crippled' Campuses.* Retrieved October 23, 2013, from http://www.theguardian.com/education/2004/feb/25/highereducation.students

——— (April 2, 2008). *NUS Drops Free Education Doctrine.* Retrieved October 23, 2013, from http://www.theguardian.com/education/2008/apr/02/highereducation.uk2

——— (October 20, 2010). *Universities Alarmed by 40% Cut to Teaching Budgets.* Retrieved October 14, 2013, from http://www.theguardian.com/education/2010/oct/20/spending-review-university-teaching-cuts

——— (November 10, 2010). *Demo 2010 Student Protests – Live Coverage.* Retrieved October 14, 2013, from http://www.theguardian.com/uk/blog/2010/nov/10/demo-2010-student-protests-live

Guzman-Concha, C. (2012). The Students' Rebellion in Chile: Occupy Protest or Classic Social Movement? *Social Movement Studies, 11*(3–4), 408–415.

Haenfler, R., Johnson, B., & Jones, E. (2012). Lifestyle Movements: Exploring the Intersection of Lifestyle and Social Movements. *Social Movement Studies, 11*(1), 1–20.

Hale, S. A., Margetts, H., & Yasseri, T. (April 18, 2012). *Petition Growth and Success Rates on the UK No.10 Downing Street Website.* Retrieved October 15, 2013, from Social Science Research Network: http://papers.ssrn.com/sol3/papers.cfm?abstract_id=2041856

Hallward, P. (June 1, 2012). *Quebec's Student Protesters Give UK Activists a Lesson.* Retrieved September 4, 2016, from The Guardian: https://www.theguardian.com/commentisfree/2012/jun/01/quebec-protests-student-activists

Hancox, D. (2011). *Fight Back! A Reader on the Winter of Protest.* London: Open Democracy.

Hands, J. (2011). @ *Is for Activism.* London: Pluto Press.

Hanna, E. (2008). The English Student Movement: An Evaluation of the Literature. *Sociology Compass, 2*(5), 1539–1552.

Hansard Society (2004–2016). *Audit of Political Engagement.* London: Hansard.

Hay, C. (2007). *Why We Hate Politics.* Cambridge: Polity.

Heath, A., & Park, A. (1997). Thatcher's Children? In G. Evans, & P. Norris (Eds.), *Critical Elections: British Parties and Voters in Long-Term Perspective.* London: Sage.

Henn, M., & Foard, N. (2012). Young People, Political Participation and Trust in Britain. *Parliamentary Affairs, 65*, 47–67.

Henn, M., Weinstein, M., & Wring, D. (2002). A Generation Apart? Youth and Political Participation in Britain. *British Journal of Politics and International Relations, 4*(2), 167–192.

Hensby, A. (2014). Networks, Counter-Networks and Political Socialisation: Paths and Barriers to High-Cost/Risk Activism in the 2010/11 Student Protests against Fees and Cuts. *Contemporary Social Science, 9*(1), 92–105.

——— (2015). Networks of Non-Participation: Comparing 'supportive', 'unsupportive' and 'undecided' Non-Participants in the UK Student Protests against Fees and Cuts. *Sociology* (pp. 1–18). DOI: 10.1177/0038038515608113.

——— (2016a). Open Networks and Secret Facebook Groups: Exploring Cycle Effects on Activists' Social Media Use in the 2010/11 UK Student Protests. *Social Movement Studies* (pp. 1–13). DOI: 10.1080/14742837.2016.1201421.

——— (2016b). Campaigning for a Movement: Collective Identity and Student Solidarity in the 2010/11 UK Protests against Fees and Cuts. In R. Brooks (Ed.), *Student Politics and Protest.* London: Routledge.

———, Sibthorpe, J., & Driver, S. (2012). Resisting the 'protest business': Bureaucracy, Post-Bureaucracy and Active Membership in Social Movement Organizations. *Organization, 19*(6), 809–823.

Hercus, C. (2005). *Stepping Out of Line: Becoming and Being Feminist.* New York: Routledge.

HESA (2012). *Statistics – Students and Qualifiers at UK HE Institutions.* Retrieved October 15, 2013, from http://www.hesa.ac.uk/content/view/1897/239/

Hirsch, E. L. (1990). Sacrifice for the Cause: Group Processes, Recruitment, and Commitment in a Student Social Movement. *American Sociological Review, 55*(2), 243–254.

Hiscock, D. (May 9, 2001). *The Apathy Generation.* Retrieved October 16, 2013, from The Guardian: http://www.theguardian.com/lifeandstyle/2001/may/09/familyandrelationships.election2001

Hoefferle, C. M. (2013). *British Student Activism in the Long Sixties.* New York: Routledge.

Holloway, J. (2010). *Crack Capitalism.* London: Pluto Press.

Holmwood, J. (Ed.) (2011). *A Manifesto for the Public University.* London: Bloomsbury Academic.

Hopkins, P., Todd, L., & Newcastle Occupation (2011). Occupying Newcastle University: Student Resistance to Government Spending Cuts in England. *The Geographical Journal, 178*(2), 2–6.

Howker, E., & Malik, S. (2010). *Jilted Generation: How Britain has Bankrupted its Youth.* London: Icon.

Hughes, C. (2015). *Young Lives on the Left: Sixties Activism and the Liberation of the Self.* Manchester: Manchester University Press.

Ibrahim, J. (2011). The New Toll on Higher Education and the UK Student Revolts of 2010–2011. *Social Movement Studies, 10*(4), 415–421.

———— (2014). The Moral Economy of the UK Student Protest Movement 2010–2011. *Contemporary Social Science, 9*(1), 79–91.

Ibrahim, Y. (2010). Between Revolution and Defeat: Student Protest Cycles and Networks. *Sociology Compass, 4*(7), 495–504.

Inglehart, R. (1977). *The Silent Revolution.* Princeton: Princeton University Press.

———— (1997). *Modernization and Postmodernization: Cultural, Economic and Political Change in 43 Societies.* Princeton: Princeton University Press.

————, & Baker, W. E. (2000). Modernization, Cultural Change, and the Persistence of Traditional Values. *American Sociological Review, 65*(1), 19–51.

Ipsos-MORI (May 21, 2010). *How Britain Voted in 2010.* Retrieved October 15, 2013, from http://www.ipsos-mori.com/researchpublications/researcharchive/poll.aspx?oItemId=2613&view=wide

Jasper, J. M. (1997). *The Art of Moral Protest.* Chicago: University of Chicago Press.

———— (2006). Motivation and Emotion. In R. Goodin, & C. Tilly, *Oxford Handbook of Contextual Political Studies.* Oxford: Oxford University Press.

Jordan, G., & Maloney, W. (1997). *The Protest Business.* Manchester: Manchester University Press.

———— (2006). 'Letting George Do It': Does Olson Explain Low Levels of Participation? *Journal of Elections, Public Opinion & Parties, 16*(2), 115–139.

———— (2007). *Democracy and Interest Groups.* Basingstoke: Palgrave MacMillan.

The Journal (October 27, 2010). *No Tuition Fees under Us, Say SNP.* Retrieved December 19, 2013, from http://www.journal-online.co.uk/article/7010-no_tuition_fees_under_us_say_snp

Juris, J. S. (2005). Violence Performed and Imagined: Militant Action, the Black Bloc and the Mass Media in Genoa. *Critique of Anthropology, 25*(4), 413–432.

———— (2012). Reflections on #Occupy Everywhere: Social Media, Public Space, and Emerging Logics of Aggregation. *American Ethnologist, 39*(2), 259–274.

Kaldor, M. (2000). Civilizing Globalization? The Implication of the 'Battle in Seattle'. *Millennium, 29*, 100–114.

Kavada, A. (2009). Email Lists and the Construction of an Open and Multifaceted Identity. *Information, Communication & Society, 12*(6), 817–839.

———— (2015). Creating the Collective: Social Media, the Occupy Movement and Its Constitution as a Collective Actor. *Information, Communication & Society, 18*(8), 872–886.

Kerton, S. (2012). Tahrir, Here? The Influence of the Arab Uprisings on the Emergence of Occupy. *Social Movement Studies, 11*(3–4), 302–308.

Kimberlee, R. (2002). Why Don't Young People Vote at General Elections? *Journal of Youth Studies, 5*, 85–97.

Kirbiš, A. (2013). Political Participation and Non-Democratic Political Culture in Western Europe, East-Central Europe and Post-Yugoslav Countries. In K. N. Demetriou (Ed.), *Democracy in Transition Political Participation in the European Union* (pp. 225–251). Heidelberg: Springer.

Klandermans, B. (1992). The Social Construction of Protest and Multiorganizational Fields. In A. D. Morris, & C. M. Mueller (Eds.), *Frontiers in Social Movement Theory*. New Haven: Yale University Press.

———— (1997). *The Social Psychology of Protest*. Oxford: Blackwell.

Klemenčič, M. (2012). The Changing Conceptions of Student. In A. Curaj, P. Scott, L. Vlasceanu, & L. Wilson (Eds.), *European Higher Education at the Crossroads – Between the Bologna Process and National Reforms* (pp. 631–653). Heidelberg: Springer.

———— (2014). Student Power in a Global Perspective and Contemporary Trends in Student Organising. *Studies in Higher Education, 39*(3), 396–411.

Lawson, R., & Barton, S. E. (1980). Sex Roles in Social Movements: A Case Study of the Tenant Movement in New York City. *Signs, 6*(2), 230–247.

Lefebvre, H. (1996). The Right to the City. In E. Kofman, & E. Lebas (Eds.), *Writing on Cities*. Oxford: Blackwell.

Lievrouw, L. (2011). *Alternative and Activist New Media*. Cambridge: Polity.

Loncle, P., Cuconato, M., Muniglia, V., & Walther, A. (Eds.) (2012). *Youth Participation in Europe*. Bristol: Policy Press.

Luescher-Mamashela, T. (2013). Student Representation in University Decision-Making: Good Reasons, a New Lens? *Studies in Higher Education, 38*(10), 1442–1456.

Lukianoff, G., & Haidt, J. (September 2015). *The Coddling of the American Mind*. Retrieved September 4, 2016, from The Atlantic: http://www.theatlantic.com/magazine/archive/2015/09/the-coddling-of-the-american-mind/399356/

Madianou, M. (2013). Humanitarian Campaigns in Social Media: Network Architectures and Polymedia Events. *Journalism Studies, 14*(2), 249–266.

Marsh, D., O'Toole, T., & Jones, S. (2004). *Young People and Politics in the UK*. Basingstoke: Palgrave MacMillan.

Mason, P. (2008). *Live Working or Die Fighting: How the Working Class Went Global*. London: Vintage.

—— (February 5, 2011a). *Twenty Reasons Why It's Kicking Off Everywhere.* Retrieved October 14, 2013, from BBC Newsnight: http://www.bbc.co.uk/blogs/newsnight/paulmason/2011/02/twenty_reasons_why_its_kicking.html

—— (2011b). *Why It's Kicking Off Everywhere: The New Global Revolutions.* London: Verso.

—— (July 1, 2012). *The Graduates of 2012 Will Survive Only in the Cracks of Our Economy.* Retrieved October 15, 2013, from The Guardian: http://www.theguardian.com/commentisfree/2012/jul/01/graduates-2012-survive-in-cracks-economy

McAdam, D. (1982). *Political Process and the Development of Black Insurgency.* Chicago: University of Chicago Press.

—— (1986). Recruitment to High Risk Activism: The Case of Freedom Summer. *American Journal of Sociology, 92*(1), 64–90.

—— (1988). *Freedom Summer.* Oxford: Oxford University Press.

——, & Paulsen, R. (1993). Specifying the Relationship Between Ties and Activism. *American Journal of Sociology, 99*, 640–667.

——, & Rucht, D. (1993). The Cross-National Diffusion of Movement Ideas. *The Annals of the American Academy of Political and Social Science, 528*, 56–74.

McCarthy, J. D., & McPhail, C. (1998). The Institutionalization of Protest in the United States. In D. S. Meyer, & S. Tarrow (Eds.), *The Social Movement Society: Contentious Politics for a New Century.* Lanham: Rowman & Littlefield.

McCarthy, J. D., & Zald, M. N. (1977). Resource Mobilization and Social Movements: A Partial Theory. *American Journal of Sociology, 82*, 1212–1241.

McDonald, K. (2002). From Solidarity to Fluidarity: Social Movements Beyond 'Collective Identity' – the Case of Globalization Conflicts. *Social Movement Studies, 1*(2), 109–128.

McGettigan, A. (2013). *The Great University Gamble.* London: Pluto Press.

McKay, G. (Ed.) (1996). *DiY Culture: Party & Protest in Nineties Britain.* London: Verso.

McPherson, J. M., Popielarz, P. A., & Drobnic, S. (1992). Social Networks and Organizational Dynamics. *American Sociological Review, 57*(2), 153–170.

Melucci, A. (1988). Getting Involved: Identity and Mobilization in Social Movements. *International Social Movements Research, 1*, 329–348.

—— (1996). *Challenging Codes: Collective Action in the Information Age.* Cambridge: Cambridge University Press.

Meyer, D. S., & Tarrow, S. (Eds.) (1998). *The Social Movement Society.* Lanham: Rowman & Littlefield.

Molesworth, M., Scullion, R., & Nixon, E. (Eds.) (2010). *The Marketisation of Higher Education and the Student as Consumer.* London: Routledge.

Morley, L. (2003). Restructuring Students as Consumers. In M. Slowey, & D. Watson (Eds.), *Higher Education and the Lifecourse* (pp. 79–92). London: SRHE and Open University Press.

Morozov, E. (September 5, 2009). *From Slacktivism to Activism.* Retrieved October 14, 2013, from Foreign Policy: http://neteffect.foreignpolicy.com/posts/2009/09/05/from_slacktivism_to_activism

—— (2011). *The Net Delusion: How Not to Liberate the World.* London: Allen Lane.

Nah, S., Veenstra, A. S., & Shah, D. V. (2006). The Internet and Anti-War Activism: A Case Study of Information, Expression, and Action. *Journal of Computer-Mediated Communication, 12*, 230–247.

NCAFC (November 12, 2010). *Press Release: 24th November National Walkout and Day of Protest against Tuition Fees.* Retrieved December 19, 2013, from http://anticuts.com/2010/11/12/press-release-24th-november-walkout-and-day-of-action/

Norgaard, K. M. (2006). 'People Want to Protect Themselves a Little Bit': Emotions, Denial, and Social Movement Nonparticipation. *Sociological Inquiry, 76*(3), 372–396.

Norris, P. (2001). The Apathetic Landslide: The 2001 British General Election. *Parliamentary Affairs, 54*, 565–589.

——— (2002). *Democratic Phoenix: Reinventing Political Activism.* Cambridge: Cambridge University Press.

——— (2003). Young People and Political Activism: From the Politics of Loyalties to the Politics of Choice? *Council of Europe Symposium, Young People and Democratic Institutions: From Disillusionment to Participation.* Council of Europe: Strasbourg.

Norwich Evening News (November 24, 2010). *Norwich Students Protest Tuition Fees Hike.* Retrieved December 19, 2013, from http://www.eveningnews24.co.uk/news/norwich_students_protest_tuition_fees_hike_1_736756

NUS (2010a). *1000 Candidates Sign Vote for Students Pledge to Oppose Tuition Fee Hike.* Retrieved October 16, 2013, from http://www.nus.org.uk/en/news/news/lib-dem-and-labour-mps-would-vote-together-to-oppose-tuition-fee-rise/

——— (2010b). *Initial Response to the Report of the Independent Review of Higher Education Funding and Student Finance.* NUS: London.

O'Byrne, D. J., & Hensby, A. (2011). *Theorizing Global Studies.* Basingstoke: Palgrave MacMillan.

Oegema, D., & Klandermans, B. (1994). Why Social Movement Sympathizers Don't Participate: Erosion and Nonconversion of Support. *American Sociological Review, 59*(5), 703–722.

Olson, M. (1965). *The Logic of Collective Action.* Cambridge, MA: Harvard University Press.

Opinion Panel (2010). *Tuition Fees and Student Protest.* Retrieved October 14, 2013, from http://www.opinionpanel.co.uk/2010/11/25/tuition-fees-and-student-protest/

Opp, K.-D. (2009). *Theories of Political Protest and Social Movements.* London: Routledge.

O'Toole, T., Lister, M., Marsh, D., Jones, S., & McDonagh, A. (2003). Turning Out or Left Out? Participation and Non-Participation among Young People. *Contemporary Politics, 9*(1), 45–61.

Palacios, L. C. (June 4, 2013). *Quebec's Student Movement: Learning from Britain and the Globe.* Retrieved October 15, 2013, from Open Democracy: http://www.opendemocracy.net/ourkingdom/lena-carla-palacios/quebec%E2%80%99s-student-movement-learning-from-britain-and-globe

Palmieri, T., & Solomon, C. (Eds.) (2011). *Springtime: The New Student Rebellions.* London: Verso.

Parry, G., Moyser, G., & Day, N. (1992). *Political Participation and Democracy in Britain.* Cambridge: Cambridge University Press.

Passy, F., & Monsch, G.-A. (2014). Do Social Networks Really Matter in Contentious Politics? *Social Movement Studies, 13*(1), 22–47.

Patel, R. (2007). *Avaaz.org's Ricken Patel on BBC World's HARDtalk.* Retrieved October 16, 2013, from http://vimeo.com/369614

Pattie, C., Seyd, P., & Whiteley, P. (2004). *Citizenship in Britain.* Cambridge: Cambridge University Press.

Penny, L. (January 31, 2011). No Drugs. No Sex. And No Leaders. *New Statesman,* pp. 24–29.

Pickerill, J., & Chatterton, P. (2006). Notes Towards Autonomous Geographies: Creation, Resistance and Self-Management as Survival Tactics. *Progress in Human Geography, 30*, 730–46.

Pickerill, J., & Krinsky, J. (2012). Why Does Occupy Matter? *Social Movement Studies, 11*(3–4), 279–287.

Poletta, F., & Jasper, J. M. (2001). Collective Identity and Social Movements. *Annual Review of Sociology, 27*, 283–305.

Power, N. (2012). Dangerous Subjects: UK Students and the Criminalization of Protest. *South Atlantic Quarterly, 111*(2), 412–420.

Purkis, J. (2001). Leaderless Cultures: The Problem of Authority in a Radical Environmental Group. In C. Barker, A. Johnson, & M. Lavalette (Eds.), *Leadership and Social Movements.* Manchester: Manchester University Press.

Putnam, R. (2000). *Bowling Alone.* New York: Touchstone.

Raine, L., & Wellman, B. (2012). *Networked: The New Social Operating System.* Cambridge: MIT Press.

Rhoads, R. A. (1998). *Freedom's Web: Student Activism in an Age of Cultural Diversity.* Baltimore: Johns Hopkins University Press.

Roberts, H., & Sachdev, D. (Eds.) (1996) *Young People's Social Attitudes – Having Their Say: The Views of 12–19 Year Olds.* Ilford: Barnardo's and Social and Community Planning Research.

Rootes, C. A. (1980). Student Radicalism: Politics of Moral Protest and Legitimation Problems of the Modern Capitalist State. *Theory and Society, 9*(3), 473–502.

——— (1997). Environmental Movements and Green Parties in Western and Eastern Europe. In M. Redclift, & G. Woodgate (Eds.), *The International Handbook of Environmental Sociology* (pp. 319–347). Northampton, MA: Edward Elgar.

——— (2012). Student Movements. In D. A. Snow, D. Della Porta, B. Klandermans, & D. McAdam (Eds.), *Wiley-Blackwell Encyclopedia of Social and Political Movements* (Vol. 3). Oxford: Blackwell.

Runciman, D. (2008). *Political Hypocrisy.* Princeton: Princeton University Press.

Salter, L., & Kay, J. B. (2011). The UWE Student Occupation. *Social Movement Studies, 10*(4), 423–429.

Sanderson-Nash, E. (2011). *Obeying the Iron Law? Changes to the Intra-Party Balance of Power in the British Liberal Democrats since 1988.* Retrieved September 4, 2016, from http://sro.sussex.ac.uk/7467/1/Sanderson-Nash%2C_Emma.pdf

Saunders, C. (2008). Double-Edged Swords? Collective Identity and Solidarity in the Environmental Movement. *British Journal of Sociology, 59*(2), 227–253.

————— (2010). Does Broad Participation Make De-Radicalisation Inevitable? The Case of Climate Camps in the UK. *PSA Annual Conference.* Edinburgh: PSA.

Savage, M., Barlow, J., Dickens, P., & Fielding, T. (1992). *Property, Bureaucracy and Culture: Middle-Class Formation in Contemporary Britain.* London: Routledge.

Savage, M., Silva, E., & Warde, A. (2010). Dis-Identification and Class Identity. In E. Silva, & A. Warde (Eds.), *Cultural Analysis and Bourdieu's Legacy* (pp. 60–74). London: Routledge.

Schein, R. (2012). Whose Occupation? Homelessness and the Politics of Park Encampments. *Social Movement Studies, 11*(3–4), 335–341.

Schweisfurth, M., & Gu, Q. (2009). Exploring the Experiences of International Students in UK Higher Education: Possibilities and Limits of Interculturality in University Life. *Intercultural Education, 20*(5), 463–473.

Sherkat, D. E., & Blocker, T. J. (1994). The Political Development of Sixties' Activists: Identifying the Influence of Class, Gender, and Socialization on Protest Participation. *Social Forces, 72*(3), 821–842.

————— (1997). Explaining the Political and Personal Consequences of Protest. *Social Forces, 75*(3), 1049–77.

Sims, J. M. (2007). *Not Enough Understanding? Student Experiences of Diversity in UK Universities.* Retrieved April 27, 2015, from http://www.runnymedetrust.org/uploads/file/Not%20Enough%20Understanding%20-%20final.pdf

Skeggs, B. (1997). *Formations of Class and Gender.* London: Sage.

Skocpol, T. (2003). *Diminished Democracy: From Membership to Management in American Civil Life.* Norman: University of Oklahoma.

Snow, D. A. (2001). Collective Identity and Expressing Forms. In N. J. Smelser, & P. B. Baltes (Eds.), *International Encyclopedia of the Social and Behavioural Sciences.* London: Elsevier Science.

—————, Rochford, E. B., Worden, S. K., & Benford, R. D. (1986). Frame Alignment Processes, Micromobilization, and Movement Participation. *American Sociological Review, 51*(4), 464–481.

—————, Zurcher, L. A., & Ekland-Olson, S. (1980). Social Networks and Social Movements: A Microstructural Approach to Differential Recruitment. *American Sociological Review, 45,* 787–801.

Solomon, C. (2011). We Felt Liberated. In T. Palmieri, & C. Solomon (Eds.), *Springtime: The New Student Rebellions.* London: Verso.

Spanier, G. (October 17, 2008). *Is Campus Activism Dead – or Just Misguided?* Retrieved September 4, 2016, from The Chronicle of Higher Education: http://www.chronicle.com/article/is-campus-activism/3970

Stoker, G. (2006). *Why Politics Matters.* Basingstoke: Palgrave MacMillan.

The Sun (November 11, 2010). *Student Demo Thugs' Tory HQ Riot.* Retrieved December 19, 2013, from http://www.thesun.co.uk/sol/homepage/news/3222200/Top-cop-I-did-not-predict-a-riot.html

Sunstein, C. R. (2009). *Going to Extremes: How Like Minds Unite and Divide.* Oxford: Oxford University Press.

Swain, D. (2011). The Student Movement Today. *International Socialism, 130,* 95–112.

Taft, J. K. (2006). 'I'm Not a Politics Person': Teenage Girls, Oppositional Consciousness, and the Meaning of Politics. *Politics & Gender, 2,* 329–352.

Tarrow, S. (1989). *Democracy and Disorder: Protest and Politics in Italy, 1965–1975.* Oxford: Oxford University Press.

———— (1992). Mentalities, Political Cultures, and Collective Action Frames: Constructing Meanings through Action. In A. D. Morris, & C. M. Mueller (Eds.), *Frontiers in Social Movement Theory.* New Haven: Yale University Press.

———— (1995). Cycles of Collective Action. In M. Traugott (Ed.), *Repertoires and Cycles of Collective Action.* London: Duke University Press.

———— (1998). *Power in Movement: Social Movements and Contentious Politics* (2nd ed.). Cambridge: Cambridge University Press.

————, & McAdam, D. (2005). Scale Shift in Transnational Contention. In D. Della Porta, & S. Tarrow (Eds.), *Transnational Protest and Global Activism* (pp. 121–147). Lanham, MD: Rowman & Littlefield.

Theocharis, Y. (2012). Cuts, Tweets, Solidarity and Mobilisation: How the Internet Shaped the Student Occupations. *Parliamentary Affairs, 65*(4), 162–194.

THES (January 24, 2012). *HE Bill 'To Be Shelved Indefinitely'.* Retrieved October 15, 2013, from Times Higher Education Supplement: http://www.timeshighereducation.co.uk/418801.article

Tilly, C. (1969). Collective Violence in European Perspective. In H. D. Graham, & T. R. Gurr (Eds.), *The History of Violence in America* (pp. 4–44). New York: Praeger.

———— (1976). Major Forms of Collective Action in Western Europe 1500–1975. *Theory and Society, 3*(3), 365–375.

———— (1995). *Popular Contention in Great Britain, 1758–1834.* Cambridge, MA: Harvard University Press.

———— (2004). *Social Movements 1768–2004.* Boulder: Paradigm Publishers.

Touraine, A. (1971). *The Post-Industrial Society. Tomorrow's Social History: Classes, Conflicts and Culture in the Programmed Society.* New York: Random House.

———— (1981). *The Voice and the Eye.* Cambridge: Cambridge University Press.

Toynbee, P. (November 5, 2010). *Sorry, Students, But You're Low in the Pain Pecking Order.* Retrieved December 21, 2013, from The Guardian: http://www.theguardian.com/commentisfree/2010/nov/05/students-low-pain-pecking-order

UCL Occupation (2010). *Our Demands.* Retrieved December 19, 2013, from http://web.archive.org/web/20101212230110/http://blog.ucloccupation.com/demands/

Van Dyke, N. (1998). Hotbeds of Activism: Locations of Student Protest. *Social Problems, 45*(2), 205–220.

———— (2003). Crossing Movement Boundaries: Factors that Facilitate Coalition Protest by American College Students, 1930–1990. *Social Problems, 50*(2), 226–250.

Verba, S., & Nie, N. H. (1972). *Participation in America.* Chicago: University of Chicago Press.

Verba, S., Schlozman, K. L., & Brady, H. E. (1995). *Voice and Equality: Civic Voluntarism in American Politics.* Cambridge, MA: Harvard University Press.

Warde, A. (1994). Consumption, Identity-Formation and Uncertainty. *Sociology, 28*(4), 877–898.

Whiteley, P., & Seyd, P. (2002). *High-Intensity Participation: The Dynamics of Party Activism in Britain.* Ann Arbor: University of Michigan Press.

Williams, J. (2013). *Consuming Higher Education. Why Learning Can't Be Bought.* London: Bloomsbury.

——— (2016). *Academic Freedom in an Age of Conformity: Confronting the Fear of Knowledge.* Basingstoke: Palgrave MacMillan.

Wolfreys, J. (2011). *Universities for Hire: The Higher Education White Paper and the Marketisation of Academia.* London: Education Activist Network.

Yang, G. (2000). The Liminal Effects of Social Movements: Red Guards and the Transformation of Identity. *Sociological Forum, 15*(3), 379–406.

Yettram, P. J. (1981). Contrary Imaginations: Student Activism and Beliefs in England in the Mid-1970s. In P. G. Altbach (Ed.), *Student Politics: Perspectives for the Eighties.* Metuchen: The Scarecrow Press.

Yulia, Z. (2010). Social Movements through the Gender Lens. *Sociology Compass, 4*(8), 628–641.

Index

About the Author

Alexander Hensby is Research Associate at the School of Social Policy, Sociology, and Social Research at the University of Kent, UK. His research and teaching interests include civic engagement, political socialisation, social networks, and higher education. He has written numerous articles on participation and social movements, and is the author of *Theorizing Global Studies* (with Darren O'Byrne).

Lightning Source UK Ltd.
Milton Keynes UK
UKOW03n1523220217
295065UK00001B/33/P